Fabulous FABRIC

Edited by
Laura Scott
and
Vicki Blizzard

No-Sew Decorating in a Snap!™

HOUSE of
WHITE
BIRCHES

PUBLISHERS
SINCE 1947

Fabulous Fabric
No-Sew Decorating in a Snap!

Executive Editors: Laura Scott, Vicki Blizzard
Managing Editor: Lisa M. Fosnaugh
Technical Editor: Läna Schurb
Copy Editors: Michelle Beck, Nicki Lehman, Mary Martin
Publication Coordinator: June Sprunger

Photography: Tammy Christian,
Kelly Heydinger, Christena Green
Photography Assistant: Linda Quinlan
Photography Stylist: Tammy Nussbaum

Publishing Services Manager: Brenda Gallmeyer
Graphic Arts Supervisor: Ronda Bechinski
Art Director: Brad Snow
Book Design: Amy S. Lin
Graphic Artist/Cover Design: Erin Augsburger
Production Assistants: Janet Bowers, Marj Morgan
Traffic Coordinator: Sandra Beres
Technical Artists: Liz Morgan,
Mitchell Moss, Chad Summers

Chief Executive Officer: John Robinson
Publishing Director: David McKee
Book Marketing Manager: Craig Scott
Editorial Director: Vivian Rothe
Publishing Services Director: Brenda R. Wendling

Printed in the United States of America
First Printing: 2003
Library of Congress Number: 2003100518
ISBN: 1-59217-017-X

Credit: No-Sew Bathroom Decor, page 169,
Myers Plumbing, Heating & Cooling, 6242 South 000 Road, Berne, IN 467111.

Every effort has been made to ensure the accuracy and completeness of the instructions in this book.
However we cannot be responsible for human error or for the results when using materials
other than those specified in the instructions, or for variations in individual work.

1 2 3 4 5 6 7 8 9

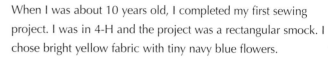

Fabulous Fabric
No-Sew Decorating in a Snap!

Dear Friend,

When I was about 10 years old, I completed my first sewing project. I was in 4-H and the project was a rectangular smock. I chose bright yellow fabric with tiny navy blue flowers.

I have no memory of what the smock was actually for, and I know I never actually wore it in public. What I do remember is struggling to get the tension just right on my mother's sewing machine, and how the bobbin kept slipping through my fingers and dropping to the floor time and time again.

I guess I discovered at an early age that I was "sewing-machine challenged." If only all the great products for working with fabrics without a sewing machine had been available then!

Needless to say, I was absolutely thrilled when the idea for this book came along. At last—a book of truly beautiful home decor items, made with great fabrics, that wouldn't require me to thread a sewing machine!

Because the techniques in this book require much of the same background knowledge used for sewing, I consulted an accomplished and skilled sewing expert and friend, Carol Zentgraf. Carol applied her knowledge of sewing to the many wonderful no-sew products available today, such as fusible webbing, fabric glue and no-sew home decor kits. You'll find lots of valuable information and tips throughout the pages of this book, along with dozens of creative, no-sew home-decorating patterns.

We've arranged the chapters in this book to go room by room through your home. That way, you can tackle redoing just one room at a time. Before you begin, however, I suggest you browse through the entire book. You may find ideas in one chapter that would suit a room covered in a different chapter.

And for those of you who love your sewing machines, rest assured that all the patterns in this book will work equally well with your skilled hands guiding the fabric through your sewing machine!

Warm regards,

Laura Ashley

Fabulous Fabric
No-Sew Decorating in a Snap!

Bedroom Makeovers

Make your bedroom warm and cozy by creating pillows, coverlets and so much more, all without making a stitch.

Bathroom Accents

A little fabric is all you need to create stunning bathroom accessories for your home.

Holiday Home

Decorate your home in comfortable style with these lovely no-sew holiday accessories.

Casual Living

Your living room will be one of the most personal and relaxed areas in your home, complete with high-quality, handmade decor and accents. Add your stylish flair and personal touch to everything from lamp shades and rugs to pillows and outlet covers.

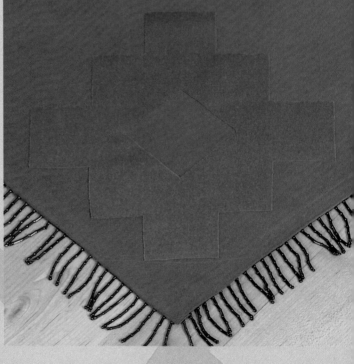

Southwest Set

No matter what your location, bring the feel of the sunny Southwest to your home with a coordinating throw, footstool and table runner. Beaded fringe is the only embellishment you need to tie these pieces together.

Designs by Bev Shenefield

Materials

- 45-inch-wide suede cloth: 4 yards rust, 1 yard turquoise
- 9 (1-yard) packages brown bead fringe
- ½-inch-wide double-stick fusible tape
- 2 yards fusible web
- 1 yard muslin
- 45-inch x 60-inch piece batting
- Recycled wooden footstool with legs and foam top or kit to make one
- Fine-point black permanent marker
- Heavy-duty stapler and staples
- Acrylic craft paints: burnt sienna, burnt umber
- Satin-finish varnish
- Flat #10 paintbrush

Throw

1. Trim rust suede cloth to 45 inches x 61 inches. Press under selvage along sides; turn ends under ½ inch and press.

2. Referring to manufacturer's instructions throughout, apply fusible tape under edges of side hems. Cut a piece of fusible tape as long as hemmed edge; cut tape in half lengthwise. Trim end hems to ¼ inch; apply cut fusible tape to secure hems.

3. Central motif: Enlarge pattern for throw 125 percent on photocopier. One-quarter of pattern for central motif is given; referring to photo, join pieces along dashed lines to form complete pattern. Use black marker to trace one central motif on paper backing of fusible web. Following manufacturer's instructions throughout, fuse web to back of turquoise fabric; cut out design, remove backing and fuse turquoise motif in center of throw.

4. End motifs: For each end motif, join two pattern pieces along dashed lines; trace, fuse and cut patterns from turquoise fabric. Referring to photo, fuse motifs along ends of throw.

5. Apply fusible tape over hem ends; iron bead fringe onto tape.

Table Topper

1. Cut 45-inch square from rust fabric. Press under selvage along sides; turn other edges (ends) under ½ inch; press.

2. Referring to manufacturer's instructions, apply fusible tape under edges of side hems to hold hems in place. Cut a 44-inch piece of fusible tape in half lengthwise. Trim end hems to ¼ inch; secure with cut fusible tape.

3. Use photocopier to enlarge pattern for table topper and footstool 111 percent. Then use black marker to trace four complete motifs onto backing of fusible web. Fuse web to back of turquoise fabric; cut out designs, remove backing and adhere turquoise shapes in corners of table topper, positioning them 2 inches from corners and aligning points with corners.

4. Cut fusible tape in half lengthwise; apply along hems on wrong side of table topper. Position ribbon edge of fringe on tape and adhere all around, making sure ribbon edge covers cut edges on two ¼-inch sides.

Footstool

1. Remove existing cover and legs from footstool; replace foam, if needed (cut to size with an electric knife). Place double layer of batting over foam; pull over edges of stool base and staple all around. Cover batting with muslin; staple. To fit corners, cut 7-inch diamond from each corner of muslin and batting and fold under edges.

2. Paint legs burnt sienna. Referring to instructions for dry-brushing in Painting Techniques (General Instructions, page 174), dry-brush with burnt umber. Let dry, then coat with one or two coats satin varnish. Let dry.

3. Cut 36-inch square rust fabric.

4. Use photocopier to enlarge pattern for table topper and footstool 111 percent. Then use black marker to trace one complete motif on backing of fusible web. Trace also four half-motifs, adding ½ inch fabric outside dashed lines to allow extra for tucking under edge.

5. Fuse web to back of turquoise fabric; cut out designs, remove backing and adhere motifs to right side of rust fabric, positioning complete motif in center and half-motifs on sides, centering them and aligning edges with edges of rust fabric.

6. Lay fabric over muslin, right side out, adjusting until it is centered. Fit corners as described in step 1; staple fabric edges to bottom of stool.

7. Staple fringe to underside of footstool, stapling all around stool and making sure fringe hangs down. Reassemble footstool and attach legs, taking care not to catch fringe. ✂

Laced Looks

Use lacing to add a decorative edge or to attach two leather or suede edges. Punch or cut small holes along the edge, then lace with ribbon or leather lacing strips.

Southwest Throw
Enlarge pattern 125% before cutting
One-fourth of center pattern is given;
match pieces along dashed lines to
construct complete center motif.
Match 2 quarters of pattern along
dashed lines to make each motif
for ends of throw.

Hang In There

A wide variety of window treatments lend themselves beautifully to no-sew techniques. Draped panels and swags require only edge finishes and no seaming at all; simply combine them with a gorgeous rod and finials for a dazzling effect.

Perfect Panels

Prefer panel treatments? Panels with rod pockets, decorative tabs or ties are all easy to make, or you can simply finish the upper edges and hang them with clip-on drapery rings. Also consider adding grommets along the upper edge to lace onto the drapery rod.

Rods & Finials

Drapery rods are available in a wide range of sizes and include round and flat metal or wooden rods. PVC pipe and heavy cardboard tubes padded with fusible batting and covered with fabric also make interesting rods when paired with fabric-covered finials.

The rod should extend at least 3 inches beyond the window on each side.

Always decide on the drapery rod and the hanging technique you'll use before you cut the panels from fabric.

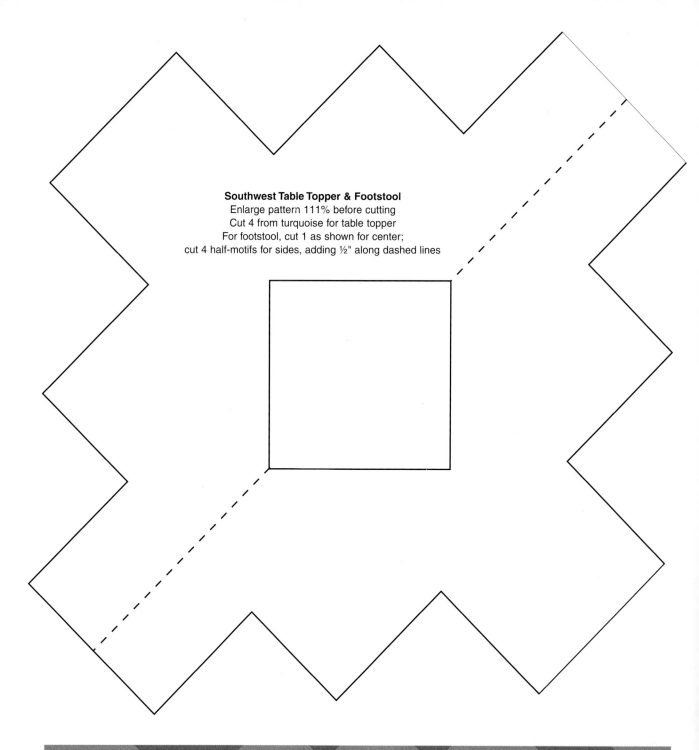

Southwest Table Topper & Footstool
Enlarge pattern 111% before cutting
Cut 4 from turquoise for table topper
For footstool, cut 1 as shown for center;
cut 4 half-motifs for sides, adding ½" along dashed lines

Directional Do's

Many fabric prints and plaids are directional, with one edge of the design intended to be at the top. Some home decor fabrics will have the direction marked with an arrow on the selvage, and sometimes it's obvious.

For prints or plaids where it isn't obvious, pick a direction and stick with it. To prevent cutting or piecing mistakes, use a fabric marker or pin to indicate the top edge of each piece as you plan and cut.

The color of napped fabrics, such as velvet and corduroy, will look different depending on which way the nap is running. Be sure to cut all pieces in the same direction.

Fabric Magic

Fabric selection is an important element in great decorating—and half the fun. The way you combine color, texture and pattern within a room gives it character and makes it uniquely yours.

Does whimsical or fun-loving suit your personality and the room's purpose? Consider mix-and-match fabrics in bright prints, gingham checks or plaids and stripes. Add lots of trims and you have a room that's guaranteed to make people smile.

Perhaps you prefer a room with a serene French country or English garden feel. Choose from the wonderful selection of toile fabrics or cabbage roses and coordinating checks and stripes.

How about a nautical look or an elegant, formal ambience? They're also easy to achieve through the magic of fabric.

Small Touches, Big Results

It isn't even necessary to redecorate an entire room to give it new life. Often a new window treatment or a bevy of throw pillows is all it takes.

Also consider your room's size and use when selecting fabric. Warm colors add coziness while cool colors can make a room feel larger. A large floral print used for a window treatment will have a different effect than subtle damask used for the identical treatment. And while warm, fuzzy fleece makes cozy pillows for a casual room, you may prefer elegant silk dupioni for a formal room.

Check Out Home Decor Fabrics

Most fabrics offered in home decor fabric departments can be used for the no-sew projects featured in this book.

You can also create your own fabric design with paint, dye, stamps, stencils and photo transfers as suggested on page 13.

Some fabrics are more compatible with some gluing and fusing products than others, so keep the following tips in mind for selecting what's best for your chosen no-sew technique.

To ensure success, it's always a good idea to test the technique on a swatch of your chosen fabric before purchasing the entire yardage.

Fused Seams, Edges & Drapery Tapes

Light- to medium-weight natural-fiber fabrics, such as cotton and linen, work best for fusible seamed techniques. Heavyweight fabrics may be too bulky or may not hold a permanent bond when used with some fusible adhesives.

For example, a heavyweight fabric applied to a fusible drapery tape may pull away from the tape once the window treatment is hung and the fabric weight responds to gravity.

The fabric must be able to withstand the heat required for fusing. Some silks, synthetics and cotton blends with a high percentage of synthetic fibers may shrink, melt or otherwise be damaged by high heat. Using a lower iron temperature may result in an insufficient bond.

Select fabric with a smooth surface to ensure an even bond. Fusing textured fabrics may result in unfused areas or lumpy seams.

Avoid fabrics treated with finishes such as Scotchgard or vinyl coating; these slick finishes will not bond well.

Select woven fabric with a close weave. The adhesive may show through

loosely woven fabrics or lace.

Glued Seams & Hems

Medium- to heavyweight fabrics are most suitable for gluing techniques. Adhesives may bleed through or show on very lightweight fabrics.

Non-fraying fabrics, such as some felt and real or faux leather and suede also are good candidates for projects with overlapping glued seams.

Because heat sensitivity isn't a problem, fabrics of most fiber contents can be glued, although adhesives and glues may stain some fabrics such as silk. Be sure to test on scrap fabric first.

Wrapped, Draped & Loosely Gathered Treatments

Medium- to heavyweight home decor fabrics that have body without being stiff are best for these treatments. They will also support the weight of heavier trims often used to finish the edges.

Consider fabrics that have an attractive wrong side, such as damask or tapestry, for unlined projects where both fabric sides will show.

Treatments With Exposed Edges or Laced Seams

Non-fraying fabrics such as fleece, felt, boiled wool, wool melton, vinyl and real or faux suede and leather are ideal for edges that will be decoratively cut or left unembellished, and for seams that will be laced together.

Fabrics that ravel easily and evenly, including tapestry, homespun cotton and linen are ideal for fabrications with fringed edges.

Embellished Lamp Shades

Jazz up an old lamp by embellishing a plain shade. Funky or elegant, you can create one for any mood or decor.

Designs by Carol Zentgraf

Materials

Floral Lamp Shade

- Self-adhesive lamp shade
- Fabric yardage indicated in lamp shade label
- Trim yardage indicated on lamp shade label
- ⅜-inch-wide fusible tape
- Permanent fabric adhesive

Plain Lamp Shade

- Paper lamp shade
- Fabric (see step 1)
- Double-sided adhesive (see step 1)
- Trim yardage to fit along upper and lower edges
- Tracing cloth or plain paper
- Permanent fabric adhesive

Plain Lamp Shade

1. Determine fabric yardage needed: Draw lamp shade pattern (see Lights On!, page 117). Measure pattern height and width to determine yardage. Purchase same amount of double-sided adhesive.

2. Trace pattern onto paper backing of adhesive; cut out. Remove paper backing and adhere adhesive to wrong side of fabric. Cut fabric along pattern edges. Remove remaining backing and turn under a single ⅜-inch hem along one straight edge of fabric.

3. Align raw straight edge of fabric with seam of lamp shade. Carefully wrap fabric around the shade, smoothing as you wrap. Glue hemmed edge in place.

4. Cut and glue trims around upper and lower edges of shade.

Floral Lamp Shade

1. Following manufacturer's instructions throughout, trace outline of shade onto wrong side of fabric; cut out along traced lines.

2. Fuse a single ⅜-inch hem along one straight edge of fabric.

3. Align raw straight edge of fabric with seam of lamp shade and carefully wrap fabric around the shade, smoothing as you wrap. Glue hemmed edge in place.

4. Cut and glue trims around upper and lower edges of shade. ✄

Measuring Windows

Window treatments can be mounted inside or outside the window, depending on the window frame and your preference.

Inside Mount

An inside-mount treatment fits between the outer edges of the window frame; the frame must have enough depth to allow for the depth of the mounting hardware and the treatment. Measure between the inside edges of the window frame to determine yardage (Fig. 1).

Outside Mount

An outside-mount window treatment can vary in its placement outside the window frame and give the effect of a wider or higher window. For treatments with rods, hang the rods first before measuring for yardage (Fig. 2).

Artistic Elements

You're already an artist when you create fabrications for your home, so why not take it one step further? Fabric surface treatments such as painting, stamping, stenciling and embossing are easy to learn and fun to apply.

For most projects, it's easiest to apply these treatments to the fabric pieces before you assemble them into a project.

Fabrics First

Natural fiber fabrics such as cotton, linen, and silk with a smooth surface are easiest to stamp and paint and hold the paint best. You can also achieve interesting effects by stamping or painting suede, faux suede and velvet.

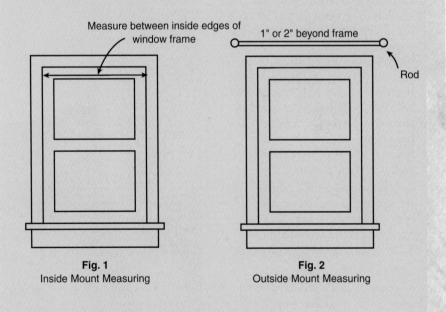

Fig. 1
Inside Mount Measuring

Fig. 2
Outside Mount Measuring

"Frayed" Not

Seam sealant is a liquid that prevents fabric threads and edges from fraying or unraveling. It can be used to prevent a fringed edge from unraveling farther than desired, to seal the edges of unhemmed appliqués, to prevent knots from coming untied, and for a multitude of other fray-preventing purposes.

Flower Power Throw Pillow

Add warmth and sunshine to your home on even the cloudiest of days.
Use your leftover fabric scraps to create this inviting flowery pillow.

Design by June Fiechter

Materials

- 16-inch square pillow
- Scrap fabrics in 7 complementary colors
- Fabric glue
- Pinking shears
- Dark chocolate soft fabric paint
- Fine writing tip for paint bottle

Instructions

1. Using photocopier with enlarging capabilities, enlarge pattern for central design 125 percent. (Pattern for corner does not need to be enlarged.) Referring to instructions for Using Transfer & Graphite Paper (General Instructions, page 174), trace patterns onto fabrics. **Note:** *On sample, dark blue is used for corners; light green for frame; light blue for background; rust for flower; red for flower center; dark green for leaf; and gold for vase.*

2. Using pinking shears throughout, cut out background piece about ½ inch outside traced lines. Cut out remaining pieces on traced lines.

3. Glue pattern pieces to pillow as shown.

4. Attach paint writer tip to bottle of fabric paint; embellish fabric pieces as desired. ✂

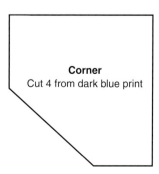

Corner
Cut 4 from dark blue print

Flower Pillow
Enlarge 125% before cutting

Woven Heart Accent Pillow

Luscious velvet is put together patchwork-style to create a soft, no-sew accent pillow.

Design by Bev Shenefield

Materials

- Panne velvet fabric: ½ yard each in complementary purples and greens
- 1½ yards fusible web
- ½ yard prewashed medium-weight muslin
- 2 yards cord trim in lavender, white and sage
- 2½ yards narrow ruffled lace
- 1¼ yards ivory ¼-inch-wide satin ribbon
- Additional assorted coordinating laces, trims and ribbons
- 1¼ yards flat pearl trim (optional)
- Purple and ivory ribbon roses (optional)
- Assorted coordinating shank buttons (optional)
- Craft clippers
- Polyester stuffing
- Fabric glue
- Jewel glue (optional)
- Water-soluble marking pen
- Back fine-point permanent marker
- Carpenter's square
- Clothespins

Instructions

1. Use photocopier to enlarge pattern to 143 percent. Use enlarged pattern to draw two hearts on muslin using water-soluble marker. Cut out ½ inch outside traced lines.

2. Iron fusible web onto back of each piece panne velvet. Using black permanent marker and carpenter's square, mark sections onto fusible web in a variety of rectangles and squares; cut out.

3. Place velvet pieces right side up on muslin hearts, arranging them in a random diagonal pattern with nap running in same direction. Remove backing and fuse pieces to muslin, following manufacturer's instructions. Make sure edges of pieces are against each other.

4. Turn under ½-inch margins around edges of hearts; press, then trim to ¼ inch. Lay cord along inside edge of one heart; glue cord backing in place with fabric glue. Secure with clothespins until glue is dry.

5. Remove clothespins; trim cord

backing to first stitching, about ¼ inch. Place other heart with wrong side against cord backing, making sure edges are against cord. (Cord should appear to cover seam between two hearts.) Glue hearts together around edges, using fabric glue through step 8, and leaving a 6-inch opening along one side. Secure edges with clothespins until dry.

6. Check both sides for any areas that did not adhere. Glue any loose pieces in place and secure with clothespins until dry.

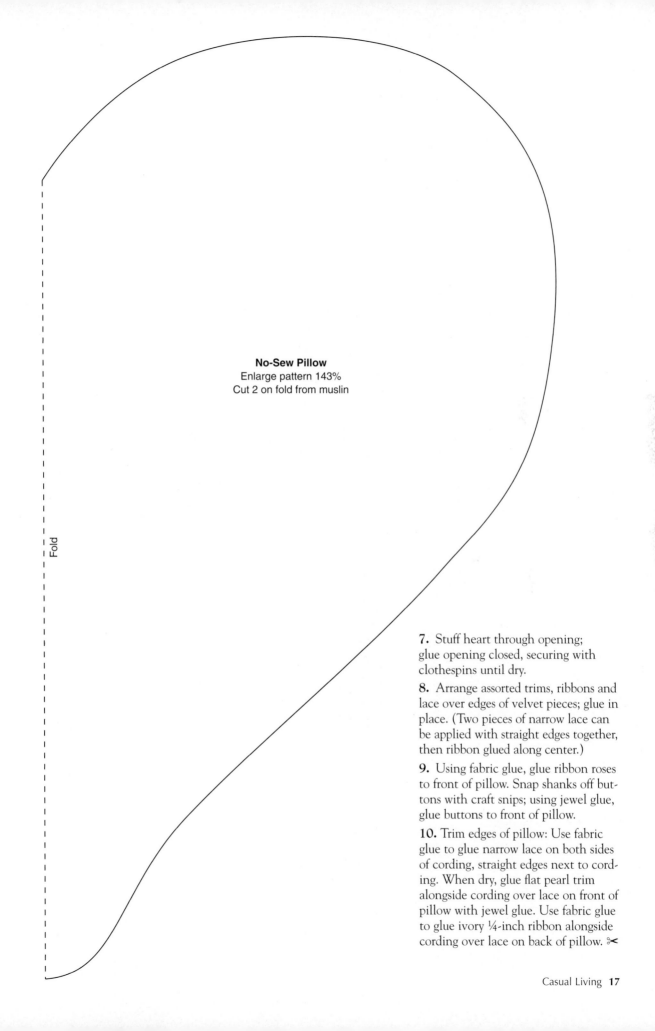

No-Sew Pillow
Enlarge pattern 143%
Cut 2 on fold from muslin

Fold

7. Stuff heart through opening; glue opening closed, securing with clothespins until dry.

8. Arrange assorted trims, ribbons and lace over edges of velvet pieces; glue in place. (Two pieces of narrow lace can be applied with straight edges together, then ribbon glued along center.)

9. Using fabric glue, glue ribbon roses to front of pillow. Snap shanks off buttons with craft snips; using jewel glue, glue buttons to front of pillow.

10. Trim edges of pillow: Use fabric glue to glue narrow lace on both sides of cording, straight edges next to cording. When dry, glue flat pearl trim alongside cording over lace on front of pillow with jewel glue. Use fabric glue to glue ivory ¼-inch ribbon alongside cording over lace on back of pillow. ✂

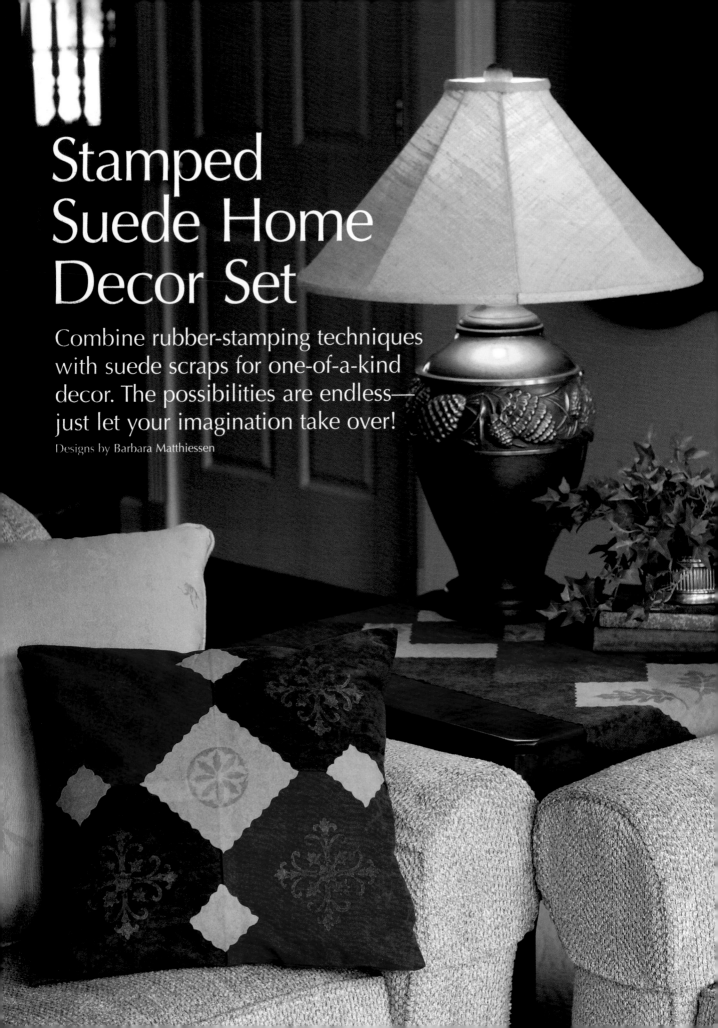

Stamped Suede Home Decor Set

Combine rubber-stamping techniques with suede scraps for one-of-a-kind decor. The possibilities are endless— just let your imagination take over!

Designs by Barbara Matthiessen

Materials

- 60-inch-wide suede cloth: 1 yard olive green; ½ yard each burgundy and gold
- 16-inch pillow form
- Leaves and medallions rubber stamps
- Metallic gold acrylic paint
- 2 packages fusible web
- ½-inch fusible tape
- Rotary cutter with tiara blade
- Rotary-cutting mat
- Ruler
- Makeup sponge or other fine-grained sponge
- Press cloth

Pillow

1. Cut 19-inch square burgundy cloth for back; cut two 10-inch squares from burgundy and two more from olive for front.

2. Referring to manufacturer's instructions, apply fusible web to wrong side of gold and remaining burgundy fabrics.

3. Using rotary cutter with specialty blade, cut one 5-inch square and four 2¼-inch squares from gold fabric.

4. Stamping: Lay gold squares and 10-inch burgundy and olive squares flat on protected work surface. Pour gold paint onto palette. Use sponge to apply paint to rubber stamps, then press stamp down firmly to make image, pulling stamp straight up. Practice stamping on a scrap of fabric or paper first to make sure you are applying sufficient paint— but not too much—to the stamp. Reload stamp with paint for each stamping. When you are comfortable with the process and satisfied with the practice results, stamp a round medallion in the center of the 5-inch gold square; stamp the largest medallion design on all 10-inch squares. Let dry.

5. Join olive and burgundy squares with fusible tape: Apply tape along one edge of 10-inch burgundy square on right side. Lay olive square over burgundy square, right sides facing; following manufacturer's instructions, press along tape to join. Repeat with remaining burgundy and olive squares. Referring to photo, apply tape along one long edge of one burgundy/olive unit; join to remaining pair of squares.

6. Add gold pieces: Peel backing off gold squares. Place 5-inch gold square in center of pillow top as shown; position 2¼-inch squares on seams 1 inch from central motif. Cover with press cloth; iron.

7. Lay pillow front right side up. Apply fusible tape around edges on right side. Place pillow back on pillow front right sides facing. Press together to fuse along three sides. Turn pillow right side out; insert pillow form. Push pillow form next to fused seam opposite open side. Fold under remaining edges; press to close pillow.

Runner

1. Using rotary cutter fitted with specialty blade throughout, cut 14-inch x 43-inch piece olive fabric. Fold in half lengthwise, then pin at sides 4 inches from each end. Lay ruler at the pin, then angle to end of fabric next to fold; cut along this line to form points in ends of runner.

2. From gold fabric, cut two 7¾-inch squares and one 9¾-inch square; from burgundy, cut two 7¾-inch squares, one 5-inch and two 2-inch squares.

3. Lay gold and burgundy squares flat on protected work surface. Pour gold paint onto palette. Use sponge to apply paint to rubber stamps, then press stamp down firmly to make image, pulling stamp straight up. Practice stamping on a scrap of fabric or paper first to make sure you are applying sufficient paint—but not too much—to the stamp. Reload stamp with paint for each stamping. When

you are comfortable with the process and satisfied with the practice results, stamp squares as follows:

Gold 7¾-inch squares—Stamp oak leaves in adjacent corners.

Burgundy 7¾-inch squares—Stamp maple leaves and round leaves in opposite corners.

Gold 9¾-inch square—Stamp oak leaves on opposite sides.

Burgundy 5-inch square—Stamp maple leaf in center.

Let paints dry.

4. Referring to photo, lay stamped squares on runner, removing paper backing. (Gold oak-leaf squares are on ends with burgundy leaf squares overlapping both end squares and center gold square.) Place 5-inch square in center of gold square and 2-inch squares on outer corners. Lay press cloth on top; iron into place. ✄

Floral Elegance Doily

Stencils and a premade doily make it easy to add elegant touches to your home. Choose a color that coordinates with your decor, or update your home with an entirely different color scheme.

Design by Debbie Williams

Project Note

Before beginning, refer to General Stenciling Instructions on page 71.

Instructions

1. Prewash doily in cool water using mild detergent and no fabric softener. Tumble-dry on low setting or air-dry.

2. Steam-press doily. Remove all water from iron, then dry-press. Allow

Materials
- 10-inch round fabric and Battenburg lace doily
- Vine frames and accents stencil
- Transparent tape
- Double-sided tape
- Cream-type stencil paints in assorted floral colors
- ¼-inch and ⅜-inch stencil brushes
- Brush cleaner

fabric to dry completely.

3. Position stencil flower that has two blooms on center of doily. Apply double-stick tape near cutout areas on back of stencil; tape stencil in place. Mask edge of other nearby flower.

4. Stencil as follows:

Blossoms—Stencil with amethyst purple; shade with additional purple and black cherry; paint center sunflower yellow.

Stem, leaves and vines—Stencil with dark hunter green; shade with additional dark hunter green; tint with assorted bloom colors.

5. Remove stencil. Mask back of used

portion of stencil to prevent smearing. Mask stenciled area on fabric with freezer paper.

6. Mask three outer leaves on one corner of the square vine frame stencil. Position remaining frame corner between center circle on one quarter of Battenburg lace edge and the three embroidered leaves on the fabric. Tape stencil in place. Stencil vine.

7. Clean brushes. Allow fabric to dry for 10 days before washing or applying heat, such as ironing. After 10 days, wash in cool water with mild soap. Tumble-dry on low setting or line-dry. Press with an iron as needed. ✂

Reversible Table Runner

Pick a side to match your mood and dress up your dinner table or hutch with this elegant reversible runner. Go from formal to classic just by the fabrics and embellishments you choose.

Design by Marian Shenk

Materials

- ¾ yard each of two coordinating fabrics
- 3½ yards of 4-inch-wide fabric border to coordinate with one of the fabrics
- 3 yards 2-inch-wide flat antique-style lace
- Metallic gold fusible bias tape
- Adhesive spray
- Washable fabric glue
- Fabric-marking pencil
- ¼-inch-wide fusible tape

Instructions

1. From each of the two fabrics cut a rectangle 36 inches x 21 inches. Fold each piece in half lengthwise; trim corners to make a point at each end. Make sure pieces match.

2. Side A: Fold under ¼-inch hem along one long edge of fabric border; press. Lay on top of matching fabric section, raw edges even; use pins to baste border along edges all around, folding under corners as you come to them. Trim excess fabric at fold points; secure with fabric glue. Fold under ¼ inch around edge of runner (border and underlying fabric); press.

3. Using fabric glue, glue inner edge of border to background fabric; let dry. Remove pins.

4. Side B: Using fabric-marking pencil, mark fabric for reverse side 2 inches from edge all around. Pin lace to fabric, aligning scalloped edge of lace with marked line and folding lace at corners.

5. Following manufacturer's instructions, iron bias tape over straight edge of lace; glue lace in place with fabric glue. Let dry; remove pins.

6. Lay Side A—with border stripe—wrong side up on work surface. Spray center portion with aerosol adhesive. Lay lace-trimmed Side B on top, wrong sides facing; smooth out and press.

7. Fold under raw edges of Side B to match folded edge of Side A. Fuse halves of runner together along their edges by sandwiching ¼-inch fusible tape between edges of fabric and ironing according to manufacturer's instructions.

8. Let runner dry and cool; press. ✄

Fabric Armchair Caddy

The never-ending search for remotes will end with this lovely toile fabric-covered organizer. Simply add fabric and embellishments to a premade piece and you'll have an armchair accessory the whole family will love.

Design by Barbara Woolley

Materials
- Natural-color fabric armchair organizer
- Adhesive-backed iron-on adhesive
- Jewel cement
- 7-inch "hook" section from hook-and-loop tape
- Fabrics: 2 (7½-inch x 13-inch) pieces toile or other desired fabric; 12-inch x 23-inch piece complementary small check
- 2 yards ½-inch complementary trim
- 10 (½-inch) buttons
- Complementary sewing thread or embroidery floss
- Hand-sewing needle

Instructions
1. Launder, dry and iron all fabrics. Fold under and press ½-inch hems around all edges.
2. Referring to manufacturer's instructions throughout, cut iron-on adhesive to fit backs of all fabric pieces; fuse to fabric.
3. Referring to photo throughout, position checked fabric across top of organizer and down into pockets; iron to fuse in place.
4. Position toile fabric on pockets; fuse in place.
5. Tie thread or floss through holes in each button so they'll appear to be sewn on; glue buttons on top of seams between small pockets with jewel cement.
6. Glue trim around edges of organizer.
7. Glue hooked tape to underside of organizer in center. This will hold organizer in place on arm of chair. ✂

Tapestry Rug

Stenciling a rug with colors of your choice is a quick way to add pizzazz to a room. You may even want to make one for a gift!

Design by Carol Zentgraf

Materials

- 54-inch-wide home decor fabrics: ¾ yard tapestry, 1 yard heavyweight cotton in complementary solid color
- ⅜-inch-wide heavy-duty fusible adhesive tape
- Quilter's template plastic
- Stencil crème paint in complementary color
- Stencil brush
- Fine-tip permanent marker
- Craft knife
- Rug backing (optional)

Instructions

1. From tapestry fabric, cut one piece 36 inches x 26 inches for center. From heavyweight cotton fabric, cut two strips 13 inches x 36 inches and two strips 13 inches x 38 inches for borders.

2. Press under ½ inch along long edges of each border strip. Press each strip in half lengthwise, wrong sides facing and edges even. On each strip, fuse adhesive tape to each seam allowance close to fold, but do not remove paper backing.

3. Overlapping ½ inch, sandwich each 36-inch edge of tapestry rug center between edges of a 36-inch border strip. Remove paper backing from adhesive tape and fuse borders in place; trim ends of border even with center as necessary.

4. Repeat to add remaining border strips to ends of rug center and side borders. Turn under short edges of border strips; fuse closed with adhesive tape.

5. Make stencil: Lay template plastic over selected motif(s) in tapestry. Trace motif(s) onto plastic with marker; cut out with craft knife.

6. Stencil motifs evenly spaced along fabric borders: Follow manufacturer's instructions to remove film from stencil crème. Dip brush in crème; blot excess onto folded paper towel. Holding brush perpendicular to surface, use a circular motion to apply paint to each opening, working from edges to center.

7. Let paint dry overnight; heat-set following manufacturer's instructions.

8. If desired, add rug backing to wrong side of rug to prevent slipping and add stability. ✂

Living Room Cornice

Make an existing window the focal point of your living room by adding a fabric and foam cornice. Decorative fringe and colors that complement your existing decor make a project that really pulls together the look of the room.

Design by Annabelle Keller for Dow Chemical

Materials

- 3 (12-inch x 36-inch x 1-inch) sheets Styrofoam® brand foam
- 42 (3-inch) wooden floral picks with wires removed
- Heavy paper
- Twin-size piece of polyester batting
- Fabrics: 1⅛ yards striped 56-inch-wide home decorator fabric; 1¾ yards 44- to 45-inch-wide solid cotton in coordinating color for lining
- 1¾ yards 1-inch-wide fringe in color to coordinate with home decorator fabric
- 2 (5-inch) angle brackets with screws
- 6 large T-pins
- Plastic-foam adhesive
- Permanent fabric adhesive
- Fine-tip permanent marker
- Serrated knife
- Small piece paraffin
- Table saw (optional)
- Hot-glue gun with needle nozzle
- Seam sealant
- Rotary cutter and self-healing mat

Plastic Foam Cornice

1. Referring to layout diagram, cut pieces for cornice ends, top and front from two sheets of Styrofoam using a serrated knife waxed with paraffin or a table saw. The third piece of Styrofoam is not cut.

2. Assemble front: Apply hot glue to three wooden picks; insert into one edge of 12-inch square cut from one piece of Styrofoam, leaving ¾ inch protruding. Apply plastic-foam adhesive to edge between the picks and hot glue to the picks themselves, then press end securely onto one end of the uncut Styrofoam sheet; let dry.

3. Assemble top: Referring to step 2, follow same procedure to attach a 5-inch edge of the 12-inch x 5-inch piece cut from one Styrofoam sheet to one 5-inch edge of the 36-inch x 5-inch piece cut from the second sheet; let dry.

4. Make pattern for curve: Use photocopier to enlarge pattern to 400 percent. Fold a piece of heavy paper in half. Position pattern's dashed line on fold; trace and cut out. Open paper pattern. Use pattern to mark and cut curves across bottom edge of cornice front.

5. Assemble ends and top: Referring to Fig. 1, apply hot glue to three wooden picks and insert into edge of top, leaving ¾ inch protruding. Apply plastic-foam adhesive to edge between the picks and hot glue to the picks themselves, then press end securely onto top; let dry. Repeat to assemble other end of cornice.

6. Attach front to top/end assembly, gluing picks into edges of plastic foam every 3 inches. Apply plastic-foam adhesive to spaces between the picks; partially press into top/end assembly. Apply hot glue to a few spots along edge between picks and quickly press front and top/end together securely; let dry.

Covering & Final Assembly

1. Cut a piece of batting 23 inches x 66 inches. Wrap batting from 1½ inches inside top to inside bottom and 1½ inches inside from side to side. Trim away excess batting at mitered corners. Hot-glue batting inside cornice near edge.

2. From striped fabric, cut two 9½-inch x 12½-inch pieces to cover ends and one 23½-inch x 49-inch piece to cover top and front. Press ½-inch hems in short sides.

3. Glue ½ inch of end pieces to top and front. Wrap remainder of end pieces to inside bottom and back, mitering corners and gluing to inside.

4. Pin 1½ inches of top/front fabric inside top, centering and aligning pressed edges at corners; wrap over top and down front, over bottom edge and 1½ inches up inside. Adjust pressed hems at sides as necessary. Trim any excess fabric at bottom inside front to 1½ inches. Glue fabric inside top, under hems at top and front, and to inside bottom of front.

5. Lining: From lining fabric, cut one strip 61¼ inches x 5¼ inches to line top and sides, and one strip 46½ inches x 11¼ inches to line front. Press ¼-inch hems along two short edges and one long edge of top/side lining, and along all edges of front lining. Center and pin top/side lining with pressed hem approximately 1 inch from open back of cornice. Glue in place at edges. Glue front lining in place at edges, covering raw edges of top/side lining.

6. Trim: Pin trim along ends and front of cornice ¼ inch from edge. Apply seam sealant to trim where it will be cut at ends; let dry for 30 minutes, then cut. Use fabric adhesive to glue trim to cornice; when dry, remove pins.

7. Mount angle brackets on wall; rest completed cornice on brackets. ✂

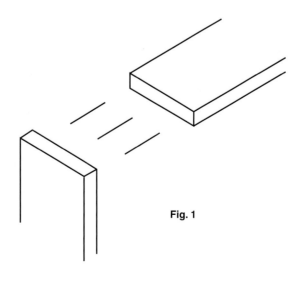

Fig. 1

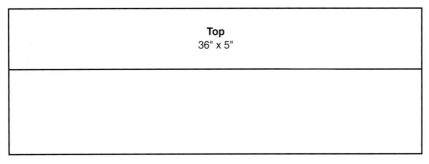

Front
12" x 12"

Top
12" x 5"

End
5" x 9"

End
5" x 9"

Top
36" x 5"

Layout Diagram

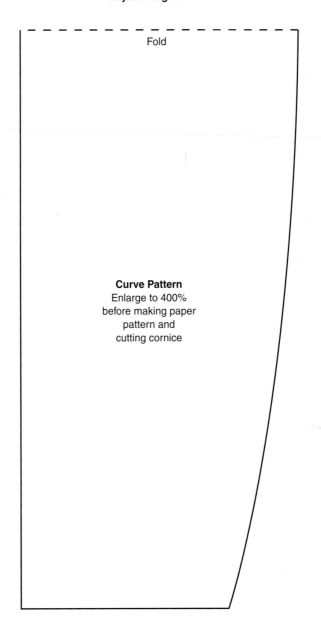

Fold

Curve Pattern
Enlarge to 400%
before making paper
pattern and
cutting cornice

Decorative Outlet & Switch Plate Covers

Let your imagination take flight as you select motifs to cover switch plates and outlet covers. Add embellishments like cord or braid for flashier results.

Designs by Carol Zentgraf

Materials
Each Piece

- Plastic or wooden switch plate or outlet cover
- Double-sided adhesive measuring 1 inch longer and 1 inch wider than cover
- Fabric the same size as double-sided adhesive
- Coordinating trims: gimp, rickrack, prepleated grosgrain ribbon (optional)
- Matching thread or narrow ribbon
- Iron-on transfer (optional)
- Coordinating paint
- Small paintbrush
- Permanent fabric adhesive

Iron-On Transfer Cover

1. Referring to manufacturer's instructions, fuse transfer to fabric.

2. Proceed with instructions for other pieces.

Other Pieces

1. Remove paper backing from one side of adhesive; adhere to wrong side of fabric.

2. Remove remaining paper backing from adhesive. Place fabric right side down on flat surface. Center front of plate to be covered on adhesive; use fingers to press in place smoothly and firmly. Wrap edges to back of plate; press in place.

3. Referring to photo throughout, glue trims to covers:

Plaid cover—Glue rickrack around edges.

Bugs cover—Glue bound edge of prepleated ribbon to back edges.

Grapes cover—Lay gimp trim diagonally across corners and glue ends to back of cover.

Silk cover—Glue cord around edges, securing ends with matching thread or narrow ribbon at lower right corner; unravel and fluff ends, trimming as desired.

4. Paint heads of screws to match or complement cover. ✂

Fall Harvest Pumpkins

Fabric bandannas and soft foam balls combine to make a wonderful tribute to nature. Great for fall celebrations or year-round decor, your family will love this easy-to-make project.

Designs by Bev Shenefield

Materials
- Child's foam balls: 4-inch and 8-inch
- Fabrics or bandannas: assorted oranges, dark greens
- Batting
- Assorted flat orange buttons, ½ inch and larger
- Heavy cord
- Large-eye needle
- Tapestry needle
- White crochet cotton

- Rust sewing thread
- 14-inch double-ended crochet hook
- Size F crochet hook
- Pinking shears
- Wooden twig, about ½ inch in diameter
- Pruning shears or craft clippers
- Craft glue
- Fabric glue
- Jewel glue
- Raffia: terra-cotta and basil

Large Pumpkin
1. Cut 22-inch square orange fabric or bandanna. Find center of square. Use tapestry needle and one strand of cord to fasten button to center of fabric on outside. This will be bottom of pumpkin.
2. Tie ends of cord to one end of double-ended hook. Force other end through center of 8-inch ball. Bring it out on the other side, pulling cord through as close to center as possible. (Hitting the exact center isn't necessary; just get as close as you can. Most real pumpkins aren't perfect, either!)

3. Cut cord from crochet hook. String each end of cord through larger button; tie once and push button as far into ball as possible, pulling tightly on cord. When satisfied, continue tying knot. This will be top of pumpkin.

4. Stem: Cut branch to desired length. Apply craft glue in center of button on top. Place larger end of branch on glue; let dry completely.

5. Measure enough terra-cotta raffia to go around pumpkin four times, allowing for extra to tie at the top and go around button. Wrap fabric up around pumpkin, then wrap raffia once around pumpkin, passing it under bottom button and pulling it as tightly as possible; tie in a knot. Wrap raffia around pumpkin three more times to make a total of eight segments. Adjust fabric until satisfied, then tie the terra-cotta raffia around stem.

6. Referring to patterns, use pinking shears to cut two of each larger leaf shape from green bandanna; cut two of each shape from batting, cutting ⅛ inch smaller all around. Using fabric glue, glue matching batting pieces together in layers. Sandwich batting between corresponding fabric leaves; glue fabric leaves together around edges, enclosing batting.

7. Using white crochet thread and large-eye needle, sew running stitch around edges of leaves; add veins with long straight stitches.

8. Turn back edges of fabric around pumpkin stem; glue in place with fabric glue, trimming excess fabric as needed. Glue leaves to pumpkin around stem; pin in place to hold until dry. Glue on buttons as desired with jewel glue. Hold several lengths of basil raffia together; tie around stem in a bow.

Small Pumpkin

Follow instructions as for large pumpkin, except cut 15-inch circle from orange fabric or bandanna; substitute size F crochet hook for double-ended hook; use smaller patterns for leaves and cut leaves from green fabric; sew around leaf edges and add veins with rust thread and hand-sewing needle. ✄

Don't Skimp

When it comes to planning your window treatment, it's important to plan on enough fullness to give your finished results a professional look. Generally the fullness should be 1½ to 3 times the length of the rod.

Equally important is the treatment length. A floor-length panel should be ½ inch above the floor, and a windowsill-length treatment should either stop ½ inch above the sill or extend several inches below. Also allow for a 2- to 4-inch doubled hem—proportionate to the treatment length—when planning the window panel length.

Determining Length

A rod pocket with a header is an easy-to-make hanging treatment and is suitable for valances, curtains and draperies. Rod pockets can be made with or without a header above the pocket.

The depth of the rod pocket is determined by the drapery rod size, plus an ease allowance so the fabric will slide easily across the rod.

Measure for Depth

To determine the depth, add 1–2 inches to the diameter of a round rod, or ½–1 inch to the width of a flat rod. Use the smaller allowance for small rods, increasing it with the size of the rod.

Adding a Header

If you want to add a header above the rod pocket, consider the style and size of the window treatment. A 1- to 2-inch header is standard for most valances and basic panels, but you can make it up to 4 inches deep for large windows or very full gathered curtains.

Panel Length

To figure the cut panel length, double the determined rod pocket depth or the total rod pocket/header depth and add 1 inch. Add this measurement, plus the hem allowance to the panel body length (Fig. 1).

Making Rod Pockets

1. For each panel, fuse ½-inch single hem along the upper edge. If the fabric is soft, fuse a strip of interfacing to the wrong side of the header.

2. Press the upper edge under the combined header and rod pocket depth, plus ½ inch. Pin or use basting tape to secure the hemmed edge to the panel wrong side. Use chalk to mark the header depth for the rod pocket upper stitching line. Draw a parallel line to mark the rod pocket lower stitching line (Fig. 2).

3. Stitch along the marked rod pocket lines; the hemmed edge should be ½ inch below the lower stitching line.

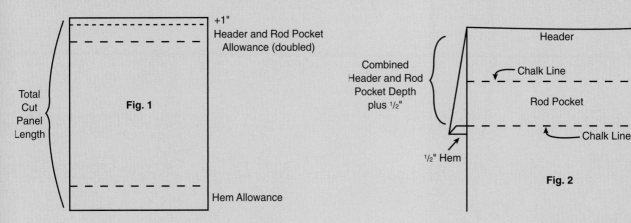

+1"
Header and Rod Pocket Allowance (doubled)

Total Cut Panel Length

Fig. 1

Hem Allowance

Combined Header and Rod Pocket Depth plus ½"

½" Hem

Header

Chalk Line

Rod Pocket

Chalk Line

Fig. 2

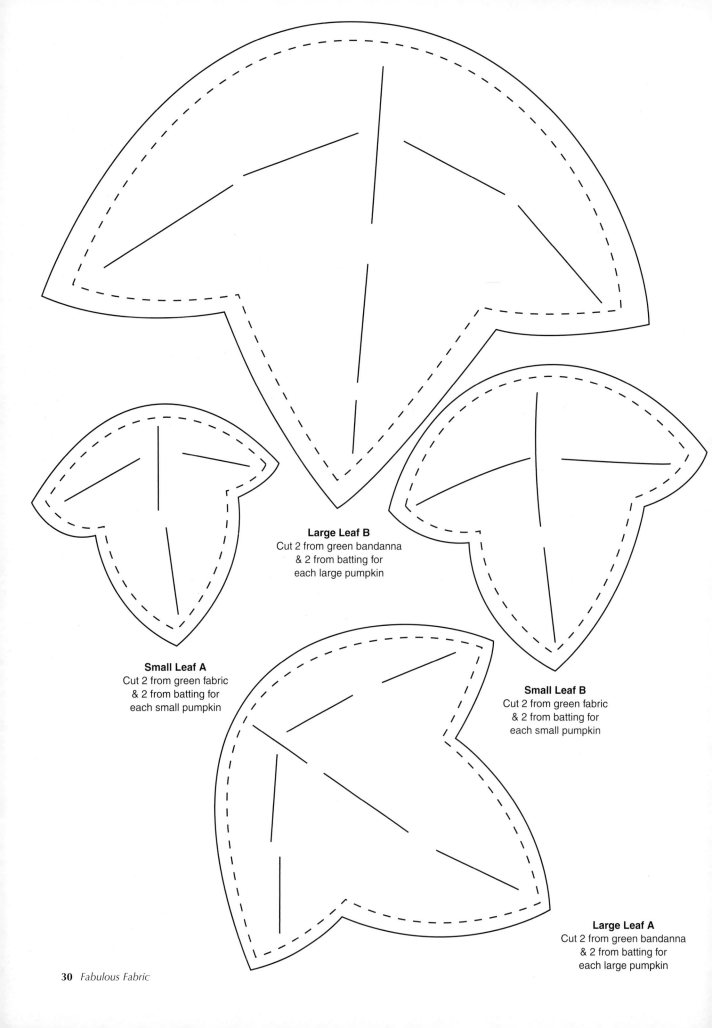

Large Leaf B
Cut 2 from green bandanna
& 2 from batting for
each large pumpkin

Small Leaf A
Cut 2 from green fabric
& 2 from batting for
each small pumpkin

Small Leaf B
Cut 2 from green fabric
& 2 from batting for
each small pumpkin

Large Leaf A
Cut 2 from green bandanna
& 2 from batting for
each large pumpkin

raw end, glue fabric band around edge of box lid.

Medium Box

1. Cover bottom of box with leaf-print fabric as in step 1 for large box.

2. From leaf print and black fabrics, cut a strip 1 inch longer than box's circumference, and 1 inch wider than depth of box side from top to bottom. Following manufacturer's instructions, apply fusible web to wrong side of leaf print. About halfway into strip, trim along top edges of leaves to give the illusion of a pile of leaves. Matching straight edges, fuse trimmed leaf strip to right side of black strip.

3. Press under ½-inch hem along one end and bottom straight edge of fused fabric. Apply bead of glue along bottom edge of box. Press hemmed edge of strip along bottom of box, overlapping raw end with hemmed end; glue hemmed end in place. Apply a bead of glue inside box along upper edge; fold excess fabric over to inside, and press to glue fabric edge in place.

4. Cover and line lid and box with black fabric as for large box.

Small Box

1. Apply fusible web to wrong side of leaf-print fabric; cut eight or nine leaf shapes from fused fabric—three for the top and five or six for bottom edge.

2. Cover and line box and lid with black fabric as for large box, fusing three complete leaves onto black fabric circle for top of lid, and fusing remaining leaves—including some cut in half to give the illusion of falling—evenly spaced to strip for covering sides of box. ✂

Tab Talk

Hanging tabs look best when they're used on flat window treatments or treatments that are gathered only 1½–2 times the window width; the tab effect is lost on very gathered edges. You can make the hanging tabs from matching fabric, wide ribbon or cord.

To determine the cut length of the fabric panels, install the rod so the upper edge of the panels will be at least 2 inches above the window frame. This prevents light from the window from showing above the panels.

Tab Size

For each cut fabric panel, also cut a 6-inch-deep facing equal to the panel upper edge. Fuse a ½-inch doubled hem on one long edge of each facing piece.

Keep the tab size in proportion to the panel size and style. To determine the cut length for the tabs, wrap a fabric scrap loosely around the rod and pin it to the panel. Make sure the tab slides easily; adjust the fit as needed. Mark the determined tab length on the fabric scrap and remove it from the rod and panel. Measure the tab length on the scrap and add 1 inch for seam allowances (Fig. 1).

Tab spacing depends on the look you want to achieve. If the tabs are spaced far apart, the panels will have a drooping or draping effect. Closely spaced tabs will result in a straight edge.

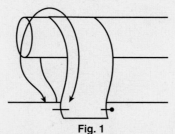
Fig. 1
Measure tab and add 1" to seam allowance.

Making Hanging Tabs

To make and attach hanging tabs:

1. For each tab, cut two fabric strips in the desired width plus 1 inch for seam allowances by determined length.

2. Fuse long edges together. Trim seam allowances. Turn tabs right side out and press.

3. Fold each tab in half and use double-sided basting tape to baste raw edges together. This prevents them from shifting when fusing them to the panel.

4. Space tabs evenly on the right side of one panel, aligning raw edges. Begin and end ¾ inch from the ends of the panel. Baste the tab edges in place (Fig. 2).

5. With right sides together and raw edges even, fuse the facing in place. Turn the facing to the wrong side of the panel and press the edge.

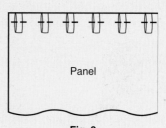
Fig. 2
Baste tabs to panel.

Seams & Edges

Sometimes a plain seam just won't do. Trims, cord and welting add a designer touch, whether they're sewn into the seam or fused onto the surface.

On the Edge

Edge finishes for home decor projects vary widely. You can choose an unembellished single or doubled hem, a hem embellished with fringe or other trims with a header, a bound edge, corded edge or decoratively cut edge.

Rose-Covered Memory Box

Felt has never been prettier than these beautiful roses adorning this fabric-covered memory box. Create this to match your personal home decor and style.

Design by Mary Cosgrove

Materials

- Papier-mâché heart-shaped box 8¾ inches x 8 inches x 3⅝ inches
- 2 (36-inch x 5-inch) strips yellow print fabric
- Felt: 2 sheets hunter green, 1 sheet each ruby and deep rose
- Mello yellow acrylic craft paint
- 1 yard wine ⅞-inch chenille gimp
- 18-inch strand 3mm gold pearls
- Stencil sponge
- Glue

Instructions

1. Using stencil sponge and a pouncing technique, cover inside of box lid with an even, opaque coat of yellow paint; let dry. Paint exterior of box in the same manner; let dry.

2. Trace around bottom of box onto hunter green felt; cut out heart shape. Repeat with second piece of green felt. Reserve felt scraps.

3. Starting at back of heart, glue fabric strip along side of box, leaving ¼ inch of fabric protruding beyond bottom edge and ½ inch protruding beyond top edge. When you reach back of box, overlap ends about ½ inch and trim off excess; fold under top end ¼ inch and glue in place. Fold over protruding edges of fabric and glue to box bottom and along inside top edge.

4. Fold under long edges of second fabric strip to fit along sides inside box; glue fabric in place, lining box and concealing edge of first strip.

5. Glue one felt heart to bottom of box. Test fit of second heart inside box; trim as needed and glue in place in bottom of box.

6. Cut gimp trim to fit around rim edge of lid (30 inches for this size box). Starting at back of box, glue gimp to lid, folding end under ¼ inch and overlapping ends at back of box.

7. Roses: Cut three 6-inch x 1-inch strips each of deep rose and ruby felt for small roses and a 12-inch x 2-inch strip each from deep rose and ruby felt for large roses. Run bead of glue along bottom edge of strip. Wrap strip in a circle, pinching bottom edges together to secure. Fold under some of the top edges to form looser petals as desired. Repeat to make rose from each felt strip. On some roses, add glue to the bottom as you shape the petals around the rose to make a more open blossom.

8. Glue bottoms of large roses in center of box lid as shown. Glue small roses as shown, about 1 inch from edge of box and leaving about 1 inch between small roses, starting at top of box and working toward front (point of heart).

9. Trace and cut nine leaves from hunter green scraps. Tack ends only of leaves to lid with glue, leaving centers slightly elevated. Glue two leaves behind large roses; glue remaining leaves between small roses as shown.

10. Tack gold pearls randomly over leaves as shown. ✂

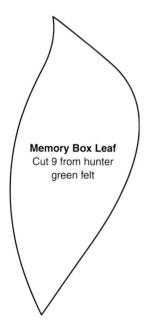

Memory Box Leaf
Cut 9 from hunter
green felt

The Bottom Line on Hems

Use a single hem for fabrics that are too bulky or heavy for doubled hems, or for non-fraying fabrics with a smoothly cut edge. Use fusible web or adhesive tape in the same width as the desired hem depth.

Fuse the tape to the wrong side of the fabric lower edge, leaving the paper backing in place. Press the hem to the wrong side along the edge of the tape. Remove the backing and fuse in place.

Narrow Doubled Hems

For some projects, such as table linens, ruffles and sheer or slippery fabrics, a narrow doubled hem has the nicest finished appearance and is easy to achieve.

Fuse ½-inch-wide adhesive or web tape ¼ inch from the edge to be hemmed. With the paper backing still in place, press the fabric edge onto the tape, then fold at the edge and press again to create the doubled hem. Open the folds to remove the tape. Carefully refold and press the hem in place.

Deeper Doubled Hems

For larger projects, a doubled hem that's 1–2 inches deep usually looks best, depending on the size of the project.

To make the doubled hem, press the desired hem depth to the wrong side. Fuse adhesive or web tape along the folded edge on the inside of the project.

With the paper backing still in place, press the entire hem depth to the wrong side again. Remove the backing and fuse the edge in place.

Home Office Ensemble

Livening up your home office space is simple when you create and personalize your own desk set. Add embellishments to coordinate with the room or have fun and go for a completely new look.

Designs by Carol Zentgraf

Materials

Blotter
- 54-inch-wide home decor fabrics: ¾ yard each of two coordinating prints
- Foam core board: 19-inch x 25-inch piece ¼-inch-thick; two 5-inch x 19-inch pieces ½-inch-thick
- 10-inch x 19-inch piece batting
- ⅝-inch-wide fusible adhesive tape
- Permanent fabric adhesive

Memo Board
- 54-inch-wide home decor fabrics: ¾ yard each of two coordinating prints
- Foam core board: 16-inch x 20-inch piece ½-inch-thick; 17-inch x 21-inch piece ¼-inch-thick
- 16-inch x 29-inch piece batting
- 5 yards ⅜-inch-wide coordinating satin ribbon
- 13 upholstery tacks
- Staple gun
- Permanent fabric adhesive

Letter Tray
- 54-inch-wide home decor fabrics: ⅓ yard each of two coordinating prints
- 10-inch x 12-inch x 2-inch lid from a box of stationery or envelopes
- 10-inch x 14-inch piece lightweight cardboard
- Permanent fabric adhesive

Pencil Holder
- ¼ yard 54-inch-wide home decor fabric
- ¼-inch-thick foam core board: 2 (3-inch x 4½-inch) pieces for front and back; 2 (2½-inch x 4½-inch) pieces for sides; 3½-inch square for bottom.
- 10-inch piece 2½-inch-long bullion fringe
- Permanent fabric adhesive

Blotter

1. From one fabric, cut two 20-inch x 26-inch pieces for front and back. From remaining fabric, cut two 14-inch x 25-inch pieces for padded sides.

2. Blotter front: Center one piece of fabric around ¼-inch-thick foam core board; glue to edges at back of board.

3. Padded sides: For each, glue edges of batting strip to top of ½-inch-thick foam core board piece. Place fabric wrong side up on flat surface, then place foam core board batting side down on fabric, centered between long edges and 6 inches from one short edge. Wrap the 6 inches of fabric over the board and glue edges in place (Fig. 1).

4. To attach right side piece, turn board over and place on the right edge with covered side pad edge toward center. Align the upper, lower and outside edges of the two boards with the excess fabric toward outside. Wrap fabric side edge to back of blotter and glue in place. Repeat for upper and lower fabric edges. Reverse and repeat to attach left side edge.

5. To finish back, use fusible tape to hem edges on back piece of fabric in a single hem. Glue fabric edges to back of blotter.

Memo Board

1. To cover base board, cut one 23-inch x 27-inch piece fabric. Center ¼-inch-thick foam core board on wrong side of fabric. Wrap fabric edges to the front, folding neatly at corners; glue edges in place.

2. Memo board: Glue batting to ½-inch-thick foam core board along edges. Cut 20-inch x 24-inch piece of second fabric and wrap it over the padded side of the board, gluing edges to back of board.

3. Referring to photo throughout, begin in center and cut ribbon strips long enough to cross board diagonally each way and wrap around the edges to back with a 2-inch overlap. Plan five rows each way with approximately 4½ inches between rows. Wrap ribbon lengths across board; staple ends to back.

4. Dip point of each tack in adhesive; press into board at ribbon intersection.

5. Glue memo board to center of base with covered side of base in back.

Letter Tray

1. From one fabric, cut one strip 6 inches x 36 inches for sides and back; two strips 3 inches x 11 inches for front and front facing; and one piece 11 inches x 13 inches for bottom. From second fabric, cut one piece 11 inches x 13 inches for tray surface.

2. Referring to photo throughout, cut a 6½-inch x 1-inch curved cutout in center of one box lid short edge; this will be tray front.

3. Center the 6-inch x 36-inch fabric strip over upper edge of lid sides and back with ends overlapping the front corners. Wrap fabric around lid sides; glue edges in place on top and bottom of lid.

4. Trace lid front onto cardboard and cut out to make template and facing; trim as needed to fit inside front of lid. Using cardboard template, trace lid front onto fabric twice; cut out 1 inch outside traced lines.

5. Cover lid front: Turn under and fuse fabric edges even with box sides. Center fabric over front; wrap edges over top and bottom; glue all edges in place.

6. Tray bottom: Fuse edges in a single hem; glue to bottom of lid.

7. Tray top: Trim lightweight cardboard as needed to fit inside lid. Wrap remaining fabric over cardboard; glue edges in back. Glue covered piece inside lid.

Pencil Holder

1. Construct pencil holder: glue foam core board side pieces between front and back, aligning edges.

2. Cut fabric: Cut two pieces 3 inches x 9½ inches for sides; two pieces 5 inches x 9½ inches for front and back; and two 5-inch squares for base. Glue 3-inch x 9½-inch pieces centered over sides of holder, overlapping ends inside bottom edge.

3. Press under and glue a ½-inch hem along each long edge of front and back fabric pieces. Glue to front and back of holder with edges overlapping sides and ends overlapping inside lower edge.

4. Wrap one piece of fabric over base foam core piece; glue ends in back. Press under and glue all edges of remaining fabric piece to make a 3¼-inch square; glue to bottom of base, covering edges of first fabric piece.

5. Center and glue holder to covered base.

6. Glue fringe around top of holder, overlapping ends. ✂

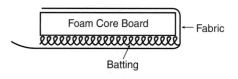

Fig. 1

Blue Leather Adornments

This trendy set is the perfect way to modernize your home. Wire and leather give each piece an upbeat look in keeping with today's styles.

Designs by Barbara Matthiessen

Materials

Each Design

- Bag of leather trimmings including lots of blues, purples and black
- Leather cement
- Craft stick
- Jet black solvent ink pad
- Rubber stamps: leaf pattern, swirl border

Ball

- Black acrylic craft paint
- Small paintbrush
- 4-inch plastic foam ball
- Silver 18-gauge wire
- Wire cutters
- Needle-nose or round-nose pliers

Flowerpot

- 5-inch terra-cotta rose pot
- Black acrylic craft paint
- Small paintbrush

Candle Band

- 3-inch x 6-inch pillar candle
- Beads: 5 iridescent beads with large holes; 6 black "E" beads
- Silver 18-gauge wire
- Wire cutters
- Needle-nose or round-nose pliers
- Awl

Stamping

Work on a firm surface. Tap stamp on ink pad, then press firmly onto surface of leather without twisting or rocking. Stamp a variety of leather pieces with both stamps in this manner. Let dry for a few minutes. Stamping leather pieces in this manner will provde a subtle look.

Ball

1. Paint foam ball black; let dry.
2. Cut pieces of black leather to cover foam ball (if leather is thick, cut small pieces to conform to shape of ball); cement in place, applying and spreading cement with craft stick.
3. Cut random pieces of plain and stamped blue leather, then cement onto ball, allowing black leather to show around edges. Let dry.
4. Crisscross silver wire around ball, leaving 10 inches at top for hanger. Fold wire in half up 4 inches, then twist wires together. Form twisted wire into a ring; wrap base of ring with

2-inch wire tail. Poke end of wire down into ball next to hanger.

Flowerpot

1. Paint pot black; let dry.

2. Cut a strip of black leather to cover pot rim; cement in place.

3. From blue and purple leathers, cut rectangles of random width and almost the height of pot rim. Use at least three colors of leather, and alternate widths. Cement leather rectangles onto black leather rim.

4. From lighter blue or turquoise leather, cut a rectangle the height of the pot (4 inches). Cut and arrange black, purple and blue leather pieces on light blue rectangle; cement arrangement in place, then cement rectangle to side of pot.

Candle Band

1. Cut a 1-inch-wide strip of black leather long enough to wrap around candle with ½-inch overlap. Cement in place, cementing ends where they overlap.

2. Cut a piece of black leather in an irregular shape approximately 2 inches x 3 inches. Cut a piece of stamped blue leather in an irregular shape slightly smaller than the black piece; cement the blue piece to the black piece.

3. Using awl, randomly poke holes in irregular leather shapes for attaching pieces of wire cut 6–10 inches in length. Begin and end wires with spirals. Form spirals by tightly grasping wire with pliers, then rotating wire in a circle. Twist and bend wires in zigzag patterns; wrap around each other here and there.

4. Poke a hole near top of leather pieces and another near bottom. Thread beads onto 8 inches of wire, alternating iridescent and "E" beads and beginning and ending with "E" beads. Thread ends of wires through awl holes, then wrap and spiral wire ends.

5. Cement bead- and wire-enhanced leather piece to leather ring where ends overlap.

Note: To create small ornament, attach leftover pieces of leather to a piece of plastic foam cut in a freeform shape using the same instruction as for the large ball. Decorate as desired with scraps of wire and beads. ✂

Cutting Up

When it comes to timesaving tools for cutting perfectly straight fabric edges, a rotary cutter, cutting mat and clear plastic ruler top the list of must-have notions.

Not only does using a rotary cutter and its companion products ensure straight lines, it also enables you to cut through multiple layers of almost any fabric at once. It's also an easier way to cut silky fabrics that slide around when you cut them with scissors.

Rotary cutters are available in several blade sizes and handle styles, some with ergonomic considerations. Blades are available in straight shapes for basic cutting techniques and in several novelty shapes for cutting decorative edges (see On the Edge, page 33). The larger the blade, the more easily it will cut through multiple fabric layers.

Choose Your Mat

Cutting mats are available in sizes ranging from small craft mats to oversized mats designed for home decor and quilting projects. All mats are marked with 1-inch grids and fractions in between.

Clear plastic rulers and cutting guides are available in several widths and lengths, as well as 12-inch and 14-inch squares. They're conveniently marked in a grid to use as both a measuring guide and straight edge to roll the rotary cutter against. Many are also marked with commonly used angles.

Cutting Tips

Stand straight. For the best cut, always stand directly above the blade and hold the blade perpendicular to the mat. Working at an angle can cause an inaccurately cut edge.

Stay sharp. Change the blade of your rotary cutter on a regular basis, and be careful to avoid rolling it across pins. Small nicks or a dull blade will lead to incomplete cutting.

Using a dull blade will also force you to apply more pressure, which can damage the mat or cause your hand to slip and incorrectly cut the fabric—or your fingers.

Safety first. The rotary-cutter blade is razor sharp, especially when new. Be sure to keep your fingers away from the ruler or cutting guide edge and get in the habit of engaging the safety guard immediately after each use. Always store a rotary cutter in a high, safe place away from children.

Easy Appliqués

Fairly new on the market is a handy shape cutter with a built-in, razor-sharp blade. Use it on stabilized cotton fabric to create freeform appliqués, or with its companion templates to create shapes such as circles, stars, hearts and more.

Like a rotary cutter, the shape cutter should be used with a cutting mat.

Leather-Trimmed Boxes

If you've always been afraid to try crafting with leather, these simple no-sew boxes are for you! They're easy for crafters of all skill levels, yet they look like they took hours to complete.

Designs by Barbara Matthiessen

Materials

- Papier-mâché boxes in various sizes and shapes (samples are 8 and 2½ inches square and 7-inch x 5-inch oval)
- 2 bags of leather trimmings
- Leather cement
- Black or brown round leather lacing
- Hook-and-loop tape (optional)
- Jet black solvent ink pad
- Rubber stamps: square stripes, spiral
- Assorted large-hole beads including faux bone, wooden and silver spacers
- Rotary cutter, mat and ruler
- Rotary punch
- Bamboo skewer
- Craft stick

General Instructions

1. Cutting: Using rotary cutter, mat and ruler, cut assorted square, rectangular and triangular leather shapes. Fit and cut larger strips and pieces to cover sides and tops of boxes as desired, allowing some of box to remain visible around edges. Cut circles and curved shapes with heavy shears.

2. Stamping: Work on a firm surface. Tap stamp on ink pad, then press firmly onto surface of leather without twisting or rocking. Let dry for a few minutes.

3. Gluing: Using craft stick, spread cement across backs of top and side leather pieces; press onto sides of boxes. Position any seams down center backs of boxes. Layer and cement all pieces except those that will have buttons attached.

4. Flat leather buttons: Stack and glue assorted leathers together. Use rotary punch to punch a pair of holes through all layers, ¼ inch apart.

5. Rolled buttons: Stamp 1½-inch x ½-inch piece leather; let dry. Roll up strip around bamboo skewer; apply cement to wrong side on end, then tape to hold until cement sets.

6. Add beads, spacers, buttons, etc.: Thread lacing through large beads or through holes in leather buttons from bottom of stack to top; knot on top. Add beads, spacers, etc. to ends of lacing as desired. Tie overhand knots in ends of lacing.

7. Hinges, etc.: If desired, use leather strips to create hinges, gluing one end to side of box and remainder to lid. Create buttonholes for box closures by punching slit in one end of leather large enough to accommodate leather or bead button. Or, use button for decorative effect only and apply squares or rounds of hook-and-loop tape for closure.

Large Square Box

1. Cut 7-inch leather square for top; glue 2¾-inch-wide strip around sides. Place lid on box.

2. From contrasting leathers, cut 11-inch x 3¼-inch strip and 11-inch x 2-inch strip. Stamp larger strip with four-square pattern; glue over top and down sides of box, gluing it in place on back to form hinge; top with narrower leather strip. On front of box, cut slit in strip hinge ½ inch from front tip.

3. Cut an assortment of leather circles and squares measuring 1–1½ inches. Plan arrangement of stacks of leather shapes on top and on sides of box.

4. Punch holes in top piece of each stack; thread through lacing and attach assortment of rolled leather beads, silver spacers, faux bone and wooden beads, etc.

5. Glue stacks together; when dry, glue across top and on sides of leather strip. Glue a rolled bead with base under strip hinge on front of box so bead can go through slit.

Small Square Box

1. Cut 2-inch leather square for top; stamp with four-square pattern. Let dry, then glue to lid; glue 1-inch-wide strip around sides. Place lid on box.

2. From contrasting leather, cut 1 ¼-inch square for top; stamp with spiral pattern and let dry. Punch holes and thread through lacing. Thread on bone bead; tie to surface of leather. Thread assorted wooden beads onto ends of lacing; finish with overhand knots. Glue leather square to lid on diagonal.

3. Cut assorted small leather shapes and glue onto leather on sides of box, covering seam where ends of strip meet.

Oval Box

1. Cut 6½-inch x 4½-inch oval for top; glue 2⅛-inch-wide strip around sides. Place lid on box.

2. From contrasting leathers, cut 3¼-inch x 2⅝-inch rectangle and 2-inch square for top; cut also a 4½-inch x 2⅛-inch rectangle and a 1¾-inch square for front. Stamp both squares with four-square pattern; let dry.

3. Punch holes in squares and thread through lacing. Thread on bone bead; glue ends to back of leather squares.

4. Glue larger rectangle and square to top of lid; glue remaining rectangle and square to side over seam in leather strip. ✂

Sharp As a Tack

Upholstery tacks are ideal for adhering one or more layers of fabric to wooden surfaces and are available in a variety of metal tones and head styles. Apply them with a hammer for decorative as well as practical effects on footstools, chairs and wooden cornices.

Entertaining in Style

Bringing friends and family into your home for a special occasion or simply to get together creates one of life's more rewarding and memorable events. Make those times extra special by decorating your kitchen and dining room with unique accents to suit the occasion—from everyday trivets made with a favorite fabric to special holiday table settings with seasonal trims.

Leaf Ensemble

Serve up the delightful splendor of fall with this colorful no-sew dining set. Affordably decorate your home for the seasons with this set that uses fusible web and adhesive tape.

Designs by Judith Sandstrom

Materials

- 7 fall-print bandannas
- ¼ yard fabric in each of 5 complementary colors to coordinate with bandannas: orange, red, gold, green, brown
- Tablecloth (sample is 52-inch x 70-inch rectangular cloth made from cotton/polyester blend)
- 4 plain cream-color cotton fabric place mats
- 2½ yards paper-backed fusible web
- 8 yards ½-inch-wide fusible adhesive tape
- 1¾ yards 1½-inch-wide coordinating fabric ribbon
- ⅞-inch clip-on rings
- Black extra-fine-point permanent marker

Tablecloth & Place Mats

1. Launder and iron fabrics, and tablecloth without using fabric softener.

2. Cut 10 (9-inch x 17-inch) pieces fusible web. Following manufacturer's instructions, iron two pieces to the wrong side of each color fabric. Remove paper backing from one piece of fusible web. Trace three of each leaf pattern onto paper side of remaining piece of fusible web.

3. Pin together the two layers of like-color fabric with traced side of fusible web on top. Cut through both layers along traced lines. Unpin and remove paper backing to make a total of six of each leaf design in each color.

4. Place mat: Select one leaf of each color, choosing a variety of shapes. Arrange leaves in center of place mat, touching but not overlapping, as shown in photo, and arranging leaves

differently on each place mat. Fuse leaves permanently in place following manufacturer's instructions.

5. Center of tablecloth: Select two leaves of each color, choosing a variety of shapes, for a total of 10 leaves. Arrange in center of tablecloth as desired; fuse permanently in place.

6. Divide remaining leaves into two equal piles. Measure each long side of tablecloth; mark center with a pin. Arrange half the leaves as desired along edge on one side; fuse permanently in place. Repeat with remaining leaves on other side. (You may have a few leaves leftover.)

Valance

1. Launder three bandannas without using fabric softener; iron, pressing edges so that they lie flat. Place bandannas side by side; try to position them so that motifs align as much as possible.

2. On center bandanna, iron a piece of fusible tape down both side edges on right side of fabric. Remove paper backing. Lay bandanna for right end of valance on top of center bandanna, right sides facing and edges even; fuse bandannas together along right edge only. Open up and press seam toward right. Repeat with bandanna for left end of valance, fusing them together along left edge of center bandanna; press seam toward left.

3. Hem side edges of valance: Iron a piece of fusible tape to wrong side along edge of each side bandanna. Remove paper backing; fold over fabric edge along tape and fuse.

4. Hem bottom of valance: Iron a piece of fusible tape to wrong side of valance along bottom edge. Remove paper backing; fold edge up 1½ inches and fuse.

5. Iron fusible tape to right side of top edge. Remove paper backing. Measure across valance top. Cut a piece of 1½-inch-wide ribbon and another piece of fusible tape that length; fuse tape to wrong side of ribbon along one edge; do not remove paper backing.

6. Place wrong side of ribbon edge without fusible tape over right side of valance top so that ribbon just covers tape on valance; fuse. Remove paper backing from ribbon edge. Fold ribbon over to wrong side of valance and fuse into place, forming a stiffened edge for valance (see photo below).

7. Squeeze clip-on rings onto valance approximately 5 inches apart. Hang valance on narrow decorative rod. Use four bandannas for napkins. Pinch in center of bandanna and pull through napkin rings to set table.✂

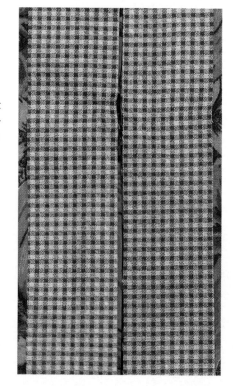

Leaf Ensemble
Cut 6 of each variety
from each color

Autumn Twist Table Covering

Celebrate the spirit of autumn by sponge-painting a fabulous leaf motif on a purchased tablecloth. This is a simple way to add seasonal accents to your home.

Design by Annie Lang

Materials

- 60-inch round flannel-backed plastic tablecloth
- DecorArt outdoor paints: pansy purple, pinecone brown, sprout green, tiger lily orange
- Paintbrushes: #10 round, #0 liner, #10 flat shader
- 4-inch x 5-inch piece compressed sponge
- Gold leafing pen
- Coated paper or plastic foam disposable plates

Instructions

1. Referring to instructions for Using Transfer & Graphite Paper in the General Instructions (page 174), transfer pattern for leaf onto compressed sponge; cut out.

2. Measure and mark a line around tablecloth 6 inches from hem. Measure and mark a second line around tablecloth 16 inches from first line.

3. Pour puddle of orange paint onto one plate and green on another. Dip sponge leaf into orange; work paint into sponge by tapping it up and down on palette. Dip leaf tip only into green; work color into sponge. Positioning sponge along inner line, press gently and then lift it straight up to create multicolored leaf.

4. Repeat to sponge leaves all around tablecloth, leaving ½ inch between leaves and making all leaves go in the same direction. If leaves start to look "muddy," wash out sponge and reload with fresh color.

5. Referring to Leaf Painting Diagram throughout, repeat to sponge leaves around outer line, making them go in the opposite direction and staggering each leaf to follow both above and below line.

6. Using flat brush, paint lines between leaves with brown: Lay brush on side edge and "squiggle" loaded brush along line, giving it the look of a tree branch.

7. Load liner with green; paint squiggly, curly vines along branches, making sure they follow in same direction as leaves.

8. Using tip of round brush, dot large purple berries here and there as desired between painted vines and leaves.

9. When paints have dried, outline each leaf with gold leafing pen. ✄

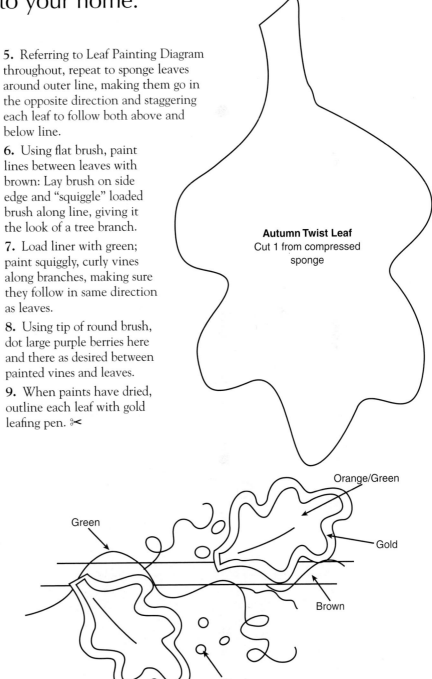

Autumn Twist Leaf
Cut 1 from compressed sponge

Green

Orange/Green

Gold

Brown

Purple

Reversible Place Mats

No-sew crafting has never looked so fancy. With so many fabric choices available, you can make mats to coordinate with any decor or occasion.

Designs by Marian Shenk

Materials
Set of Two

- 2 purchased preprinted fabric place mats
- Complementary fabrics: ½ yard each solid color and print
- 2½ yards gold braid trim
- Aerosol cement
- Fabric adhesive

Instructions

1. From solid fabric, cut one piece the same size as place mat. Turn under all edges ¼ inch on solid fabric and place mat; press.

2. Spray cement on the wrong side of solid-color fabric; lay place mat on top, wrong sides facing, and smooth out all wrinkles.

3. Using fabric adhesive, glue outer edges together; let dry, then press.

4. Measure length and width of place mat. Subtract 2 inches from each dimension and cut a rectangle to match that measurement from print fabric. Use spray cement to glue rectangle in center of place mat on solid side, smoothing as you go.

5. Use fabric adhesive to glue gold braid around rectangle to conceal raw edge.

6. Repeat steps 1–5 to make second place mat. ✄

Bias Bonanza

The fabric bias is the 45-degree angle between the two grains. Pieces cut on the bias will stretch, making bias-cut strips ideal for covering cording.

No-Sew Fabric Trivets

Add a decorative yet functional touch to your dinner table with classic trivets made from mat board and fabric. Tacky glue and batting give these projects their delicate, quilted look.

Designs by Janice McKee

Materials

Nine-Patch Trivet
- Stiff mat board: 6-inch and 9 (2-inch) squares
- Cotton batting: 6-inch and 9 (2-inch) squares
- 3-inch square of each of 9 black cotton prints
- 8-inch square of black cotton print fabric
- Tacky glue

Stamped Trivet
- Stiff mat board
- Cotton batting
- Cotton fabrics: 8-inch square solid black plus scraps of complementary gray, black and beige
- Tacky glue
- Rubber stamps: chives and vine
- Black permanent ink
- Small flat paintbrush

Nine-Patch Trivet

1. Glue 2-inch batting square on top of each 2-inch square of mat board; let dry.

2. Cover batting–mat-board squares: Lay square batting side down on wrong side of a 3-inch print cotton square. Fold excess fabric smoothly over to wrong side (mat board) of square and glue fabric edges to mat board, finishing corners neatly. Let dry. Repeat with remaining squares.

3. Repeat steps 1 and 2 with 6-inch squares of mat board and batting, and 8-inch fabric square.

4. Glue 2-inch squares to 6-inch square in nine-patch pattern, wrong sides facing; let dry.

Stamped Trivet

1. Cut 6-inch square from batting and mat board; glue batting on top of mat board; let dry.

2. Cover batting–mat-board square: Lay square batting side down on wrong side of 8-inch black cotton square. Fold excess fabric smoothly over to wrong side (mat board) of square and glue fabric edges to mat board, finishing corners neatly. Let dry.

3. Referring to patterns, cut four triangles A, one square B and four triangles C from mat board; cut matching pieces from batting. Glue each piece batting to matching piece of mat board.

4. Cover batting–mat-board pieces: Lay triangle A batting side down on wrong side of gray fabric; cut around shape adding ½ inch on all sides. Fold excess fabric smoothly over to wrong side (mat board) of shape and glue fabric edges to mat board, finishing corners neatly. Let dry. Repeat with remaining triangles A.

5. Repeat step 4 to cover square B with beige fabric and triangles C with black fabric.

6. Referring to photo, stamp chives in center of beige square and vines in gray triangles A as shown using black permanent ink. Use small paintbrush to apply light strokes of ink around chives.

7. Glue stamped pieces to 6-inch backing piece, wrong sides facing. Let dry. ✂

Stamp Smarts

- When selecting a stamp for a fabric project, keep the fabric texture and weave in mind.

A stamp with a large design area can be attractive on a slightly textured or loosely woven fabric, but a smaller stamp or one with a detailed design is best used on a tightly woven fabric with a smooth surface.

- Use rubber, foam or clear polymer stamps on fabric. Clear stamps are especially designed for fabric and make it easy to see the placement of your design.

Selecting Paints & Inks

It's best to use paints and inks specifically formulated for textiles to paint, stencil or stamp your fabric. These products provide good coverage without stiffening the fabric, and are permanent after heat-setting.

- If you want to use acrylic paints, add textile medium following manufacturer's instructions.

- Colors of the same brand of both paint and ink can be mixed to create new colors.

- Fabric paint is thicker than ink. The opacity and thickness of the paint varies among brands. Thicker paints adhere best to stamps, while thinner paints are easier to brush on.

- Fabric inks are used with ink pads. They are available in pre-inked pads as well as bottled inks to be used with blank ink pads.

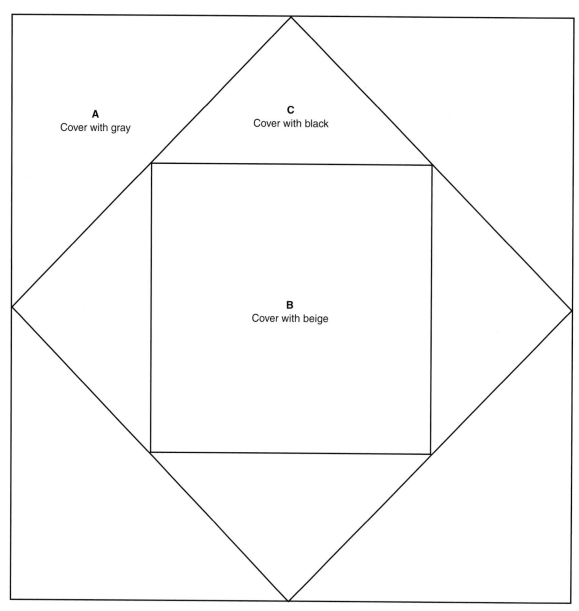

A
Cover with gray

C
Cover with black

B
Cover with beige

Stamped Trivet

Stamping a Design

1. Wash and dry washable fabrics to remove any sizing.

2. Place the fabric flat on a paper-covered, smooth, hard surface.

3. To stamp with paint, pour fabric paint into a small container tray. Use a brush or a small roller intended for fabric paint to apply a thin, even coat of paint to the stamp surface. Check to make sure there is no excess paint in crevices or along the edges, removing any if necessary. Press the stamp firmly onto the fabric, then lift straight up without sliding the stamp.

4. To stamp with ink, press the stamp onto the ink pad, then press it onto the fabric. Lift the stamp straight up without sliding.

5. Let stamped design dry for 24–48 hours. Follow paint or ink manufacturer's instructions to heat-set the design.

Burgundy Satin Table Ornament

Beads and flowers add a classy touch to this accent piece. Match this ornament with fresh flowers for an elegant coordinated look for your dinner table.

Design by Janice McKee

Materials

- Stiff mat board
- ¼ yard burgundy embroidered satin fabric
- ¼ yard cotton batting
- 2½ yards ¼-inch-wide burgundy satin ribbon
- 10 yards fine decorative gold cord
- Assorted burgundy, metallic and luster beads
- Assorted silk flowers, leaves and berries
- Hot-glue gun
- Tacky glue
- Glue stick
- Masking tape

Instructions

1. Cut four 4-inch squares from mat board and from batting; glue one piece batting to each mat-board square.

2. Cover batting–mat-board squares: Lay square batting side down on wrong side of satin. Cut around square adding 1 inch on all sides. Fold excess fabric smoothly over to wrong side (mat board) of square and glue or tape fabric edges to mat board, finishing corners neatly. Repeat with remaining squares.

3. Hot-glue fabric-covered squares together along edges to form sides of box, holding pieces together tightly to achieve a good bond and working as neatly as possible.

4. Measure box to get dimensions for box top and bottom; cut squares of mat board and batting to fit. Referring to steps 1 and 2, assemble and cover squares.

5. Cut eight 6-inch pieces of ribbon; glue them down each side of each corner of open-ended box, gluing or taping raw ends inside box.

6. Cut several 7-inch lengths gold cord for each corner of box; knot together in the middle. Glue knots

inside corners at top of box.

7. Thread various burgundy, metallic and luster beads onto another strand of gold cord as desired to hang down from each corner of box, leaving a tail long enough to glue inside box and allow ¼ inch between top of box and beads; attach at each corner.

8. Hot-glue box top and bottom onto box, weighting as necessary to achieve a good bond.

9. Cut two 17-inch pieces burgundy ribbon. Glue one around top of box just below lid, covering knots of cord. Glue other piece around bottom of box. Hot-glue silk flowers, leaves and berries on top of box. ✄

Treasure Balls

Have a party and delight your guests as they discover the hidden treasures in these exquisite Victorian handcrafts. Variations in fabric motifs make this simple project appropriate for a variety of occasions.

Designs by Samantha McNesby

Materials
Each Ball

- ¼ yard 45-inch-wide fabric
- Ribbon: 1 yard narrow ribbon or cord for wrapping around ball, 1 yard wider ribbon for topper
- Small treasures to fill ball: candies, buttons, charms, stickers, jewelry, hair accessories, etc.
- Hot-glue gun or thick white craft glue

Project Notes

Read entire general instructions before beginning. Refer to directions that follow for suggestions for materials and toppers for individual designs.

1. Cutting across the width of the fabric, cut two 4-inch strips and one 1-inch strip.

2. Choose a variety of small items to enclose in treasure ball (see specific instructions that follow).

3. Wrap ball: Begin with largest treasure; lay it at one end of a 4-inch strip of fabric. Fold fabric over item and begin rolling it into a ball. Add small items as you wrap, placing them so as to maintain the ball shape. When you reach the end of the first fabric strip, place the ball on the end of the second 4-inch strip and resume rolling and adding treasures to the ball.

4. Finish ball: Wrap ball with 1-inch strip of fabric, tucking in any loose ends. When you reach the end of the strip, tuck it under one of the previous wraps to hold it securely.

5. Ribbon trim: Wrap the completed ball with narrow ribbon. Choose the top of the ball and leave a 3-inch ribbon tail. Wrap ribbon around the ball once and knot it at the top. Repeat until entire ball is wrapped (about four times total). Do not trim tails, as you will use them to attach the topper.

6. Topper: Follow the instructions for individual designs to make the topper; attach to ball with the tails of narrow ribbon left from step 5. Or, glue topper in place with hot glue or thick white craft glue.

Sports/Soccer Ball

Materials: All-over sport-print fabric with red background; ⅛-inch green satin cord for wrapping; 1½-inch wire-edge blue satin ribbon and 1¼-inch soccer ball or other miniature sports ball for topper

Treasures: Candy, stickers, small stamps, buttons, pins, whistle, small stopwatch

Topper: Fold blue satin ribbon accordion-style into 5-inch folds. Tie folded ribbon to top of treasure ball using tails of green cord. Knot cord tightly, then fluff out ribbon folds with your fingers. Glue mini soccer ball in center of bow.

Traditional Victorian Treasure Ball

Materials: All-over small floral print fabric with pale pink background; ⅛-inch ivory satin ribbon with flowers for wrapping; 1½-inch ivory shantung ribbon and 3 (¾-inch) pink rosebuds with wire stems for topper

Treasures: Vintage jewelry, gift certificates, pretty mint or candy tins, stickers, buttons, charms

Topper: Fold shantung ribbon accordion-style into 5-inch folds. Tie folded ribbon to top of treasure ball using tails of ivory flowered ribbon. Knot ribbon ends tightly, then fluff out ribbon folds with your fingers. Twist rosebud stems together and tuck into bow. ✄

Lace Candle Mats

These elegant ribbon-and-lace-adorned mats look fabulous as candle centerpieces. Premade doilies make this project a snap to complete.

Designs by Marian Shenk

Materials

Round Candle Mat

- 11-inch round lace doily
- Fabric: 14-inch circle pink moire; ¼ yard off-white fabric for backing
- 1½ yards 1½-inch to 2-inch-wide off-white lace for border
- Ribbon: ¼-inch-wide pink; ⅛-inch-wide deep rose

Oval Candle Mat

- 14-inch x 8-inch oval lace doily
- Fabric: 12-inch x 18-inch off-white brocade; ¼ yard off-white fabric for backing
- 2 yards 1½-inch to 2-inch-wide off-white lace for border
- Ribbon: ¼-inch-wide lavender; ⅛-inch-wide purple

Each Candle Mat

- Aerosol cement
- Fabric adhesive
- 2-inch-wide strips fusible adhesive

Round Candle Mat

1. Weave pink and deep rose ribbons around round doily through openings in designs. On sample, pink ribbon is woven around center; the narrower deep rose ribbon is woven around design closer to edge.

2. Spray wrong side of doily with aerosol cement; place on top of pink moire; press in place.

3. Trim edges of pink circle evenly all around, trimming about 2 inches from outside edge of doily.

4. Iron 2-inch-wide strips of adhesive around outer edges of candle mat. Peel off paper backing.

5. Pin border lace around edge of fabric over adhesive strips, easing along the inner edge and stretching outer edge. Fuse in place.

6. Cut backing fabric ½ inch larger all around than mat; turn under edge of backing ½ inch and press so that edges of top and backing match.

7. Lay mat top and backing together wrong sides facing; squeeze fabric adhesive between layers and press together with fingers. Let dry completely; press.

Oval Candle Mat

1. Weave lavender and purple ribbons around oval doily through openings in designs. On sample, lavender ribbon is woven around center; the narrower purple ribbon is woven around design closer to edge. Also weave lavender and purple ribbon through openings in 2-inch-wide border lace.

2. Repeat steps 2–7 for round candle mat, substituting materials for oval candle mat. ✄

Floral Motif Kitchen Set

Beads and a variation on floral designs will brighten any kitchen. Decorating with handcrafted projects is the perfect way to personalize your home.

Designs by Mary Ayres and Linda Wyszynski

Materials

Apron & Dish Towel
- White apron
- White dish towel
- Cotton fabrics: ⅛ yard each blue print and green solid
- Bright blue embroidery floss
- Hand-sewing needle
- 2 (¾-inch) flat pink buttons
- Heavy-duty iron-on adhesive

Beaded Valance
- Pale yellow chintz window topper 16 inches x desired length
- Violet rubber stamp
- Brushable fabric paints: black, cornflower, grape, holiday green, royal blue, white
- Painting sponges
- #4 shader fabric-painting brush
- 3 packages royal beaded fringe trim
- Waxed paper
- Scrap fabric

Project Note
Launder and dry apron, dish towel and all fabrics without fabric softener as directed on care tag; press as needed.

Apron
1. Flower: Cut 4-inch x 5-inch piece iron-on adhesive for leaves and 5-inch x 10-inch piece for petals. Following manufacturer's instructions, fuse smaller piece to wrong side of green fabric and large piece to wrong side of blue print. Referring to pattern, cut five petals from blue print and two leaves from green.
2. Peel paper backing from pieces and position on center front of apron; fuse in place.
3. Using 3 strands bright blue floss throughout, work buttonhole stitch around edge of each fabric piece.
4. Transfer flower stem to apron; embroider with buttonhole stitch. Sew pink button in center of flower with floss.

Dish Towel
Follow instructions as for apron to fuse and embroider flower on center front of dish towel.

Beaded Valance
1. Place waxed paper inside valance to keep paint from bleeding through; lay valance on clean, hard surface.
2. Mix paints: For flowers, mix 2 parts each cornflower and royal blue; add 3 parts grape and one small drop black; blend well. For leaves, mix 3 parts green with ½ part white and a tiny drop of black; blend well.
3. Use large flat end of sponge to apply paints to stamp. Be sure entire stamp is evenly covered with paint. Test stamp and paint on fabric scrap to check for proper placement and how much paint to use for a sharp, even image. Place stamp straight down on fabric, press down gently, and remove stamp.
4. When satisfied with results, stamp flowers across valance, beginning approximately 1 inch from left edge, 2½ inches above hemmed edge of valance. Randomly place stamp across valance at different heights and turn stamp so leaves point in a different direction each time. Position stamps 3½–4 inches apart, adjusting stamped images as needed as you approach the right edge.
5. Use shader to touch up large areas that don't receive enough paint from stamp; don't worry about tiny spots.
6. Allow paints to dry for 24 hours.

Trim Time
It's easy to capture a designer look when you add lavish trims to your decorating projects. In addition to beautiful fabrics, it's one of the things that most expensive accessories sold at retail have in common.

Many trims are available in coordinating colors and styles for your mixing and matching pleasure, and in a variety of in-seam or surface applications. Following are some of the most widely available and often used trims.

Cording
Cording is available in assorted sizes, either with a lip (for inserting in a seam by fusing it to a seam allowance) or without a lip (for gluing onto the fabric surface).

Welting
Welting is cording or piping covered with fabric. You can purchase it already made, but it's easy to make your own with bias-cut fabric strips that match your project (see Creating Bias Strips on page 146 and Making Welting on page 117).

Fringe
Fringe is available with a lip for in-seam applications or with a decorative header for gluing on or applying with fusible tape. The fringe itself is available in a variety of lengths and styles, including cut, looped, beaded and tasseled.

Tassels & Chair Ties
Tassel loops can be inserted in a seam, and both tassels and chair ties can be used as decorative ties or accents on a variety of home decor accessories.

7. Following instructions accompanying beaded fringe, attach to back of valance, aligning blue ribbon with edge of valance. Press down firmly. As you place fringe, check to be sure ribbon is not showing on front. ✂

Floral Apron/Dish Towel
Cut petals from blue print
and leaves from green

Flower Button Coasters & Basket Liner

Impress your family and friends with this attractive floral and denim set. Dress up an ordinary meal or save these for special-occasion brunches with friends.

Designs by Carol Dace

Materials

- ½ yard lightweight denim fabric
- Scrap of solid green fabric
- ¼ yard felt-type batting
- ⅓ yard heavy-duty iron-on adhesive
- Permanent fabric adhesive
- Flat yellow flower-type buttons: 4 (⅝-inch), 1 (1-inch)
- Large pin or needle

Coasters

1. From batting, cut eight 3½-inch squares. From iron-on adhesive, cut four 3½-inch squares and eight 4-inch squares. From lightweight denim fabric, cut eight 4½-inch squares.

2. Following manufacturer's instructions, fuse a 3½-inch adhesive square to one side of a batting square. Fuse a second batting square to other side of adhesive, making a "sandwich." Repeat with remaining batting squares and 3½-inch adhesive squares.

3. Center a 4-inch square of iron-on adhesive on wrong side of a 4½-inch square of fabric, leaving even fabric border all around; fuse. Repeat with remaining fabric and adhesive squares.

4. Center a batting "sandwich" on adhesive side of one fabric square; top with a second fused fabric square, adhesive side down, making sure fabric edges are even. Fuse top and around all edges on both sides. Repeat with remaining pieces to make four coasters.

5. Using pin or needle, pull threads on all four sides of each coaster to fringe excess fabric up to the fusing, about ¼ inch.

6. Fuse scraps of iron-on adhesive onto wrong side of green fabric. Referring to patterns, cut four small leaves from green fabric; fuse one in corner of each coaster. Glue a 5/8-inch button to center of leaves for flower.

Basket Liner

1. From lightweight denim fabric, cut one 18-inch square.

2. Using pin or needle, pull threads on all four sides to fringe edges ½–¾ inch.

3. Fuse scrap of iron-on adhesive onto wrong side of green fabric. Referring to patterns, cut one large leaves; fuse in one corner of basket liner. Glue 1-inch button to leaves for flower. ✂

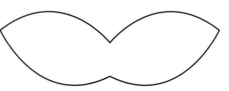

Large Leaves
Cut 1 from fused green fabric

Small Leaves
Cut 4 from fused green fabric

Fruit Kitchen Tea Set

This pretty set is the perfect way to add new life to your kitchen. It's simple to make with premade pieces and rubber stamps.

Designs by Judith Sandstrom

Materials

- Purchased valance of desired dimensions
- Purchased place mats
- Purchased waffle-weave terry-cloth dish towels
- Purchased terry-cloth pot holders
- Purchased canvas apron
- 3½-inch x 4½-inch rubber stamps: apple, grape cluster, pear cluster
- Black ink pad for stamping on fabric
- Fabric markers: black, brown, dark green, gray, lavender, light green, orange, pink, purple, red, yellow
- Straight pins
- Ruler

Project Notes

Samples were made using ready-made cotton items that are off-white or eggshell in color. Sample items are of different textures, and although the same stamps and fabric markers are used throughout, each texture yields a somewhat different effect. Try several test images on various textures to get the feel of the stamp before working on the kitchen ensemble.

Take care not to apply ink to the edges of the stamp, which may give your image "halos." You may want to place a small piece of a T-shirt or thin cotton batting under the fabric to be stamped to help clarify the center portion of the stamp.

Note that the rubber stamps are used in sets of three on all items except the pot holders, on which only one motif is stamped.

It is best to use one stamp at a time, stamping all the intended surfaces, and then clean it as recommended by the manufacturer before progressing to the next one.

Valance

1. Press as needed, then measure its width.

2. Plan placement of stamped images. Allow 10½ inches for each grouping of three stamped motifs, plus another 3–4 inches between groupings and at each end of valance. (Sample valance is 72 inches wide and comfortably accommodates five groupings of the three motifs. On a 48-inch valance, three groupings will fit nicely.) Using ruler, measure and mark the center of each three-stamp grouping with a pin. Stamp grape cluster—the center motif in each group of three—at each of these markings about 3 inches below top of valance. Clean grape stamp; allow motifs to dry.

3. Determine placement of apple stamp: Place clean, dry grape stamp over stamped grape image. Prepare apple stamp with ink, then place it so that it touches left side of grape stamp 2½ inches below top of grape stamp. Stamp apple motif and repeat for all apple motifs. Clean apple stamp after all images are completed.

4. Pear cluster stamp: Place grape stamp over stamped grape image again. Prepare pear stamp with ink and place it touching right side of grape stamp 2½ inches below top of grape stamp. Stamp all pear motifs; clean stamp.

5. Using black marker throughout, draw slightly curved vine connecting grapes with apple and pears. Redefine any lines in stamped motifs that are difficult to see.

6. Color in dry stamped motifs: Using brown marker, fill in vines and stems. Color leaves light and dark green with gray or black shading. Use purple, lavender, gray and touches of yellow to color in grapes. Use red, pink, yellow and gray for apple; use yellow, light green, orange and gray for pears. Use your finger to blend colors slightly as desired.

7. Iron over colored motifs using iron set at appropriate temperature for fabric.

Place Mat, Towel & Apron

1. Refer to instructions for valance throughout. Find center of each piece; mark with a pin, and position grape cluster stamp at this point, about 4 inches from top of place mat, and 5–6 inches from bottom of towel and apron.

2. Apply apple and pear cluster stamps as described in steps 2 and 3 for valance.

3. Repeat steps 5–7 for valance; on towel, it is best to dab on colors for a somewhat impressionistic effect.

Pot Holder

1. Mark center of pot holder with a pin. Position desired stamp at this point, turning it on point so hanging loop is at top. Stamp fruit in center of pot holder; let dry.

2. Using black marker, accentuate any portions of stamped design that are difficult to see. Let dry.

3. Referring to step 6 for valance, color in dry stamped motif, dabbing on colors for an impressionistic effect.

4. Iron over colored motif using iron set at appropriate temperature for fabric. ✂

Appliquéd Fruit Towels

Using fabric scraps and iron-on adhesive, it's simple to decorate your kitchen with these appliqué-look towels. Choose fabric shades that coordinate with your existing decor.

Designs by Chris Malone

Materials

- 3 coordinating 20-inch x 28-inch tan-and-cream tea towels
- ⅛ yard coordinating tan-and-cream print fabric
- Coordinating fabric scraps: red, gold, brown, three shades of purple, two shades of green
- ¼ yard heavy-duty iron-on adhesive
- 2 yards ⅞-inch-wide ecru trim
- Permanent fabric adhesive

Instructions

1. On paper side of iron-on adhesive, draw three 4½-inch x 6-inch rectangles for appliqué backgrounds. Referring to patterns, trace fruit shapes onto paper side of remaining adhesive: one pear and one apple; three pear leaves and three apple leaves, reversing one of each; two grape leaves, reversing one; three stems; 10 large, seven medium and six small grapes.

2. Following manufacturer's instructions, fuse adhesive to wrong side of fabrics, cutting shapes apart outside traced lines as needed: Fuse rectangles onto tan-and-cream print; fuse pear onto gold and apple onto red; fuse one pear leaf and reversed pear leaf, one apple leaf and reversed apple leaf, and one grape leaf onto light green; fuse remaining leaves onto dark green; fuse stems onto brown; fuse grapes onto assorted purples.

3. Cut out rectangles on traced lines; remove backing and fuse one to short end of each towel 2½ inches from bottom edge.

4. Cut out fruit motifs and leaves on traced lines. Referring to photo, arrange fruit and their leaves on rectangles. Note that some leaves overlap edges of background print. Grapes are randomly overlapped and stacked to form a cluster. When satisfied with placement, fuse appliqués in place.

5. Measure across bottom of towel; add ½ inch, and cut three pieces of ecru trim to that measurement. Fold each end under ¼ inch; glue in place. Apply a thin line of glue across top of trim on right side. Lay bottom edge of towel over top of trim and press to secure trim to towel edge. ✂

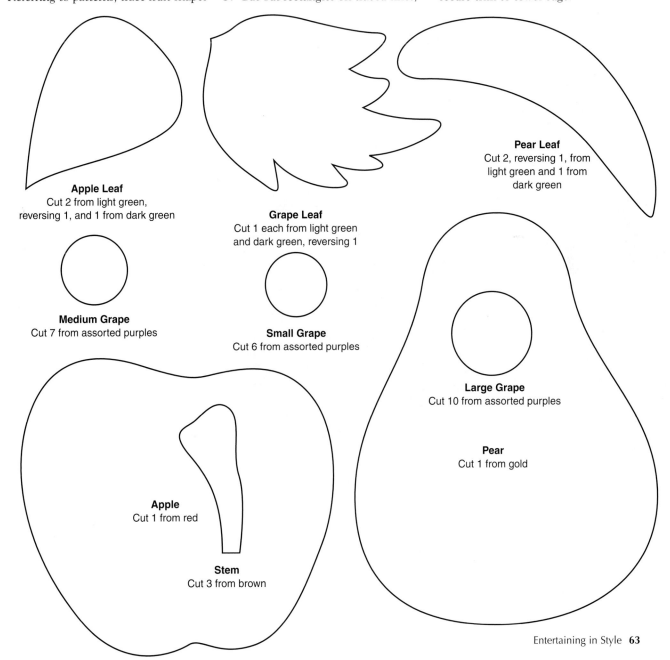

Apple Leaf
Cut 2 from light green, reversing 1, and 1 from dark green

Pear Leaf
Cut 2, reversing 1, from light green and 1 from dark green

Grape Leaf
Cut 1 each from light green and dark green, reversing 1

Medium Grape
Cut 7 from assorted purples

Small Grape
Cut 6 from assorted purples

Large Grape
Cut 10 from assorted purples

Apple
Cut 1 from red

Pear
Cut 1 from gold

Stem
Cut 3 from brown

Stenciled Fern Dish Towels

Add classy elegance to your kitchen with stencils and premade towels. Stenciling is the perfect method to quickly complete a project.

Designs by Mary Ayres

Materials

- 2 ivory linen-look dish towels
- Heavy-duty fusible adhesive
- ¼ yard cotton muslin
- 8 (½-inch) flat two-hole ivory buttons
- Green 6-strand cotton embroidery floss
- Embroidery needle
- Heavy-duty iron-on adhesive
- Fern stencils to fit in a 3 x 6-inch area
- Acrylic craft paints: antique green, dark green, jade green
- Stencil brushes
- 1 sheet white paper
- 4 tea bags
- Iron
- Pencil

Instructions

1. Tea-dye fabric: Boil tea bags for several minutes in water in a small saucepan. Remove pan from stove. Crumple muslin and place in tea; soak until desired color is achieved. Rinse muslin in cold water; dry in dryer. Press.

2. Cut 8-inch square from iron-on adhesive and muslin; fuse adhesive to back of muslin. Cut two 3½-inch x 6 ½-inch rectangles from fused fabric.

3. Referring to directions for Stenciling With Brush under Painting Techniques in the General Instructions (page 174), stencil desired fern motif in the center of each rectangle. Stencil leaves with jade; shade outer tip of each with antique green and inner tip of each with dark green. Do not stencil stems. Let dry; lay paper atop painted designs and press with iron to heat-set paints.

4. Peel paper backing from rectangles; position one on center front of one towel with bottom edge 3½ inches above edge of towel. Fuse in place. Repeat with remaining rectangle and towel.

5. Using 3 strands floss, embroider blanket stitch around each rectangle. Place plastic stencils on top of stenciled ferns and lightly draw around stem shapes with pencil. Using 1 strand green floss, embroider over penciled lines with stem stitch.

6. Sew buttons to corners of fabric rectangles with vertical floss stitches. ✂

Stamped Canvas Shelf Unit

Add a pretty accent to your home by rubber-stamping delicate ferns on a purchased shelving unit. Neutral colors and versatile canvas will fit beautifully with any kitchen decor.

Design by Lorine Mason

Materials

- 4-shelf canvas cart on wheels
- ½ yard coordinating fabric
- Soft fabric paints: light green, olive, soft sage
- Heavy-duty fusible adhesive tape: ⅜-inch and ⅝-inch
- Fancy fern rubber stamp
- 12-inch ½-inch-diameter wooden dowel rod
- 4 yards coordinating ½- to ⅝-inch ribbon
- 8-inch x 12-inch piece cardboard
- 1-inch foam brush

Instructions

1. Assemble shelf unit following manufacturer's instructions.

2. Insert cardboard inside the shelves to provide a firmer backing for stamping. Using foam brush to dab alternating colors of paint onto stamp, stamp fern images over top, back and sides of shelf unit, overlapping and changing directions of ferns as you stamp. Let dry.

3. Cut 36-inch x 14-inch piece fabric. Following manufacturer's instructions, iron ⅝-inch tape onto wrong side along all four edges. Fold over 1 inch on each long side; press to crease. Remove paper backing and fuse side hems. Repeat with bottom edge, folding over a 1½-inch hem.

4. Iron ⅜-inch tape to back of 2½ yards ribbon. Remove backing and fuse ribbon down sides and across bottom of fabric panel 1 inch from edges.

5. Insert top edge of fabric panel through top bar of shelf unit and fold

over a 1½-inch hem; hold in place while ironing. ***Hint:*** *Iron on top of the cardboard section.*

6. Insert 30-inch piece of ribbon between front cover and top of shelf unit so that one half hangs down outside fabric panel and other half hangs

behind it; glue center of ribbon to underside of shelf top, near front edge in center.

7. Insert dowel rod into pocket formed at bottom hem. Open shelf unit by rolling up front fabric panel and tying it in place with ribbon. ✂

Dining
Side Table & Linens

A premade television tray and delicate floral fabric combine to make this set. Pick a color scheme that accentuates your existing decor and marvel at the huge difference a new piece can make in your home.

Designs by Lorine Mason

Materials
- Oversize wooden TV-style folding table
- Coordinating fabrics: 3 yards print, 2 yards solid color
- Heavy-duty iron-on adhesive
- Iron-on ⅜-inch-wide tape
- 2 cabinet door handles
- Staple gun
- Masking tape
- Scalloped paper/fabric edgers or pinking shears
- Craft drill with bits
- Screwdriver
- Decorative hole punches: teardrop, ⅛-inch round

Side Table

1. Measure and cut fabrics: From print fabric cut one piece 20 inches x 28 inches for front; two pieces 15 inches x 28 inches for sides; and two pieces 11½ inches x 28 inches for back. From solid fabric cut four pieces 9 inches x 28 inches for corners.

2. Following manufacturer's instructions, press ⅜-inch tape to right side edges of all print sections of fabric, running tape along 28-inch length.

3. Join fabric sections: Remove paper backing and press seams, right sides facing, in the following order: back, corner, side, corner, front, corner, side, corner, back. Press well on both sides.

4. Create hem on sides of back sections of skirt by folding fabric edge in 1 inch; press.

5. Fold over 2-inch hem along bottom of skirt and press ⅜-inch tape along edge. Remove paper backing; press.

6. Corner pleats: Fold seam edges toward center, creating 4-inch pleat down length of skirt. Press.

7. Turn table upside down. Starting at center back, staple skirt in place, working around the table and matching corner sections.

8. Center handles 1½ inches in from side table edges; mark and drill holes. Attach handles.

Linens

1. Measure and cut fabrics: From print fabric cut two 15-inch squares and one 16-inch square. From solid fabric cut two 15-inch squares and one 16-inch square.

2. "Cutwork" square: Following manufacturer's instructions, press iron-on adhesive onto wrong side of 16-inch square of print fabric. Remove paper backing; fuse 16-inch solid square to other side.

3. Trim edges of square with scalloped edgers or pinking shears. Create a cutwork look by punching a decorative pattern in corners with round and teardrop punches.

4. Napkins: Following manufacturer's instructions, press ⅜-inch tape along edges of a 15-inch print fabric square on right side, leaving a 3-inch section open. Remove paper backing; top with 15-inch square of solid-color fabric, right sides facing. Press edges thoroughly; let cool.

5. Turn napkin right side out through opening. Press all seams. Cut 3-inch piece tape; remove backing paper and insert in opening between fabric edges. Press opening closed. Repeat with remaining print and solid-color fabric squares. ✄

Punch It Out

Use leather punches and a mallet to punch designs in suede or leather.

To punch a design, place the fabric on a punching board. Hold the punch perpendicular to the surface and hit the punch top firmly with the mallet.

Use one or more punch shapes to create random designs or a border.

French Country Picnic Set

Get the look of an expensive purchased dining set by using pretty fabric of your choice in this simple no-sew project. You'll love meals outdoors presented on coordinating handcrafted pieces.

Designs by Lorine Mason

Materials
- Coordinating fabrics: 3 yards print No. 1, 1¼ yards print No. 2, 1½ yards print No. 3
- Wire grid paper-plate holder
- Heavy-duty iron-on adhesive
- Iron-on tape: ⅜-inch, ⅞-inch
- 2 yards ¾-inch decorative cording
- 7 (1-inch) grommets and grommet-setting tool
- Waffle-weave place mats: 2 pink, 3 green
- 4 yards ½-inch-wide ribbon
- Stiff cardboard or mat board
- Hot-glue gun
- Pinking shears
- Needle
- Seam sealant

Tablecloth & Napkins

1. Measure and cut fabrics: From print No. 1 cut one piece 45 inches square for tablecloth; from print No. 3 cut four 15-inch squares for napkins.

2. Tear fabric pieces on sides to find the straight of grain. Using needle or pin, fray edges by pulling threads across and down from corners. When you achieve desired length of fringe, add a drop of seam sealant to each corner.

Picnic Bag

1. Measure and cut fabrics: From print No. 1 cut one piece 24 inches x 30 inches and one piece 13 inches square; from print No. 2 cut one piece 24 inches x 30 inches; from print No. 3 cut one piece 13 inches square.

2. Set paper-plate holder on top of cardboard; trace around bottom edge. Cut out two cardboard circles to match.

3. Lay one circle on top of one 13-inch fabric square; trace around, adding 1 inch. Cut out; set aside.

4. Following manufacturer's instructions, fuse ⅜-inch tape to right side of fabric down 24-inch length of one 24-inch x 30-inch piece. Fold fabric in half, right sides facing, and fuse to create a tube. Repeat with second 24-inch x 30-inch piece of fabric.

5. Clip ¾ inch up into fabric every 1 inch along bottom edge of each fabric bag section, creating tabs. Insert cardboard circle into No. 1 fabric tube turned right side out; glue fabric tabs around circle. Insert same cardboard circle into tube of No. 2 fabric, also right side out, and glue tabs to reverse side of cardboard circle. Turn bag right side out with No. 1 print on outside and No. 2 print as lining.

6. Center remaining cardboard circle on wrong side of fabric circle cut in step 3; clip into fabric from edge to within ¼ inch of cardboard, creating tabs. Fold fabric tabs over edges of cardboard and hot-glue in place, pulling tabs taut. Glue fabric-covered circle to bottom of bag and weight with heavy object until glue is set.

7. Press iron-on adhesive onto back of remaining 13-inch fabric square. Trace around wire grid plate holder onto fabric; cut out with pinking shears. Remove paper backing; press circle to inside of bag to cover any visible raw edges.

8. Fuse ⅞-inch tape to reverse side along top edge of bag and again 8 inches down from top edge. Remove paper backing; iron lining to outer fabric. Trim top edge with pinking shears.

9. Starting at back seam line and 8 inches down from top of bag, mark 1½ inches from either side of back seam and then every 4 inches around bag. Following package instructions, insert grommets at these marks.

10. Thread cording through grommets; knot ends to prevent fraying. Insert wire-grid plate holder.

Utensil Roll

1. Measure and cut fabrics: From print No. 1 cut one piece 14 inches x 21 inches; cut matching piece from print No. 2. Fuse fabric pieces together, wrong sides facing, with iron-on adhesive; trim edges with pinking shears.

2. Measure and cut one green place mat: one piece 6½ inches x 11½ inches for pocket; one piece 4 inches x 11½ inches for top; two pieces 3½ inches x 1½ inches for tabs.

3. Center pocket on inside of utensil roll; hot-glue in place along side and bottom edges.

4. Curved pocket top: Fold top in half and cut a curve along edge; center over top of pocket; hot-glue along top edge. Add a decorative ribbon at center of curved edge.

5. Referring to photo, glue tabs in place beside pocket, applying glue only to ends of tabs.

6. Center 1-yard piece of ribbon on outside of utensil roll; glue to roll approximately 4 inches from left side edge.

Place Mats

Trim out small sections in each place mat's weave so that ribbon can be woven through to tie napkin in place. ✄

Behind the Scenes

Add a hint of color to punched leather or suede projects when you back the leather with a brightly-colored fabric lining. Fuse or glue the fabric to the wrong side of the leather, being careful not to get glue or adhesive in the punched holes.

Bulletin Board

Post family reminders and weekly shopping lists in style on this embellished bulletin board. Fabric-covered plastic foam forms the basic bulletin board; you make it your own with creative personal touches!

Design by Annabelle Keller for Dow

Materials

- 36-inch x 12-inch x 1-inch sheet Styrofoam
- Fabrics: ⅔ yard desired print for center panel plus ⅞ yard for backing and border plus ⅛ yard coordinating fabric for buttons
- 26 (⁹⁄₁₆-inch) flat button covers
- 59 (1¹⁄₁₆-inch) ballpoint pins
- 5 (3-inch) floral picks with wires removed
- 5 yards coordinating ⅜-inch-wide grosgrain ribbon
- 2⅛ yards blue, white and yellow ³⁄₁₆-inch corded, twisted braid
- Crib-size polyester batting
- 2 sawtooth picture hangers with nails
- Plastic foam glue
- Yardstick
- Fabric adhesive
- Serrated knife
- Black fine-point permanent marker
- Pencil
- #10 artist's painting knife or 1-inch putty knife
- Hot-glue gun with needle nozzle
- Toothpicks

Project Note

Depending on fabric pattern, more fabric may be needed to center desired motif.

Instructions

1. Using a yardstick, a serrated knife and fine-point marker, measure mark and cut two 12-inch x 18-inch pieces from Styrofoam sheet.

2. Apply a little hot glue to ends of five floral picks and push glued ends into one long edge of one Styrofoam panel, spacing picks evenly.

3. Apply foam glue to edge of Styrofoam between the picks and to one long edge of the other Styrofoam panel; apply hot glue to protruding ends of picks. Working on a flat surface, push panels together firmly, joining glued edges. Let dry.

4. Mark 1¾-inch border around edges of 18-inch x 24-inch Styrofoam with fine-point marker. Draw diagonal lines from inside corners of border to outer corners of Styrofoam (draw through 1¾-inch "frame" only, not across center of Styrofoam board); score all lines with a sharp pencil.

5. From batting, cut four pieces 1½ inches x 17¾ inches and four pieces 1½ inches x 23¾ inches; cut also one piece 14¼ inches x 20¼ inches. Hot-glue a double layer of strips around border, mitering corners; hot-glue single batting panel in center. Let dry.

6. Cut 15½-inch x 21½-inch piece print fabric for center panel; cut a piece of coordinating fabric 24½ inches x 30½ inches for back and border.

7. Center fabric for center over center of Styrofoam. Working on opposite sides, tuck seam allowances into Styrofoam by using painting or putty knife to push seam allowance straight down into Styrofoam, keeping tension even. Trim fabric at corners as needed.

8. Center back side of Styrofoam over wrong side of back/border fabric and "tuck in" seam allowance, keeping tension even. Trim fabric at corners as required and tuck fabric into mitered corners.

9. Plan arrangement of ribbon; cut pieces of ribbon to length, adding ½ inch. Using a toothpick, add a dot of fabric adhesive at end of ribbon; using painting or putty knife, tuck ¼ inch into each seam. Where ribbons cross, dip pin into fabric adhesive and push pin through ribbons, into Styrofoam.

10. Cover button covers according to instructions on package; glue over pins at intersections of ribbons with fabric adhesive.

11. Cut corded, twisted braid to fit into tucked seam lines around center of panel; glue in place, applying fabric adhesive with a toothpick.

12. Position sawtooth hangers on top back edge of bulletin board 1 inch from top and 2 inches in from edges. Apply hot glue to hanger "ears" and press in place. Dip nails in glue; push through holes in hangers into Styrofoam.

13. Use additional pins to embellish printed design in fabric on center panel; do not apply glue to these pins. These pins and the ribbons can be used to hold notes, tickets, etc., on bulletin board. ✂

Stenciling

Stencils abound for home decor projects. Use them for borders on tablecloths, pillowcases, sheets and window panels or for all-over effects on almost any project.

Select a precut stencil, then choose a brush or brushes in appropriate sizes and the stencil paint crème colors of your choice. Temporary stencil adhesive spray makes it easy to securely hold the stencil in place while you work.

1. Wash and dry washable fabrics. Press the fabric to remove wrinkles.

2. Lightly and evenly spray the back of the stencil with adhesive and position it on the fabric.

3. Use a paper towel to remove the coating that forms on top of the stencil crème. Dip the stencil brush into the paint, then brush it onto a paper towel to remove the excess paint.

4. Holding the brush upright, use a circular motion to apply the paint to the stencil openings, working from the outside toward the center.

5. Let the paint dry, then heat set following the manufacturer's instructions.

Bag Holder Trio

Choose a color scheme, apply some glue and quickly craft these trendy and convenient bag holders. Store your recycled bags in style with these handy projects.

Designs by Barbara Woolley

Project Note
Use fabric adhesive unless instructed otherwise.

Tabletop Plastic Bag Keeper
1. Paint ball knobs for feet and bottom on exterior of box; let dry.

2. Put lid on box. With pencil, draw line around box along edge of lid; remove lid.

3. Apply a thin, even layer of adhesive around sides of box from bottom up to pencil line; wrap box with 21-inch strip of solid fabric so that edge of strip is even with bottom of box.

4. Apply a thin, even layer of adhesive to sides and top of lid. Place batting circle on lid. Lay 6-inch circle of checked fabric over batting, pulling edges down over sides.

5. Apply a thin, even layer of adhesive to one side of tag board strip; center 21-inch strip of checked fabric on tag board. Apply adhesive to edges on other side of strip; fold excess fabric over edges of tag board. Glue covered strip around side of lid.

6. Glue fringe around bottom edge of lid; glue two rows of braid around bottom edge of box.

7. Cover buttons with same fabric used for lid and remove shanks; using craft cement, glue buttons evenly spaced around box.

8. Using craft cement, glue ball knobs to bottom of box for feet.

9. Using craft knife, cut a 1- to 1½-inch hole in center of lid, through all layers—fabric, batting and papier-mâché. Apply fabric adhesive to glue batting and fabric around hole; glue braid around cut edges.

10. Fill box with plastic bags; pull out through hole in lid.

Hanging Plastic Bag Keeper
1. Put lid on box. With pencil, draw line around box along edge of lid; remove lid.

2. Apply a thin, even layer of adhesive around sides of box from bottom up to pencil line; wrap box with 13-inch x 17-inch piece of solid fabric so that edge of fabric is even with bottom of box.

3. Apply a thin, even layer of fabric adhesive to sides and top of lid. Place batting circle on lid. Lay one 5-inch circle of checked fabric over batting, pulling edges down over sides. Glue other 5-inch fabric circle to bottom of box.

4. Apply a thin, even layer of adhesive to one side of tag board strip; center 17-inch strip of checked fabric on tag board. Apply adhesive to edges on other

Materials

Tabletop Plastic Bag Keeper
- 6½-inch-tall, 6-inch-diameter round papier-mâché box with lid
- 4 (2-inch) unpainted wooden ball knobs
- 6-inch circle polyester batting
- Complementary fabrics: 21-inch x 5-inch strip solid; 21-inch x 2-inch strip, 7-inch circle and 6 (4-inch) circles check
- Trims: 21-inch piece 2-inch fringe and 48 inches ¼-inch cording in color(s) to coordinate with fabrics
- Acrylic craft paint in color to coordinate with fabrics
- Small paintbrush
- 6 (1⅛-inch) shank buttons to cover
- 21-inch x 1½-inch strip tag board
- Permanent fabric adhesive
- Permanent craft cement
- Pencil
- Craft knife

Hanging Plastic Bag Keeper
- 14-inch-tall, 5-inch-diameter round papier-mâché box with lid
- 5-inch circle polyester batting
- Complementary fabrics: 13-inch x 17-inch strip solid; 17-inch x 4-inch strip, 2 (5-inch) circles and 4 (4-inch) circles check; 4-inch circle stripe

- Trims: 17-inch piece 2-inch fringe; 20-inch piece and 36-inch piece ¼-inch cording in color(s) to coordinate with fabrics
- 6 (1⅛-inch) shank buttons to cover
- 16-inch x 3-inch strip tag board
- Permanent fabric adhesive
- Permanent craft cement
- Pencil
- Craft knife

Hanging Brown Bag Keeper
- Hanging file with 2-inch-wide "placket" or "spine" across bottom
- 11½-inch x 2-inch strip strong cardboard
- Complementary fabrics: 20-inch x 11¾-inch piece of fabric A for exterior of file plus scraps for buttons; 24-inch x 11¾-inch piece and 3-inch x 12½-inch strip fabric B for interior
- Trims: 24-inch piece 2-inch fringe; 2 (26-inch) pieces ⅛-inch-wide cording in color(s) to coordinate with fabrics; 4 coordinating tassels
- 6 (¾-inch) shank buttons to cover
- Iron-on adhesive: 24-inch x 11¾-inch piece and 20-inch x 11¾-inch piece
- 16-inch x 3-inch strip tag board
- Permanent fabric adhesive
- Permanent craft cement

side of strip; fold excess fabric over edges of tag board. Using craft cement, glue covered strip around side of lid.

5. Using craft cement, glue fringe around bottom edge of lid.

6. Cover four buttons with same fabric used for lid and remove shanks; using craft cement, glue buttons evenly spaced around box near bottom. Cover remaining button

with striped fabric; glue in center of covered lid.

7. Using craft knife, cut a hole about the size of a quarter in the center of the box bottom. For attaching hanging cord, cut two small holes through sides of box, opposite each other and about ½ inch below edge of lid. Apply fabric glue to cut edges to hold fabric in place and keep it from fraying.

8. Using craft cement, glue two rows of braid from the 36-inch piece around bottom edge of box; glue a single row of braid around cutout opening in bottom.

9. Thread ends of 20-inch cord through small holes from outside to inside of box; knot ends inside to keep hanger in place.

10. Fill box with plastic bags; pull out through hole in bottom of keeper.

Hanging Brown Bag Keeper

1. Apply even layer of fabric adhesive

to one side of 2-inch x 11½-inch cardboard strip. Center cardboard, glue side down, over wrong side of 3-inch x 12½-inch piece fabric B; lay in place and smooth with fingers to smoothly cover cardboard with fabric. Wrap excess fabric to back of cardboard and glue in place.

2. Following manufacturer's instructions, apply iron-on adhesive to wrong sides of matching fabric pieces. Fuse fabric B inside folder, folding excess over top front edge. Fuse fabric A to exterior of folder.

3. Using craft cement throughout, glue fabric-covered cardboard strip (step 1) in bottom of hanging file.

4. Glue fringe trim to keeper an inch below top on front and back. Cover buttons with fabric; glue three to each side of keeper.

5. Tie cording to metal hooks on ends of hanging file; secure with cement. Glue or stitch tassels to hooks. ✄

Fraying Fun

Loosely woven fabrics such as linen and some cottons that fray evenly are perfect for finishing with frayed edges. Use them on table linens, pillows and other projects that lend themselves to this casual look.

Use a water-soluble marking pen and mark the fringe depth on the fabric wrong side. Squeeze a line of seam sealant or permanent fabric adhesive along the marked line and let it dry.

Cut to the stitching line at 2-inch intervals along the length of the edge.

Use a pin or needle to remove the horizontal threads between the cuts to make fringe.

Binding Edges

Binding is an attractive finishing technique for the raw edges of medium- to heavyweight fabrics; lightweight fabrics usually can't support the weight of the trim.

You can use purchased bias binding, ribbon or trim strips; create double-fold binding from bias strips; or use strips of a nonwoven fabric that won't fray, such as faux suede or leather, or heavyweight felt.

It's a Wrap

To bind an edge with purchased binding, ribbon or trim strips, or nonfraying fabric strips, use fusible web or adhesive tape in the same width as the trim to be applied. Fuse the tape to the trim wrong side. Evenly wrap over the fabric edge and fuse in place.

On the Double

To create double-fold binding, first determine the width of the binding you'd like to see on each side of the fabric edge, keeping it in proportion to the project size. You'll also need fusible web or adhesive tape in the same width or slightly smaller than your binding width.

Follow the instructions on pages 48 and 49 to cut bias strips. To determine the cut bias strip width, multiply the desired binding width by 4 and add $\frac{1}{8}$ inch to allow for folds and the edge depth.

For example, to make $\frac{3}{8}$-inch-wide binding, 4 x $\frac{3}{8}$ inches = $1\frac{1}{2}$ inches; add $\frac{1}{8}$ inch for a total measurement of $1\frac{5}{8}$ inches.

Press the cut binding strip in half lengthwise, with wrong sides together to mark the center. Open the strip flat with the wrong side up. Press the long edges to meet in the center. Adhere fusible tape to each folded edge (see photo below).

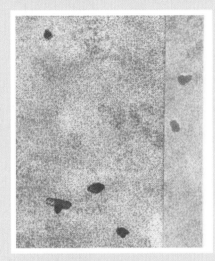

Fold the binding on the center fold and wrap over the fabric edge. Fuse in place.

Banded Edges

A band is wider than binding—usually $1\frac{1}{2}$ to 3 inches, depending on the scale of the project—and can either create an extension of an edge or be applied like a binding to cover the edge. It's a nice finishing touch for place mats, tablecloths, table or sink skirts, shower curtains, and window treatment panels.

Straight Talk

To add a band to an edge without corners, such as skirts or panels, determine the desired finished band width. Double the width and add $1\frac{1}{8}$ inches for seam and fold allowances to the measurement. Cut strips this width and seam the short ends together to equal the length of the edge, plus add 2 inches for overlapping the ends.

Press a $\frac{1}{2}$-inch seam allowance to the wrong side on each long band edge, then press the band in half lengthwise with wrong sides together. Apply fusible web or adhesive tape to each seam allowance. Position the band over the seam allowance of the edge to be banded and fuse in place.

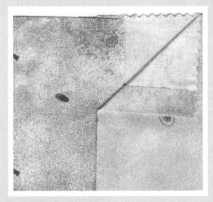

Corner Concerns

If your banded project has corners, like place mats or tablecloths, mitering is the neatest way to finish the corners.

To cut the band strips, double the desired finished width and add $1\frac{1}{8}$ inches for seam and fold allowances to the measurement.

For each edge to be banded, cut a strip equal to the edge length, plus the finished band width times two. For example, for a place mat with a $1\frac{1}{2}$-inch-wide finished band, cut a strip as follows for each edge: edge length + 3 inches.

Follow "Straight Talk" to press each strip and apply fusible tape. Center each band along the appropriate fabric edge and fuse in place; do not fuse the extended ends.

At each corner, insert the ends of one band strip into the fold of the adjacent strip. On the upper layer, press the edges under diagonally on each side to form a mitered look. Apply fusible tape to the edge and fuse in place.

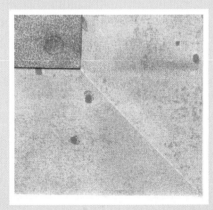

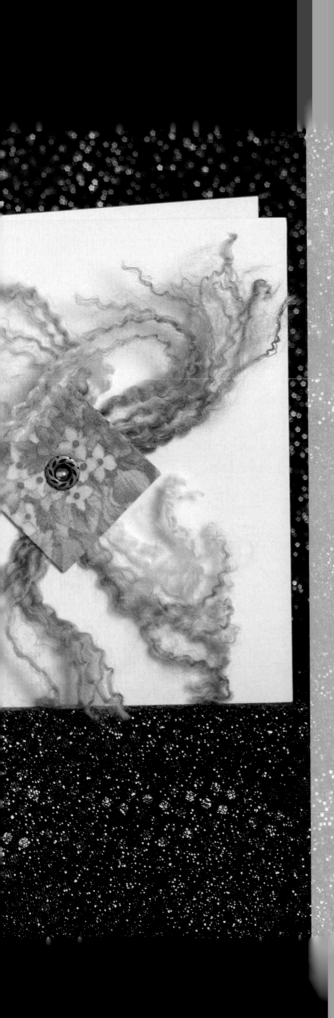

A Lifetime of Memories

As recent trends in scrapbooking have shown, there is much more to collecting and displaying memories than just taking a good photograph! Use the frames, cards, scrapbooks and other projects in this chapter to make the most of your "special moments" displays.

Fabric & Fiber Greeting Cards

Easy-to-find card stock, fabric, and embellishments of your choice are all you need to create stylish, trendy cards for friends and family. Pick colors and accents to suit each card's recipient.

Designs by Janice McKee

Opposites Attract

1. Edge front of card with a gold border using paint pen.

2. Center card stock square on back of black cotton fabric; fold over raw edges and glue to back. Repeat with remaining card stock and beige cotton fabric. Turn squares on point and glue to card as shown.

3. Carefully fray edges of 1-inch linen squares; glue beige linen in center of black square and black linen in center of beige square as shown.

4. Glue gold foil motif in center of each linen square.

5. Cut two 3-inch strands of floss; separate plies. Hold plies from one strand together and knot in center; glue knot to center of one gold foil motif. Repeat with remaining floss and other motif.

Fabric & Fiber

1. Center card stock square on back of fabric; fold over raw edges and glue to back.

2. Unravel yarn slightly and arrange attractively on front of card; using glue stick, anchor in several spots as needed. Turn fabric-covered square on point and glue to card over yarn as shown.

3. Glue button in center of square; glue bead in center of button.

Butterfly in the Fringe

1. Carefully fray edges of cotton fabric scraps along their length. Using fabrics in a variety of colors and widths, arrange them at angles in a pleasing manner on the piece of plain white paper. When satisfied with arrangement, glue scraps in place and trim any excess from edges of paper.

2. Cut a ¾-inch-wide frame from the larger piece of black card stock. Using double-stick tape throughout, attach frame first to fabric-covered paper and then, centered, to front of card.

3. Stamp and emboss butterfly in center of black card-stock square; color as desired with gel pens. Trim square with paper edgers. Center and glue square in place on top of fabric panel. ✂

Materials

Opposites Attract

- 5-inch x 7-inch blank white greeting card
- 2 (2-inch) squares card stock
- Fabrics: 1-inch square each black and beige loosely woven linen; 3-inch square each complementary black and beige print cotton
- 2 small motifs cut from a gold foil doily
- Black metallic embroidery floss
- Metallic gold paint pen
- Glue stick

Fabric & Fiber

- 5-inch x 7-inch blank white greeting card
- 2-inch square card stock
- 3-inch square multicolored cotton print fabric
- 6-inch length coordinating variegated yarn, wool roving or similar fiber
- ⅜-inch flat metal button
- Small luster bead in coordinating color
- Glue stick

Butterfly in the Fringe

- 5-inch x 7-inch blank white greeting card
- Black card stock: 4½-inch x 6½-inch piece and 2-inch square
- 4-inch x 6-inch piece plain white paper
- Scraps of 9 cotton fabrics in bright solid colors, in a variety of widths but each measuring at least 5 inches x 1 inch
- Butterfly rubber stamp
- White embossing ink
- White embossing powder
- Metallic ink or gel pens in colors to coordinate with fabrics
- Glue stick
- Double-stick tape
- Craft knife
- Decorative paper edgers

Follow the Rules

Your mother was right: "Follow the rules."

Always, yes always, adhere to the manufacturer's instructions for using any glue or fusible product, as well as recommendations for prewashing the fabric if necessary. Not doing so may result in damage to the fabric, a bond that won't hold or a sticky mess that may never dry.

Equally important are the manufacturer's recommendations for washing or dry-cleaning the finished project. Consider these factors when selecting the product. For example, you don't want to use a product that requires heat activation on heat-sensitive synthetic fabrics.

Father's Day Card

Celebrate Father's Day with love and creativity. This card is full of individuality and expression and will be cherished by that lucky dad.

Design by Jacqueline Stetter

Materials

Each Card

- 8½-inch x 11-inch piece card stock
- 5½-inch x 8½-inch envelope
- 5½-inch x 8½-inch piece metallic fabric
- 30 inches coordinating velvet trim
- Adhesive-backed fusible-web sheets
- ½-inch fusible tape
- Markers, stamps and ink pads, colored pens, and other materials as desired to complete card
- Hot-glue gun
- Photo
- Decorative paper edgers

Instructions

1. Fold card stock in half to create 5½-inch x 8½-inch greeting card. Following manufacturer's instructions, fuse web sheet to back of fabric and fuse fabric to front of card.

2. Using fusible tape, fuse velvet trim around edges of card to create frame.

3. Cut photo to size with paper edgers. Apply a few small dabs of hot glue around edge of photo and press into place on front of card.

4. Use markers, pens, rubber stamps, etc., to add message inside card. ✂

Mitten Card & Pin

Winter greetings are fun and simple with this card-and-pin set. Personal gifts like this one are always cherished and remembered.

Designs by Angie Wilhite

Materials

Card
- 4-inch x 5½-inch brown kraft card with envelope
- Fabrics: 4-inch square for mitten, 3-inch square for heart
- 5-inch x 7-inch piece heavy-weight fusible web
- Black fine-tip permanent marker

Pin
- Fabrics: 4-inch x 8-inch piece for mitten, 3-inch square for heart
- 4-inch square fusible web
- 4-inch square fusible fleece
- 3-inch square heavyweight fusible web
- ½-inch flat wooden button
- Sewing needle and natural-color thread
- Metallic fuchsia fine braid
- Permanent adhesive
- 1-inch pin back

Card

1. Following manufacturer's instructions, apply fusible web to wrong side of fabrics. Referring to patterns, trace mitten and heart shapes onto paper side of fabric. Cut out appliqués.

2. Position appliqués on front of card as shown; peel off backing and fuse in place.

3. Using marker, write "WARM HANDS, WARM HEART" on card and add outline of short dashed lines around mitten.

Pin

1. Cut mitten fabric into two 4-inch squares. Following manufacturer's instructions, apply fusible web to wrong side of one piece of fabric and fusible fleece to the other piece. Fuse fabric pieces together, wrong sides facing.

2. Referring to patterns, cut mitten from fused fabric.

3. Following manufacturer's

instructions, apply heavy-duty fusible web to wrong side of heart fabric. Trace heart onto paper side of fabric; cut out. Peel off backing and fuse heart onto mitten.

4. Using sewing thread and needle, sew button in center of heart. Using fuchsia braid, blanket-stitch around edges of mitten.

5. Glue pin back to back side of mitten. ✂

Mitten Card & Pin
For card, cut 1 mitten and 1 heart from complementary fabrics.

For pin, cut 1 mitten from fused fabric layers and 1 heart from complementary fabric.

Child's Party Invitation

Delightful playtime pals add cheer to this colorful party-time invitation. Children will love these fabric-and-paper cards. They're perfect for birthdays and other special events.

Design by Jacqueline Stetter

Materials
Each Invitation

- 10½-inch x 7-inch piece card stock
- 5¼-inch x 7¼-inch envelope
- Print fabric to correspond with party's theme
- Dimensional craft paint(s) in complementary color(s)
- Markers, stamps and ink pads, colored pens and other materials as desired to complete invitation
- Adhesive-backed fusible-web sheets

Instructions

1. Fold card stock in half to make 7-inch x 5¼-inch greeting card.

2. Following manufacturer's instructions, fuse a web sheet to back of fabric.

3. Trim desired motifs from fabric; peel backing and fuse in place on front of card. Fuse a single motif to front of envelope.

4. Enhance/accent design as desired with dimensional paint; let dry.

5. Use markers, pens, rubber stamps, etc., to add date, time, location and other information to invitation as desired. ✂

Fusible Stabilizer & Interfacing

Fusible on one side only, stabilizer or interfacing is fused to the wrong side of the fabric to add firm support and prevent raveling.

Use interfacing to add body to a drapery header, hems, place mats or a pillow closure.

Use stabilizer to back cotton fabrics that will have raw plain or decoratively cut edges, or to add stability to a fabric before fusing or gluing trims in place.

Liquid Fusible Web

Liquid fusible web is heat-activated glue that comes in a bottle and is recommended for all fabrics except sheers. Use it to apply trims, appliqués and lace, and to fuse fabrics together.

It can be applied as a thin line, dabbed on or applied with a foam brush to larger areas and open fabrics such as lace.

Baby Photo Album Covers

Make a delightful keepsake for baby memories with fabric and glue. This project makes a perfect shower gift or a wonderful way to remember your own little one.

Designs by Helen L. Rafson

Materials

- White paper
- Fusible web
- Fabrics: pink gingham check or blue print; flesh color
- Acrylic craft paints: black, red, white, pink or light blue
- Small paintbrush
- Black fine-point permanent marker
- Glue
- Light blue or pink baby rickrack
- Yellow or brown doll hair
- 6¾ inches ⅛-inch-wide white satin ribbon
- ¼-inch round hole punch
- Seam sealant
- 4⅞-inch x 6¼-inch plastic photo album
- Pin

Instructions

1. Remove original papers from photo album.

2. Cut two pieces white paper each 4⅞ inches x 6¼ inches.

3. Referring to patterns, trace head and pajamas on backing of fusible web; fuse web with head pattern to back of flesh-color fabric and web with pajamas pattern to back of pink or blue print. Cut out head and pajamas.

4. On back of remaining web, draw four strips each ⅝ inch x 4⅞ inches. Fuse to back of check fabric and cut out.

5. Using marker, draw dashed lines along sleeves and bottom of feet; add mouth.

6. Dip end of paintbrush handle into black paint; dot on two eyes. Dip handle into red; add cheeks. Let dry. Dip pin into white paint and add highlights to eyes; let dry.

7. Fuse one check strip across top of each piece of paper and another across bottom. Cut four 4⅞-inch pieces baby rickrack; glue over edges of check strips. Let dry.

8. Fuse head and pajamas in place on one piece of paper for front cover. Cut curl from doll hair; glue to forehead; let dry.

9. Tie a small bow from white satin ribbon; trim ends at an angle and treat with seam sealant. Let dry, then glue bow in place.

10. Using hole punch, punch two circles from scrap of white paper; glue to pajamas for buttons; let dry.

11. Dip end of paintbrush handle into blue or pink paint; dot background on front cover around baby; dot back cover. Let dry.

12. Insert front and back covers in front and back of album. ✄

Head
Cut 1 from flesh-colored fabric

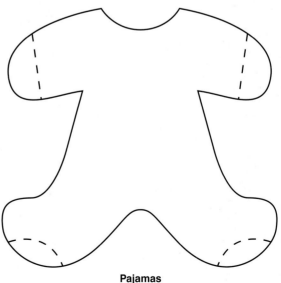

Pajamas
Cut 1 from pink or blue print fabric

Memories Set

Combine sparkly fabric and delicate lace to make a photo set that you'll cherish for years to come. Pretty rose embellishments add the perfect finishing touch.

Designs by Bev Shenefield

Materials

Both Projects
- Batting
- ⅓ yard "old rose"-color satin
- ⅓ yard ivory sparkle sheer
- Cream ruffled lace
- 2 rolls ¼-inch–wide double-sided adhesive tape
- 12 ivory rolled ribbon rosettes with green ribbon leaves
- Fabric glue

Photo Album
- 9-inch-square photo album
- Vinyl page protector

Frame
- 5⅜-inch x 7¼-inch photo frame with oval opening
- White computer paper
- Craft glue

Photo Album

1. Measure cover of photo album; add ½ inch to each dimension and cut batting to that measurement.

2. Cut strips of adhesive tape to fit along edges of album cover. Peel off backing and adhere strips to album; peel off remaining backing and press batting in place.

3. Satin album cover: Check size of your album cover, then cut satin approximately 23 inches x 12 inches, large enough to cover album with sufficient extra fabric to fold over edges and secure inside.

4. Open album and lay flat; measure cover from top to bottom. Cut two strips of tape to fit. Remove backing and press one along left edge (inside front cover) and one along right edge (inside back cover). Lay satin wrong side up; lay open album in center of satin. Fold over excess fabric at sides and secure on tape strips. (Check fit to make sure you can close album without pulling fabric too tight.)

5. Referring to step 4, apply tape along top and bottom edges of album; fold over fabric and secure, trimming corners as needed and folding edges to cover corners neatly.

6. Snip along folds in album; apply adhesive tape as before to edge above and below pages. Turn under fabric edge and adhere to tape. Or, if there is room to tuck in fabric, apply fabric glue in this space and push fabric into it.

7. Sheer cover: Cut sheer fabric same size as satin and apply it as you did in steps 4–6, covering satin. Do not pull fabric so tightly that it makes ridges in satin.

8. Line album covers: Cut two pieces satin to fit inside album, each about 8¾ inches square; fold under fabric edges all around; press.

9. Apply strips of adhesive tape inside covers, around edges; peel off remaining backing and press fabric squares in place to conceal edges of satin and sheer fabric and cover insides of fabric covers.

10. Lace trim: Apply adhesive tape along edges of front cover. Remove remaining backing and press lace onto it in one long piece, beginning at bottom, going all around cover, and overlapping ends. Cut lace, leaving enough extra to turn under and still overlap beginning end. Secure with an additional small piece of adhesive tape. Repeat to trim back cover.

11. Referring to step 10, apply lace trim along top and bottom edges of spine, tucking ends of lace under lace on front and back covers for a neat finish.

12. Referring to pattern, cut oval from sheet protector. Apply short lengths of adhesive tape along edges of oval, clipping tape around curves. Remove backing and apply a border of lace, beginning and ending at bottom of oval and turning under lace where ends overlap.

13. Apply adhesive tape to vinyl as before, omitting right edge—or, apply tape all around the oval and then remove most of the stickiness from tape on right edge by gently pressing finger to tape until most of the stickiness is gone. This will allow it to stick just enough to keep the photo from falling out without making it impossible to change the photo.

14. Glue vinyl oval to center front of photo album. Trim photo to fit, using pattern for oval; insert photo in vinyl oval.

15. Glue three ribbon rosettes in upper left corner and three more in lower right using fabric glue.

Frame

1. Remove anything that holds glass and backing in frame. Measure frame; add ½ inch to each dimension and cut batting to that measurement. Mark and remove oval from center of batting.

2. Cut strips of adhesive tape to fit along edges and around oval of frame. Adhere strips to frame; peel off remaining backing and press batting in place.

3. Satin frame cover: Check size of frame, then cut satin to fit, approximately 8¾ inches x 10¾ inches, large enough to cover album with sufficient extra fabric to fold over edges and secure on back.

4. Apply tape to edges on back of frame; remove backing. Lay satin wrong side up; lay frame in center and fold excess fabric over edges to back, securing it on tape.

5. Apply tape around edges of oval opening on back of frame. Carefully slit fabric in center of oval; slit fabric to edges of oval and fold to back of frame, covering edge of oval opening.

6. Sheer cover: Cut sheer fabric and apply it as in steps 3–5, covering satin. Do not pull fabric so tight that it makes ridges in satin.

7. Cut paper to fit inside frame to cover fabric edges. Oval can be cut out before or after gluing; cut it about ⅛ inch larger than opening in frame. Use craft glue to glue paper in place.

8. Place adhesive tape along frame's front edge and around oval, clipping curves as needed. Remove backing and press lace in place. Reassemble frame with backing and glass, inserting photo.

9. Using fabric glue, glue three ribbon rosettes in upper left corner and three more in lower right. ✂

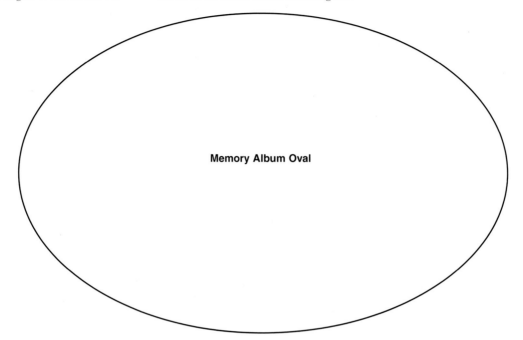

Memory Album Oval

Which Web Is Which?

Fusible web is a thin, weblike adhesive, while *fusible adhesive* is a thin sheet of solid adhesive, and both are intended for the same general purposes.

Either one may or may not have a paper backing, depending on the manufacturer.

They are available in rolls of tape, packaged sheets and by the yard. Use it to fuse together two layers of fabric, trim to fabric and even fabric to hard surfaces, such as wood. The adhesive melts when the heat of an iron is applied, creating a bond.

Look for it in light, medium and heavy weights.

Use the Right Product

Most lightweight fusible adhesives are designed for securing fabric only until the edges are sewn or otherwise sealed, and may not hold if they're not and the project is washed.

Use them for no-sew projects where the edges will be sealed with paint or secured with permanently glued trims. Do *not* use them for seams or other construction techniques.

Medium- to heavyweight fusible adhesives are usually permanent once they've been fused and allowed to cool. You can sew or seal the edges as for lightweight webs if desired, but it isn't necessary for most brands.

Use it for medium- to heavyweight fabrics and trims. Use these weights for construction techniques and appliqués.

Repositionable fusible webs are available in medium weight. They have a pressure sensitive adhesive on one or both sides that you can stick to the fabric, allowing you to remove and move one or both pieces of fabric or trim; once it's pressed, the bond is permanent.

They're ideal for the same purposes as other medium-weight webs and also for positioning appliqués, matching prints or plaids at the seamline, and for seams and other construction techniques.

Tapes Galore

Tapes of all weights are available in pre-cut widths sized to match standard seam allowance, hem, trim and ribbon widths.

They're excellent for creating straight and accurate seams and hems, for applying fabric trims and bindings, and for making fused ruffles or pleats. You can also apply fusible adhesive tape to the wrong side of regular drapery tapes to make them fusible.

Sheets & Yardage

Fusible adhesive sheets and yardage are ideal for creating and fusing appliqués or fusing large fabric areas. Most are backed with a plain or gridded paper backing and are transparent enough for you to trace a pattern or design.

Denim Scrapbook

Your treasured family memories will fit perfectly in this denim-covered scrapbook. Add a fabric-printed photo of your loved ones to the cover for the ultimate memory album.

Design by Jacqueline Stetter

Materials

- Photo album
- ¼ yard denim fabric
- Red bandanna
- 2 sizes complementary rickrack
- Printer fabric sheets
- ½-inch fusible tape
- Adhesive-back fusible-web sheets
- Alphabet stencils
- Red dimensional fabric paint
- Paintbrush
- Hot-glue gun
- Computer and printer with photo-printing capabilities

Instructions

1. Print a favorite photo onto a printer fabric sheet.

2. Measure height of notebook (top to bottom) and add 3 inches; measure width (side to side) and add 4 inches. Cut denim to match resulting measurements.

3. Fold denim under 1½ inches along both top and bottom edges. Center open album on fabric; mark sides of album on wrong side of fabric. Mark another line ¼ inch outside each side marking.

4. Using fusible tape, fuse hem top and bottom, leaving unfused the sides from each edge to marking. Fold excess fabric to inside creating sleeves into which you can slide the album's covers.

5. Slide album into sleeves; close to make sure it doesn't pull too tight. Once cover is properly fitted, place fusible tape between where hems and folded sleeves touch. Fuse with iron from outside of album.

6. Run a bead of hot glue along

unfinished edge on inside front and back covers to secure sleeves in place.

7. Beginning on inside front cover, hot-glue larger rickrack in place over unfinished edge of fabric. Continue applying rickrack all the way around outside of front cover, taking care to keep it straight. Repeat on back cover.

8. Determine placement of photo; carefully adhere it to front of album using fusible-web sheet. Using glue gun, frame picture with smaller rickrack.

9. Temporarily fuse a fusible-web sheet onto back of bandanna. Using stencils, trace desired letters on bandanna. Cut out and fuse letters in place.

10. Outline letters with red dimensional fabric paint; let dry. ✂

New Happenings

In addition to fusible web tapes, you can purchase tape specifically designed for fusing hems. It's available as a roll of iron-on adhesive without any paper backing in regular and heavy weights.

Consider using this tape for pillows, draperies, table linens, pillows and lamp shades.

Fabric-Covered Photo Album

Keep your memories close at hand with this beautiful floral motif album. This project is so pretty you won't be able to resist flipping through the pages often.

Design by Chris Malone

Materials

- 3-ring binder photo album
- Fabrics: ½ yard blue-and-white check for cover, ⅓ yard coordinating blue with white polka dots for lining
- Fabric scraps for basket and flower appliqués: light brown print; blue, red and yellow in an assortment of checks, dots and prints; green print
- Embroidery floss: black, green
- Embroidery needle
- ⅓ yard fusible fleece
- Heavy-duty fusible adhesive
- Permanent fabric adhesive
- Lightweight cardboard

Instructions

1. Open album; measure width (from side to side) and length (top to bottom). Cut a piece of fusible fleece to fit. Add 4 inches to each dimension and cut blue-and-white check fabric to size.

2. Fuse adhesive to backs of fabrics.

Referring to patterns and to photo, trace one basket onto back of brown print; trace eight assorted flower shapes and centers onto a variety of red, yellow and blue checks, dots and prints; trace nine leaves onto green print. Cut out shapes.

3. Set aside two flowers, two flower centers and four leaves to decorate insides of covers. Arrange basket with remaining flowers, flower centers and leaves on front cover; fuse in place.

4. Center fleece on wrong side of checked fabric; fuse to fabric.

5. Using 2 strands green floss, sew stem lines to leaves and flowers with running stitch. Using 2 strands black floss, outline arrangement with running stitch.

6. Center open album on wrong side (fleece side) of cover. Fold fabric corners diagonally over corners of album. Fold short edges over sides of album; glue in place. Fold long edges over top and bottom of album, trimming fabric to fit

around binder hardware; glue in place.

7. Lining: Cut two 2-inch-wide strips of lining fabric each 1 inch shorter than album's measured length (top to bottom). Press under both short ends and one long edge ¼ inch on each strip. Center and glue one long strip along each side of hardware with folded edge against metal.

8. Cut two pieces cardboard ½ inch smaller on all sides than front of album. Cut two pieces of blue polka-dot fabric 1 inch larger on all sides than cardboard. Center one cardboard piece on wrong side of one fabric piece; fold corners diagonally over corners of cardboard; glue in place. Fold fabric edges over cardboard; glue in place. Repeat with second piece of cardboard and fabric. Glue covered pieces inside front and back covers.

9. Iron one flower and two leaves on outer bottom corner inside front and back album covers. ✂

Vinyl Vibes

If you'd like to make a project water- or stain-resistant, fusible vinyl is what you're looking for. This flexible vinyl has a paper backing on one side and is designed for both sewing and no-sew projects.

Remove the paper backing to reveal the sticky surface, then adhere it to the right side of the fabric. Once pressed in place with an iron, the bond is permanent and machine washable.

Use it to laminate fabrics for projects like outdoor cushions, table covers, kitchen accessories and accents for children's rooms or playrooms. It's available in shiny or matte finishes.

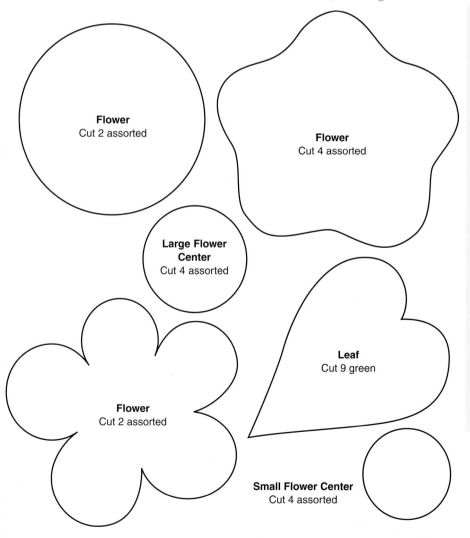

Flower
Cut 2 assorted

Flower
Cut 4 assorted

Large Flower Center
Cut 4 assorted

Leaf
Cut 9 green

Flower
Cut 2 assorted

Small Flower Center
Cut 4 assorted

A Web of Fusing

Thanks to today's technology, the array of heat-activated fusible products keeps growing, making it easier than ever to create gorgeous home decor fabrications without sewing.

Included in this product mix are webs and films for appliqué and construction techniques, liquid fusible web, stabilizers, vinyl for right side applications, fleece for wrong side applications and decor tapes.

As wonderful as it is, this vast array can also be confusing. And, products work better for certain tasks than others. Take a minute to discover what's available, then decide which product or products will best serve your needs.

Be sure to test the product on a scrap of fabric before beginning your project.

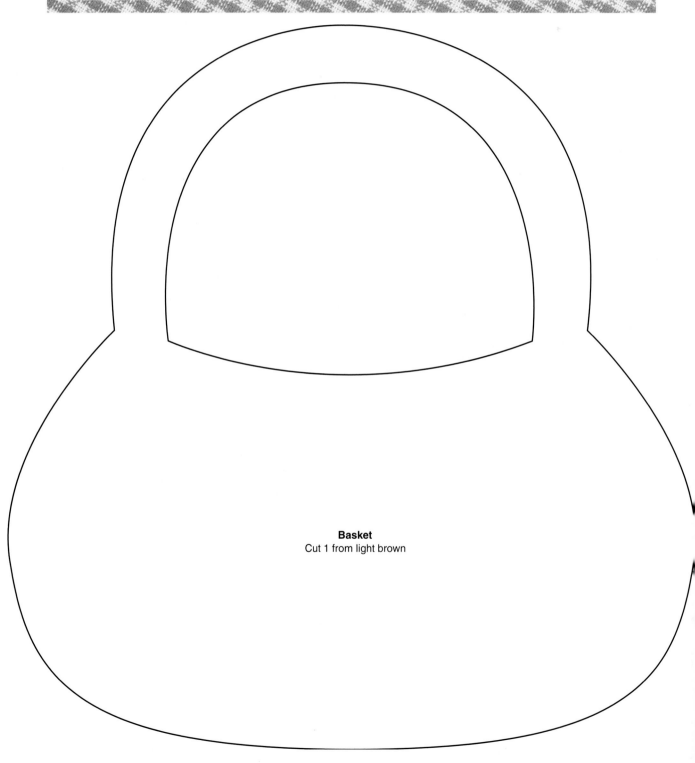

Basket
Cut 1 from light brown

French Country Frame Set

Display pictures of your loved ones proudly in these stylish frames. This French-country-style project is a quick, eye-catching piece for your home.

Design by Mary Ayres

Materials

- 2 (5-inch x 6-inch) rectangular wooden frames
- Photos to fit in frame openings
- ¼ yard heavyweight red toile decorating fabric
- 2 yards ½-inch-wide off-white trim
- 1⅝ yards ⅝-inch-wide off-white wire-edge satin ribbon
- 2 (5-inch x 6-inch) pieces off-white felt
- Permanent craft adhesive
- Permanent fabric adhesive
- Pencil

Instructions

1. Lay frames on right side of fabric, making sure sides of frame enclose a pleasing scene printed on toile. Trace frames' openings and outside edges with pencil. Cut out along traced lines.

2. Apply a thin, even coat of craft adhesive to front of one frame. Lay fabric on top; press flat, smoothing with fingers and wiping off excess adhesive. Repeat with remaining frame and fabric.

3. Using fabric adhesive throughout, glue ½-inch trim around frame openings and outer edges of frames, concealing edges of fabric and butting ends together neatly in a corner.

4. Glue photos to backs of frames in openings.

5. Lay frames facedown on work surface, one above the other, about 1 inch apart. Cut ribbon in half. With bottom end of ribbon even with bottom edge of bottom frame, glue ribbon up side of both frames about ⅜ inch from edge, extending excess over top edge of top frame. Repeat with remaining strip of ribbon, gluing it to other side of frames.

6. Round off corners of felt so that felt will not extend beyond edges of frames. Glue a piece to the back of each frame, covering ribbons; let dry.

7. Tie ribbon ends together in a bow at top of frames; trim ends even. ✂

Cork Memo Board

Never forget a thing with this elegant combination memory and corkboard. Beautiful floral fabric and silky ribbons make this a classic piece you'll enjoy for years to come.

Design by Mary Ayres

Materials

- 6½-inch x 14½-inch wooden rectangular frame
- ¼ yard heavyweight decorator fabric
- 8-inch square unbleached muslin
- 3 (5-inch squares) cotton batting
- 4½ yards ¼-inch ivory satin ribbon
- Flat ivory buttons: 2 (½-inch), 2 (¾-inch)
- 3⅞-inch x 6⅛-inch ¼-inch-thick cork sheet
- 5-inch square cardboard
- 2 thumbtacks
- Light buttermilk acrylic craft paint
- Small paintbrush
- Fine sandpaper
- Tack cloth
- Permanent craft adhesive
- Permanent fabric adhesive
- Pencil
- Sturdy craft scissors

Instructions

1. Lightly sand frame; wipe off dust with tack cloth. Paint frame with two coats of paint, letting it dry between coats.

2. Lay frame on wrong side of fabric; trace frame opening and outside edge with pencil. Cut out along traced lines.

3. Apply a thin, even coat of craft adhesive to front of frame. Lay fabric on top; press flat, smoothing with fingers and wiping off excess adhesive.

4. Cut four lengths of ribbon to fit across edges of frame. Using fabric adhesive, glue one across the top edge of the frame opening, and one across the bottom edge, concealing cut edges of fabric. Set aside remaining pieces of ribbon for now. Measure and cut four pieces of ribbon to fit from top to bottom of frame; glue two along side edges of frame opening, and up and down length of frame, concealing cut fabric edges.

5. Glue remaining ribbon strips along outer edges of frame, gluing on the longer pieces first and then the shorter pieces across top and bottom.

6. Round corners of cork with scissors; glue inside frame opening with craft adhesive.

7. Stack batting squares on top of cardboard, edges even. Place muslin square on top of batting. Wrap and glue raw edges of fabric to back of cardboard with fabric adhesive, pulling fabric taut.

8. Wrap four 8-inch pieces ribbon diagonally across muslin, forming two intersections in center as shown in photo. Glue ribbon ends to back of cardboard with fabric adhesive. Using craft adhesive throughout, glue ¾-inch buttons on top of ribbons where they intersect; let dry.

9. Glue remaining buttons on top of thumbtacks; let dry.

10. Center muslin-covered square on bottom half of memo board; glue in place. Slip photos and other mementos between ribbons or tack them to cork portion with button thumbtacks. ✂

Embellishment Escapades

In addition to trims, other embellishments play leading roles in today's home decor trends.

Button, Button

Who's got the button? Everyone does, and the selection of creative buttons is almost endless. Use wire snips to remove the shank if there is one, then use permanent fabric adhesive to adhere the button to the fabric surface.

Beads Aplenty

Like buttons, the array of beads available is stunning. Glue beads in place with permanent fabric adhesive, or thread them onto ties and lacing strips.

Studs & Stones

Available in assorted metal tones, studs and stones are easy to find in round, square and novelty shapes. Use an applicator tool and follow the manufacturer's instructions to apply the pronged versions, or use permanent fabric adhesive for styles with a flat back. Fairly new on the market is a tool that heat sets its related series of rhinestones and studs.

Iron-on Appliqués & Transfers

A walk through your favorite craft store will reveal a world of appliqués, ranging from embroidered designs to studded shapes.

Transfers, too, range in style and offer something for everyone, from cute painted looks to realistic photos. Follow the manufacturers' instructions to apply any of these to your fabric.

Extra-Hold Fusible Adhesive Film

Similar in use to fusible web and lighter weights of fusible adhesive, this sturdy sheet of adhesive film has paper backing on one side and is intended for a strong bond on no-sew projects only. It fuses at a lower temperature and in less time than webs, so it is applicable to a wider range of materials.

Available in sheets, rolls, yardage and tapes, this film specifies that fabrics should be prewashed without fabric softener. It's ideal for use with medium to heavy fabric weights, felt, suede, leather, wood and cardboard. It can be laundered, but not dry-cleaned.

Bedroom Makeovers

Finding coordinating bedding and bedroom accents that suit your taste and style isn't always easy. Turn that process into a satisfying, creative experience as you select fabrics and embellishments to fit your personal decor. Durable fabric glues and fusible web make it a snap to put together your new bedding and accent pieces!

Fringed Bedroom Ensemble

Pretty feminine fabrics and elegant embellishments are all you'll need for this no-sew bedroom set. Coordinating pillows pull the set together.

Designs by Carol Zentgraf

Project Notes

Use ½-inch seam allowances and fuse seams right sides facing unless otherwise indicated.

Duvet Cover: Before beginning, refer to Duvet Do's, page 130.

Bed Skirt: Before beginning, refer to Bed Skirts, page 101.

Pillow Sham: Materials are given in amounts for a single sham. Each finished sham measures 32 inches x 25½ inches and fits a standard-size pillow.

Materials

Duvet Cover

- 2 (54-inch-wide) home decor fabrics for top and reverse (Refer to Duvet Do's, page 100, to figure yardage needed)
- Loop fringe in length equal to duvet cover's side and bottom edges plus 2 inches
- ½-inch fusible adhesive tape
- ½ yard self-adhesive hook-and-loop tape
- Permanent fabric adhesive

Bed Skirt

- 54-inch-wide home decor fabric (Refer to Bed Skirts, page 101, to figure yardage needed)
- Flat sheet to fit top of box springs
- Fusible shirring tape in yardage to equal bed sides and end measurement
- ½-inch fusible adhesive tape
- Permanent fabric adhesive

Each Pillow Sham

- 1½ yards 54-inch-wide home decor fabric
- 3 yards tassel fringe
- 3 yards gimp trim

- ½-inch and ¼-inch fusible adhesive tape
- Permanent fabric adhesive
- Air-soluble fabric marker

Round Throw Pillow

- Home decor fabrics: 40-inch circle, 8-inch x 36-inch strip
- No-sew round pillow form
- Tassel chair tie
- 1¼ yards tassel fringe
- ¼-inch fusible adhesive tape
- Permanent fabric adhesive

Neck Roll Pillow

- ½ yard each of 2 (54-inch-wide) home decor fabrics
- No-sew neck roll pillow form
- 1 yard tassel fringe
- ¼-inch fusible adhesive tape
- Permanent fabric adhesive

Square Pillow

- Home decor fabrics: 40-inch square, 9-inch x 45-inch strip
- No-sew square pillow form
- 1 yard tassel fringe
- ¼-inch fusible adhesive tape
- Permanent fabric adhesive

Duvet Cover

1. Measure width and length of comforter to be covered. Add 1 inch to width and 4½ inches to length; these measurements determine cut dimensions of pieced cover.

2. Cover top: For center panel, cut a panel of one fabric the full width of the fabric x the length determined in step 1. Cut an identical panel of fabric in half lengthwise for side panels. Align selvage edges with each side of center panel, matching prints. Fuse half panels to full panel with fusible tape. Press seams. Trim side panels evenly so that cover top measures width determined in step 1.

3. Cover back: Repeat step 2 with second fabric.

4. Fuse cover top and back together along side and bottom edges with fusible adhesive tape.

5. Using fabric adhesive, attach loop fringe to edge of duvet cover along side and bottom edges of top, beginning at center bottom edge and working your way up sides. Hold trim in place with pins as needed until adhesive sets. Fold excess ends of loop trim to wrong side of cover top and glue in place.

6. Finish upper edges: Press under and fuse a doubled 2-inch hem on top and back. Fuse upper edges together along side panels only, leaving full edges of center panels open. Cut hook-and-loop tape into three equal pieces; evenly space and adhere tape to open edges, reinforcing them with permanent fabric adhesive if desired.

Bed Skirt

1. Referring to Bed Skirts (page 101), cut determined number of widths from fabric in required length.

2. Fuse panel short ends together using ½-inch fusible adhesive tape and press seam allowances to one side. Turn under and fuse ½-inch hem on short edges and one long edge.

3. Fuse shirring tape to wrong side of remaining long edge, 1 inch from fabric edge. Knot cords together at one end; pull cords from the other end to gather fabric to the determined length. Tie cord ends together.

4. Bed skirt deck: Measure top of box springs; add 2 inches to width measurement and 1 inch to length. Cut flat sheet to these dimensions.

5. Using 1-inch seam allowance, glue upper edge of bed skirt to sheet, aligning ends of skirt with upper edges of sheet.

Pillow Sham

1. Cut 33-inch x 26½-inch panel of fabric for front, and two 19-inch x 26½-inch panels for back.

2. Finish edges for back panel overlap: Turn under left 19-inch edge on right panel; fuse a doubled ¼-inch hem with ¼-inch adhesive tape. Repeat for left panel, turning under right edge.

3. Mark flange: Place front panel wrong side up on flat surface. Using air-soluble marker, draw line around center of panel 3¼ inches from outer edges. Adhere ¼-inch fusible tape along line but do not remove paper backing.

4. Place front panel right side up. Place back panels right side down on front panel, aligning outer edges and overlapping finished edges. Fuse outer edges of front and backs together with ½-inch seam allowance using ½-inch fusible tape. Turn sham right side out; press.

5. Remove paper backing from flange tape; press to fuse front and back panels together along flange line.

6. Using permanent fabric adhesive, glue gimp along flange line and tassel trim along sham's outer edges.

Round Throw Pillow

1. With pre-cut center slit up, center pillow form on wrong side of fabric circle. Evenly bring fabric edges to form front and tuck into center slit.

2. Bow: Press under 2¼ inches along each long edge of fabric strip; overlap and fuse edges together. Shape strip into 12-inch-wide bow; cut off excess length and reserve to use for center. Wrap center tie around bow; knot to secure. Insert ends in pillow form's center slit. Secure tie and wrap ends in slit with fabric adhesive.

3. Tie chair tie through bow loop and glue tassel fringe around edge of pillow.

Neck Roll Pillow

1. Mixing and matching fabrics as desired, cut three 8½-inch x 28-inch strips and two 8-inch circles.

2. Using ¼-inch seam allowance and ¼-inch fusible tape, fuse long edges of strips to each other, right sides facing. Trim as needed to form fused fabrics into a 24-inch x 28-inch panel. Press under a 3-inch hem along one 24-inch edge.

3. Center and glue the raw 24-inch edge across pillow form. Roll fabric snugly around form; glue hemmed edge in place. Tuck fabric ends into slits at ends of pillow form.

4. Center a fabric circle over each end and insert circle edges in slit.

5. Glue tassel fringe along fabric seam lines and around end slits.

Square Pillow

1. With pre-cut center slit up, center pillow form on wrong side of fabric square. Smoothly wrap side edges around form and tuck into center slit. Gather upper and lower edges to form an "envelope" closure and tuck ends into center slit.

2. Band: Press under 2½ inches along each long edge of fabric strip; overlap and fuse edges together. Tuck one band end in pillow form's center slit and wrap band around pillow. Form two loops at center, tucking base of loops and end of band into slit. Secure fabric in slit with fabric adhesive.

3. Glue tassel fringe along band's lower edge. ✂

Drapery Tape Talk

Fusible drapery construction tapes can make even the largest home decor project a snap to create. These tapes have premeasured folds and stitched-in pockets with cords that are pulled after the tape is fused in place.

Perfect for window treatments, dust ruffles, table skirts and sink skirts, these tapes are fusible on one side. They're available as single- or double-cord shirring tape, balloon-shade tape, pinch-pleat tape and ring tape styles.

Simple to Use

To use these tapes, finish your project edge, then fuse the tape along the edge on the wrong side. Pull the cords on the tape to form pleats or gathers.

Look for these tapes in the home decor section of your fabric store. If they are unavailable in your area, make your own with regular drapery tapes and fusible web tape. Simply fuse the web tape along the upper and lower edges of the drapery tape on the wrong side.

Floral Accent Bedroom Set

Give your bedroom a makeover with the coordinating pieces in this striking set. Taking advantage of fabric and fusible web is an easy way to redecorate.

Designs by Jane Schenck

Frame

1. Carefully open package holding glass; reserve protective cardboard to use for base of frame.

2. Trace around cardboard onto paper side of fusible web. Add 1 inch around outer edge and inside center opening.

Materials

Frame

- 8-inch x 10-inch piece of glass packaged with cardboard backing
- Fabrics: ½ yard decorator fabric plus scraps of coordinating floral print
- ½ yard paper-backed fusible web
- ½ yard fusible fleece
- Sawtooth picture hanger
- 15-inch piece 1-inch-wide hook-and-loop tape
- Hot-glue gun
- Pearl fabric paint
- Small paintbrush

Window Shade

Note: *Carefully measure window(s) and refer to instructions for cutting directions before purchasing materials.*

- New or recycled wooden shade roller, bottom slat and mounting hardware
- Decorator fabric (Medium-weight, firm, tightly woven, flat-surface fabrics look best. Consider the print: Large motifs should be centered on shade; stripes, while easy to cut and measure, may be more difficult to fuse because stripes may be pulled out of line during fusing.)

3. Trace cardboard shape onto fusible fleece; cut out.

4. Place fusible web with entire cardboard tracing adhesive side down on wrong side of decorator fabric; press in place. Cut around traced lines.

5. Iron scraps of fusible web to wrong

- Fusible backing
- ½-inch-wide fusible web tape
- Decorative coordinating ½-inch-wide trim or braid
- Coordinating ⅞- to 1-inch-wide ribbon
- Tape

Swag

Note: *Carefully measure window(s) and refer to instructions for cutting before purchasing materials.*

- Medium-weight home-decorating fabric
- ½-inch-wide fusible web tape
- Disappearing-ink marker

Wastebasket

- Fabric (stripes and plaids are not recommended)
- 1-inch-wide ribbon
- ⅝-inch-wide trim
- Heavy-weight sew-in interfacing (stabilizer)
- Fusible fleece
- Paper-backed fusible web
- Kraft paper
- Tape
- Wastebasket
- Hot-glue gun

side of floral print. Cut out flowers and leaves for trimming frame.

6. Place fusible fleece adhesive side down on cardboard base; press with steam iron.

7. Center decorator fabric right side up on top. Press lightly to hold fabric

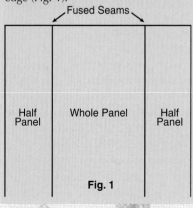

Panel Play

For duvet covers, window treatments and other projects that are wider than one fabric width, do not piece two fabric panels (widths) together with a center seam.

Instead, use a full fabric width as the center panel and two half-widths as the side panels: Cut one panel in half lengthwise and fuse it to each side of a whole panel, matching any prints or plaids.

Cut the width to the desired size by evenly cutting from each side panel edge (Fig. 1).

Fused Seams

| Half Panel | Whole Panel | Half Panel |

Fig. 1

Duvet Do's

1. Measure the width and length of the comforter that will fit inside the duvet cover. Add 1-inch seam allowances to each measurement. This gives you the cut dimensions of the pieced cover.

2. To determine the number of fabric widths needed, divide the cover cut width by the fabric width, rounding up to a whole width. Add 1 inch for each seam needed for piecing.

3. To determine the total yardage required for the cover top, multiply the number of widths by the length, then divide by 36 inches; round up to the nearest half yard.

For fabric with a print to be matched at the seam lines, measure the print repeat and add the extra length to the total yardage.

Example: The cut size for the 92-inch-wide x 95-inch-long queen-size duvet cover featured in the Fringed Bedroom Ensemble, page 126, is 93 inches x 96 inches.

92 inches divided by 54 inches = 2 widths

2 x 96 inches = 192 inches; 192 inches divided by 36 inches = 5½ yards.

Add 1 yard for repeat; total needed for the featured cover top is 6½ yards of fabric.

You will need the same amount for the duvet cover's reverse side.

in place. Fold outer edges of fabric to underside; press.

8. Arrange fabric and leaf cutouts around frame as desired; fuse in place. **Note:** *Allow some petals and leaves to extend beyond edge.*

9. Lightly paint over flowers and leaves with pearl paint; let dry. Turn frame over and paint any unfused edges; let dry.

10. On inside, glue hook-and-loop tape across bottom of frame and 2-inch pieces halfway up both sides.

Glue picture hanger to back of frame.

Window Shade

1. Careful measuring, marking and cutting are essential. Measure window's length (L) and width (W) carefully and note measurements. Then cut fabric, backing and trim:

Fabric: Cut fabric W plus 1½ inches x L plus 10 inches.

Fusible backing: Cut backing W x L plus 10 inches.

Trim: Cut a length equal to twice window's W plus 1 inch.

2. Steam-press decorator fabric to remove wrinkles and minimize shrinkage.

3. Place backing fusible side up on ironing board. Place fabric right side up on top of backing, aligning bottom edges and centering fabric from side to side. Fabric will extend on both sides of backing. Iron, following manufacturer's instructions.

4. Finish sides: Down each side, fold ¼-inch fabric hem to back; press. Place strip of fusible web tape on top of folded edge; press. Peel off paper backing; fold edge over backing, and fuse.

5. On wrong side of fabric, place strip of fusible web tape along lower edge of shade. Turn up 2-inch hem; fuse.

6. Glue ribbon and trim around hem, overlapping ends on center back.

7. Insert slat through hem. Attach shade to top of roller as directed by manufacturer.

Swag

1. Careful measuring, marking and cutting are essential. Measure and note the following:

Window's width (W)

Desired length of swag (L) **Note:** *Swag on sample is short, hanging down just 24 inches on each side of window. Longer swags may extend below windowsill or "puddle" on the floor.*

Desired depth of swag (D) **Note:** *Sample swag is 15 inches deep.*

2. Purchase fabric based on total length of swag: L + L + W + 2 inches (for hem allowances).

3. Cut fabric down its length to reduce width of fabric to 34 inches; trim fabric to square corners and ends perfectly.

4. Narrow hemmed edges: Turn under ¼-inch hem along both ends of fabric;

press. Press strips of fusible tape on top of folded edges. Fold fabric over again, using edge of a sheet of paper as a guide; press lightly to crease. Peel off adhesive's paper backing and fuse fabric in place.

5. Double-folded 1-inch hems across top and bottom: Turn under 1-inch hem across top and bottom edges of fabric; press. Press strips of fusible tape on top of folded edges. Fold fabric over again, 1 inch from edge, and press lightly. Peel off paper backing and fuse.

6. Measuring and marking: Lay fabric wrong side up. Referring to diagram, mark center of fabric from top to bottom. Using this mark as centering point, mark width of window (W) on both top and bottom edges of fabric.

7. On bottom edge only, mark a position equal to half the desired depth of swag (D) outside both W marks. Using ruler, lightly draw lines to connect these points with the W points on top edge of swag (dotted lines on diagram).

8. Using a ruler and beginning at bottom of swag, carefully mark fold lines every 6 inches along line drawn in step 7, continuing to top of swag.

9. Fold bottom edge of swag up to first fold line so that bottom mark on hem matches first pair of cross marks and a deep fold forms.

10. Bring hem and first fold up to second mark, creating a second fold.

11. Continue up swag, creating folds as you connect the marks. Pin or tie edges together.

12. Loop fabric around curtain rod or through swag hooks. Adjust pleats as needed so they are even from side to side and at sides of window.

Wastebasket

1. Make paper pattern of wastebasket: Wrap kraft paper tightly around basket; tape in place. Fold excess paper at top into container, creating a smooth fold around edge. Following bottom of basket, trim off excess paper all around. Draw straight line from top to bottom; cut along line to remove pattern from wastebasket. Trim off excess paper at top.

2. Lay paper pattern flat on stabilizer; add ½-inch seam allowance to both ends (where pattern was cut from top to bottom) and cut out shape. In same manner, cut two pattern shapes with seam allowances from fusible fleece.

3. Trace paper pattern onto fusible web. Add 1½-inch seam allowance to both ends and 1-inch seam allowances along top and bottom edges. Lay web adhesive side down on wrong side of fabric and cut out shape.

4. Fuse one piece of fleece to interfacing; lay second fleece layer on top and fuse again to form a double layer of fleece.

5. Lay fabric adhesive side down on top of fleece; press lightly. Turn under seam allowances extending beyond fleece and interfacing; press.

6. Wrap cover tightly around wastebasket, hot-gluing overlapping ends.

7. Glue ribbon around wastebasket 1 inch from top. Glue on trim on top of ribbon, with bottom edges of trim and ribbon even. ✂

Bed Skirts

1. To determine the cut depth of a bed skirt, measure from the top of the box spring to point ½ inch from the floor and add 2 inches for a hem allowance.

2. Measure the sides and end of the bed to determine the cut length.

For a gathered ruffle, double the length measurement.

For a pleated ruffle, determine the number of inches used for each pleat. Multiply the inches used by the number of pleats and add the total to the length measurement.

3. *To figure the required yardage:* Divide the cut length by the fabric width to determine the number of fabric widths required, allowing 1 inch for each seam.

Multiply the number of fabric widths required by the cut depth and divide by 36 inches to determine the number of yards needed.

Example: The cut dimensions for the gathered bed skirt featured in the Fringed Bedroom Ensemble, page 126, are 440 inches x 15 inches.

440 inches divided by 54 inches = 8.14 + 8 (1-inch) seam allowances; round up to 8½ widths.

8½ x15½ inches =127½ inches = 3.54 yards; round up to 3²/₃ yards of fabric needed.

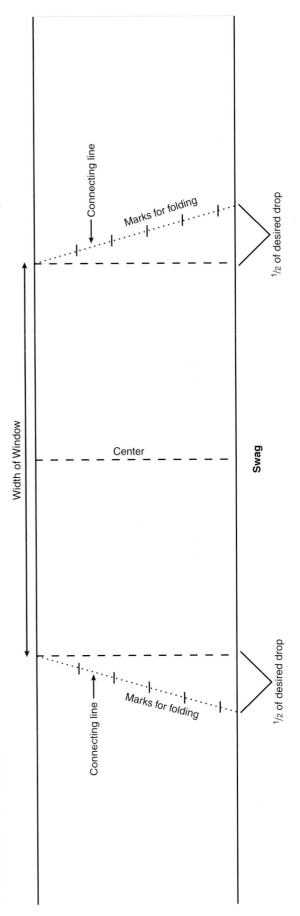

Connecting line

Marks for folding

½ of desired drop

Width of Window

Center

Swag

Connecting line

Marks for folding

½ of desired drop

Antique Crazy Quilt Set

With pretty antique-style fabrics and just a few embroidery stitches, you can create this beautiful patchwork set. It makes a wonderful gift for newlyweds.

Designs by Mary Ayres

Materials

Tissue Box Cover

- Papier-mâché or wooden boutique-style tissue box cover
- Scraps of 13 complementary pastel cotton print fabrics
- Assorted scraps of lace and crochet trim
- 2 yards narrow ⅛- to ³⁄₁₆-inch-wide ribbon or fabric or lace trim
- 3 (8½-inch x 11-inch) sheets memory book mounting adhesive
- Permanent fabric adhesive

Pillow

- 3 tea bags
- 12-inch x 14-inch heavy crochet-edged, envelope-style lingerie bag
- Scraps of 5 pastel complementary cotton print fabrics
- 2 (25-inch) pieces yellow ⅜-inch satin ribbon
- 1 skein yellow embroidery floss
- Embroidery needle
- Polyester stuffing
- Lightweight iron-on adhesive
- Permanent fabric adhesive

Tissue Box Cover

1. Lay box cover on its side on mounting adhesive; trace around it with pencil. Divide resulting rectangle into three unequal sections using ruler and pencil. Cut out sections.

2. Peel paper backing from one side of each section (make sure you peel the same side from each piece) and press each piece of adhesive onto the back of a different fabric. Cut fabric along edges of adhesive sections. Peel off paper backing and adhere fabric shapes to side of box cover, fitting pieces together like a puzzle.

3. Repeat steps 1 and 2 for each of the remaining sides, using a different fabric for each section.

4. Lay box cover on its top on mounting adhesive; trace around edge and center opening; cut out. Peel paper backing from one side and press onto back of final remnant of fabric; cut out along outer edges and opening. Peel off remaining backing and adhere fabric to top of box cover.

5. Glue assorted lace trims over inner seams of fabric scraps, trimming ends even with fabric shapes and sides of box. Glue first those pieces that end in the center of a side, and then those that end on the edges.

6. Glue narrow ribbon or trim around opening in top, around edge of top and down corners. Glue lace trim around bottom edge of box cover.

Pillow

1. Boil tea bags for several minutes in a large pot of water; remove tea bags. Submerge lingerie bag in tea, then remove and rinse in cold water. Dry in dryer; press.

2. Cut five 5-inch x 6-inch pieces from iron-on adhesive. Remove one piece of backing from each and adhere each to the back of a different fabric, following manufacturer's instructions.

3. Referring to layout diagram throughout, cut A, B, C, D and E pieces from different pieces of fused fabric, adding ¼ inch to the bottom and side edges of C, to top and bottom left edges of E, and to top left edge of B (these edges will overlap when fabrics are fused together). Cut pieces A and D as shown.

4. Position fused fabric shapes on crochet-edged flap of lingerie bag, placing C first, then E, then B, then A and D. Fuse fabrics in place.

5. Using 3 strands yellow floss, work blanket stitch along "seams" in patchwork panel, then around outer edge of patchwork panel. Add a second blanket-stitch border in seam between crochet edging and fabric; complete this border by blanket-stitching across top of patchwork panel where crochet edging ends.

6. Insert ribbons through openings in crochet at top of bag on both sides, leaving 2-inch ribbon tail inside bag; glue end to secure. Weave both pieces of ribbon through openings in crochet to meet at center bottom. Tie ribbons in a bow and trim ends evenly.

7. Stuff bag firmly and evenly with stuffing. Spread glue inside opening across top of bag and finger-press shut to keep filling securely in place. ✄

Staple Strategy

Sometimes a staple gun will work where nothing else can, especially when it comes to attaching fabric to wood or heavy cardboard.

Because staples are flat, they're easy to hide under fabric or trim. For large projects, an electric staple gun will prevent arm and hand fatigue.

Antique Patchwork Layout Diagram

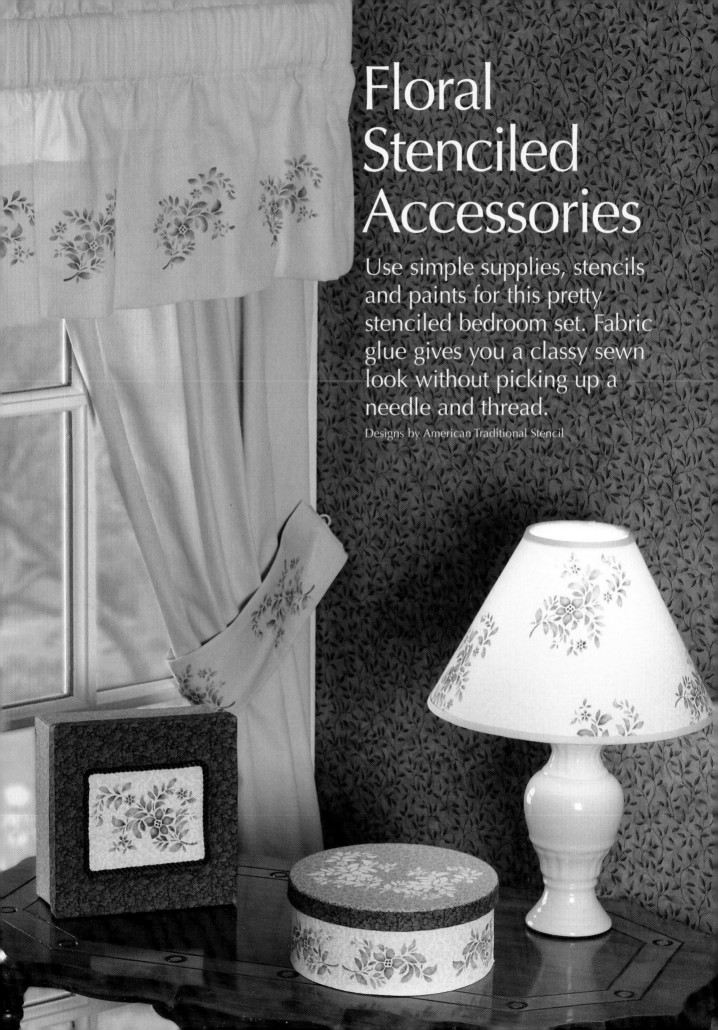

Floral Stenciled Accessories

Use simple supplies, stencils and paints for this pretty stenciled bedroom set. Fabric glue gives you a classy sewn look without picking up a needle and thread.

Designs by American Traditional Stencil

Materials

Each Project

- Flower stencil
- 3 (³/₁₆-inch) stencil brushes
- Oil-paint sticks for stenciling: azo yellow, purple, sap green
- Low-tack masking tape
- Large piece of clean cardboard

Square & Round Boxes

- 3-inch-deep papier-mâché boxes: 7-inch square box, 8-inch-diameter round box
- 1 yard each of three coordinating calico fabrics (sample used small floral prints in dark green, medium green and white-on-ivory)
- White stencil paint
- ⅝ yard ¼-inch-wide purple twisted cord or other decorative trim
- Fabric glue
- Seam sealant

Lamp Shade

- 4-inch x 11-inch x 7-inch self-adhesive lampshade
- ½ yard tone-on-tone calico print fabric (sample is white-on-ivory)
- 1¾ yards ¼-inch ecru double-fold bias tape
- Fabric glue

Window Treatments

- Purchased curtains, tiebacks and valance, or fabric and pattern to make your own

Tips for Successful Stenciling

1. Use very little paint on brush. Tap brush into paint, then swirl brush on paper towel to remove excess, leaving tips of bristles dry to the touch.

2. Use lightest color first and work to the darkest. (It's easier to add darker color over lighter than vice versa.)

3. To increase the intensity of the color, instead of adding more paint to brush, change the pressure on the brush. Changes in pressure will automatically vary the shades of color.

4. Use low-tack masking tape to mask off areas of the stencil that are not needed, or to make design elements fit in the area to be stenciled.

5. Creating mirror images: Stencil first image, then remove stencil and wipe clean. Turn stencil over and stencil second image.

Square Box

1. Measure lid, starting at bottom edge of one side, measuring up over the top and down to bottom edge on opposite side. Measure other dimension in the same manner. Add 1 inch to both dimensions and cut a piece of dark green fabric to this measurement. (For instance, a 7-inch-square top with 1-inch sides would measure 9 inches square. Adding an inch to each dimension results in a 10-inch square of fabric.)

2. Center fabric over top of lid and glue in place, mitering corners as you

fold fabric smoothly down over sides; glue fabric edges inside lid. If desired, line lid with coordinating calico, turning under raw edges near edges of sides.

3. Repeat procedures in steps 1 and 2 to cover box with medium green print.

4. Cut 4-inch x 5-inch piece ivory fabric. Tape edges onto clean cardboard to hold it smoothly and securely for stenciling.

5. Center stencil on fabric square and secure with low-tack tape. Stencil design, referring to Tips for Successful Stenciling: Tap or swirl yellow paint randomly onto leaves; repeat with green. Colors will blend in some areas, yielding a variety of leaf colors. Stencil purple onto flowers.

6. Remove stencil; let paint cure for 24 hours.

7. Heat-set paints: Cover stenciled area with a press cloth; iron.

8. Center stenciled fabric on box lid; glue in place. Measure cord to fit around edges of fabric. Wrap tape around area to be cut; cut, then dab ends of cord with seam sealant. Let ends dry before carefully peeling off tape. Glue cord in place, covering cut edges of stenciled fabric and butting cord ends neatly.

Round Box

1. Measure and cut a circle of ivory fabric the size of the box's base plus 1 inch. Glue fabric to bottom of box, gluing excess fabric smoothly up sides,

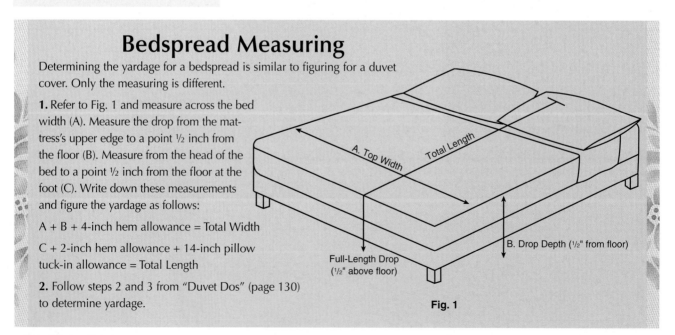

Bedspread Measuring

Determining the yardage for a bedspread is similar to figuring for a duvet cover. Only the measuring is different.

1. Refer to Fig. 1 and measure across the bed width (A). Measure the drop from the mattress's upper edge to a point ½ inch from the floor (B). Measure from the head of the bed to a point ½ inch from the floor at the foot (C). Write down these measurements and figure the yardage as follows:

A + B + 4-inch hem allowance = Total Width

C + 2-inch hem allowance + 14-inch pillow tuck-in allowance = Total Length

2. Follow steps 2 and 3 from "Duvet Dos" (page 130) to determine yardage.

Labels on figure: A. Top Width · Total Length · Full-Length Drop (½" above floor) · B. Drop Depth (½" from floor)

Fig. 1

clipping fabric edges as needed for a smooth fit.

2. Measure circumference of box; cut a piece of ivory fabric ½ inch longer than circumference and 1 inch wider than side of box from top to bottom. Tape edges onto clean cardboard to hold it smoothly and securely for stenciling. Plan arrangement of stenciled design, starting in center of fabric strip and working toward each end. Keep in mind that the lid will overlap top edge of fabric by ⅝–¾ inch, so part of the design may need to be masked off. (Sample project has three pairs of masked and mirror images.)

3. Stencil and heat-set designs on fabric, referring to steps 5–7 for Square Box.

4. Fold under raw edges of fabric; press. Glue fabric to sides of box. If desired, line inside of box with fabric.

5. Measure and cut a circle of medium green fabric the diameter of the box lid plus 2 inches. Center and glue fabric to top of lid, clipping fabric edges and gluing them down smoothly over sides.

6. Measure circumference of lid; cut a piece of dark green fabric ½ inch longer than circumference and ½ inch wider than side of lid from top to bottom. Fold under ¼ inch along all edges; press. Glue this band around edge of lid.

7. Position stencil on left half of lid so that you can stencil a mirror image on right half; secure with low-tack tape. Stencil design with white. Remove stencil, wipe off, turn stencil over and secure it on right side of lid. Stencil mirror image with white. Remove stencil; let dry completely.

Lamp Shade

1. Following manufacturer's instructions, measure and cut fabric to fit shade.

2. Tape fabric edges onto clean cardboard to hold it smoothly and securely for stenciling.

3. Referring to step 5 for Square Box, stencil a random floral pattern on fabric. Remove stencil; let paint cure for 24 hours.

4. Heat-set paints: Cover stenciled area with a press cloth; iron.

5. Attach fabric to shade following instructions on shade's label.

6. Glue bias tape around top and bottom edges of lamp shade.

Window Treatments

1. Iron curtain tiebacks and valances as needed to remove wrinkles.

2. Tape tiebacks onto clean cardboard to hold them smoothly and securely for stenciling.

3. Referring to step 5 for Square Box, secure stencil and stencil a motif in center of one tieback. Stencil additional motifs, working toward each end and spacing them evenly. On remaining tieback, reverse stencil so that tiebacks will look symmetrical on curtains.

4. Measure and plan stencil layout on valance so flowers will be positioned evenly across bottom edge. Secure with low-tack tape and stencil as for tiebacks.

5. Allow stenciled tiebacks and valance to cure for 24 hours.

6. Heat-set paints: Cover stenciled area with a press cloth; iron. ✄

Fabric Snippets

Size Matters

When selecting fabric, keep in mind that home decor fabrics are wider than fashion fabrics. This makes them more practical for large projects like duvet covers, window treatments and tablecloths, because less piecing is required.

Quality Counts

Especially for large projects, choosing a high-quality fabric will not only ensure attractive results, it may also save your sanity.

Make certain that the pattern or plaid is printed straight—aligned with or perpendicular to the selvage edges—or it will appear to run up or downhill when made into a project.

The same holds true for fabric grain. On quality fabrics, the lengthwise grain will run parallel to—and not at odd angles to—the selvage. This affects the way the fabric will drape after it's cut.

Easy Living

Consider bed sheets and table linens as sources of fabric. The wide width of sheets makes them ideal for numerous bed and window treatments, and the ready-made hems can save hemming time.

Table linens can be used for myriad projects, from pillows to window treatments.

Tune In

Whether you're decorating an entire room or just looking for a quick accessory update, it's good to begin with a plan.

Do you admire ideas you see in magazines and catalogs? Tear them out, then keep a folder or notebook of favorite decorating ideas.

Add fabric and trim swatches that you'd like to incorporate in your home, then pull it all together when you're ready to fabricate your decor accents.

Many of the sewn looks you see in decorating magazines and catalogs can be easily adapted to no-sew creations, as you'll discover through the projects in this book. And best of all, you can make any of them fit into your decor by selecting appropriate fabrics and trims.

Spring Tulips Valance

Brighten up a plain room or add yearlong springtime flair with colorful, cheery flowers. Iron-on adhesive makes this a simple project with great results.

Design by Annie Lang

Materials
- 3 (16-inch) square white napkins with Battenburg lace corners
- 3 (3-inch) yellow-orange Battenburg tulips
- 3 (5-inch) seafoam green Battenburg leaf shapes
- Heavy-duty fusible adhesive sheet
- 3 yards heavy-duty fusible adhesive tape
- Pressing paper
- Wide satin ribbon (optional)

Project Note
Sample was designed to fit a 36-inch rod. If working with a longer rod, you may need additional materials.

Instructions
1. Fold napkins in half diagonally to create triangles with lace corners in the center; iron.

2. Lay two triangles on the ironing board, folds across the top and lace facing you; arrange so that they overlap slightly. Check width against curtain rod and adjust overlap to fit. Fuse overlapping edges together with adhesive tape.

3. Place center triangle over other two; secure center triangle with fusible adhesive tape.

4. Rod pocket: Sandwich a length of tape inside folded triangles across valance with bottom edge of tape 2 inches below fold; fuse with iron.

5. Place Battenburg tulips and leaves on a piece of fusible adhesive; place pressing paper on top and fuse. Remove pressing paper and pull Battenburg shapes off adhesive.

6. Arrange tulips and leaves above lace corners in points of valance as shown in photo. Place pressing paper over pieces; iron firmly into place.

7. Optional: For a pretty, feminine touch, add bows of wide coordinating ribbon at ends of curtain rod. ✂

Wildly Floral Painted Sheet Set

Give your bedroom a splash of color with a bright and bold floral design. You can finish this must-have sheet set in less than a day!

Designs by Annie Lang

Materials
- White cotton bed linens: flat top sheet, pillowcase
- Clothesline
- Spray colors: basil, cinnabar, Sonia
- Textile markers: dark pink, green, red
- Shirt-painting board or cardboard covered with plastic

Instructions

1. Wash bedding without using fabric softener to remove sizing. Hang damp bedding on clothesline.

2. Working quickly before bedding dries, stand 15–18 inches from bedding and spray it randomly with large circular blotches of Sonia. **Note:** *Work as quickly as possible, as the damp fabric helps soften and blend the colors.* These areas will be the flowers, so loosely spray various sizes over the bedding, spacing them far enough apart so that

you can add some greenery while still allowing some of the white background to show through.

3. Continuing to work quickly, spray large, oval, leaflike shapes of basil here and there around flowers.

4. Add just a few, small, blotchy areas of cinnabar between flower and leaf shapes to help fill gaps. Do not overdo this darker color; it is intended to be an accent for the flower colors. Some white background should still be visible.

5. To pull design together, "spatter" the linens with cinnabar: Step back a bit from the bedding and spray with short blasts from the can of cinnabar, depressing the nozzle only halfway; this interrupts the spray and applies the color in spatters rather than a mist. Work your way around the bedding, "spattering" it in this manner.

6. Allow bedding to dry on the line, then take down.

7. Enhance designs with fabric markers:

Secure a section of the sheet or pillowcase over the shirt-painting board. Use brush tip on red marker to draw loose, squiggly, circular flower shapes on each of the flowers. Don't worry about making shapes identical.

8. Using scroll brush tip on green marker, loosely draw leaf shapes around flower areas. Use fine tip of green marker to add loose, fernlike shapes and squiggly, curly vines to help fill areas.

9. Using fine tip of dark pink marker, draw clusters of loosely formed mini circles; circles should not be much larger than a pencil eraser. Using brush tip of dark pink marker, transform some of the cinnabar blotches into small flowers.

10. Heat-set the paints by drying the finished bedding in a dryer on "HIGH" setting for about 15 minutes. Using an iron on the cotton setting, press bedding to remove wrinkles and set color a second time. ✂

Safari Sheet Set

Give your bedroom an exotic jungle feel by adding animal-print sheets. This wild set is easy to make with rubber stamps and paint.

Designs by Jeanne Cody

Materials

- White bed linens: top sheet, 2 pillowcases
- Flat paintbrush
- Acrylic craft paints: black, burnt sienna, terra cotta
- Fabric-painting medium
- Rubber stamps: zebra, elephant, giraffe, sun, leopard spots plus an old spiral stamp
- Craft knife

Instructions

1. Launder sheet and pillowcases without using fabric softener; dry and press as needed.

2. Blend fabric-painting medium into all paints, 1 part medium to 2 parts paint.

3. Using paintbrush to apply paint to stamps throughout, apply burnt sienna to leopard spots stamp. Reapplying paint as needed, stamp pillowcase, leaving the hem white and leaving some other white areas showing. Let dry completely.

4. Use paintbrush to add terra cotta sparingly between burnt sienna spots; let dry completely.

5. Apply black paint to zebra, giraffe, elephant and sun stamps and stamp images alternately over sheet and pillowcases; let dry completely.

6. Use a craft knife to cut a few sections out of the spiral stamp to break up the spiral pattern. Then apply black paint to the stamp and stamp images onto white hems of pillowcases. Between black images, add some terra cotta with paintbrush.

7. Using same spiral stamp and black, fill in as desired on sheet and pillowcases. Let dry completely.

8. If pillowcases have lace or eyelet, enhance the trim with small dots of black or other colors as desired.

9. If desired, use a cardboard triangle as pattern/spacer and add terra cotta between spirals on sheet. Let dry.

10. Referring to instructions accompanying fabric-painting medium, launder sheet and pillowcases before using them. ✂

Asian Influence Display Banner

Add mysterious Eastern charm to your bedroom with this banner. Bamboo, ribbon and beads combine beautifully to make a wonderful display for photos and other keepsakes.

Design by Mary Lynn Maloney

Materials

- 18-inch x 27-inch canvas banner
- 17½-inch x 26½-inch piece felt in desired color
- 4 yards ¾-inch-wide green/blue/metallic gold floral-print jacquard ribbon
- 4 yards dark salmon ⅝-inch-wide satin ribbon
- ⅝-inch shank buttons: 8 dark blue, 3 copper
- Fabric glue
- Wire snips
- Safety goggles
- Gem glue
- 28 inches amber/purple multi-colored beaded fringe
- 20½-inch ⅜-inch-diameter bamboo rod
- 4 yards multicolored/multi-textured decorative fibers
- 14 assorted decorative beads

Instructions

1. Lay banner on work surface with long edges at top and bottom. Using ruler, lightly mark five evenly spaced diagonal lines from top toward bottom, first in one direction and then the other, intersecting lines to form a diamond pattern.

2. Cut floral jacquard ribbons to lengths of first five diagonal lines plus 1 inch on each end. Repeat with salmon satin ribbons. Lay ribbons over pencil marks and weave in an over-under pattern.

3. Working from center intersection outward and using fabric glue through step 5, glue each ribbon intersection to banner. **Note:** *Apply glue only to intersections. Let dry.*

4. Turn ends of ribbons to back of banner; glue in place with fabric glue. Let dry.

5. Glue felt to back of banner, covering ribbon ends.

6. While wearing goggles, snip shanks off buttons. Using gem glue, glue copper button at each intersection in center row and blue buttons at remaining intersections.

7. Turn banner so that casing is at top. Glue beaded fringe to bottom edge of banner; turn ends to wrong side and glue in place.

8. Hanger: Slide bamboo rod through casing. Tie ends of 26-inch piece of salmon ribbon to ends of bamboo.

9. Cut decorative fibers into two approximately equal sets. Thread beads onto the fibers in a random fashion, knotting beads on fibers to secure their positions. **Note:** *Hanging the banner on a wall makes this step easier.* Tie beaded fibers so that they dangle from ends of bamboo rod. ✂

Natural Elegance Valance

Colorful trim and bright beads add style and elegance to this valance. This is a simple way to revamp existing home decor.

Design by Mary Lynn Maloney

Instructions

1. Insert a piece of mat board into each pillow cover.

2. Lay pillow cover on work surface with flap open and button facing you. Lay place mat over pillow, aligning one short end with top edge of pillow cover. Cut a small slit in place mat where pillow cover button is located; slip button through slit. Using fabric glue, glue place mat to pillow cover front; turn remainder of place mat over bottom edge of pillow cover and up back; glue in place. **Note:** *Place mat will cover only part of back.* Repeat with remaining pillow covers; let dry.

3. Button flap closed over top edge of place mat. Cut a 14½-inch piece jacquard ribbon; fold edges under so that ribbon fits width of place mat. Press folded edges under and glue ribbon across place mat at bottom edge. Repeat with salmon ribbon, gluing it to partially overlap jacquard ribbon. Repeat with remaining pillow covers.

4. While wearing goggles, snip shanks off ⅜-inch buttons. Using gem glue, glue a button to center of each pillow button. Snip shanks off ¾-inch buttons; glue one in each open end of bamboo rod. Let dry.

5. Cut decorative fibers into three sets of fibers, one for each pillow button. Thread beads onto fibers in a random fashion, knotting fibers to hold beads as desired. Loop beaded fibers behind pillow buttons and dab a bit of fabric glue between buttons and fibers to secure.

6. Lay pillow covers side by side; slide bamboo rod through top of each flap.

7. Install brackets; hang valance. ✄

Materials

- 3 (14-inch-square) natural-color envelope pillow covers
- 3 (13-inch x 13½-inch) pieces mat board
- 3 tan and black bamboo place mats
- 2 bottles fabric glue
- 2 yards ¾-inch green/blue/metallic gold floral-print jacquard ribbon
- 2 yards dark salmon ⅝-inch satin ribbon
- Copper shank buttons: 3 (⅜-inch), 2 (¾-inch)
- Wire snips
- Safety goggles
- Gem glue
- 47½-inch ⅝-inch-diameter bamboo rod
- 4 yards multicolored/multi-textured decorative fibers
- 24 assorted decorative beads
- Drapery rod brackets with hardware

French Country Toile Boxes

Special keepsakes fit beautifully in these attractive and stylish boxes. You'll love all the compliments you'll receive on these quick and easy projects.

Design by Mary Ayres

Materials

- Small round papier-mâché boxes with lids, 8 inches in diameter or smaller
- Fabrics: ¼ yard red toile print fabric, ¼ yard red satin
- ½-inch-wide off-white fabric trim
- Memory book adhesive mounting sheets
- Permanent fabric adhesive
- Scallop-edge fabric shears or pinking shears

Instructions

For each box:

1. Lay box lid top down on a sheet of mounting adhesive; trace around it with a pencil. Add ¼-inch margin all around and cut out. **Note:** *If sides of lid are deeper than ½ inch, cut the fabric circle larger or use wider trim to cover lid sides.*

2. Peel paper backing from one side and adhere shape to wrong side of toile fabric, centering a fabric motif in the circle. Cut out fabric along edge of adhesive. Peel off remaining backing and adhere fabric, centered, over top and sides of lid.

3. Measure circumference of lid; add 1 inch to measurement and cut trim to that length. Glue trim around sides of lid, butting edges together neatly.

4. Set box on adhesive sheet; trace around bottom with a pencil. Cut out.

5. Peel backing from one side and adhere shape to wrong side of satin. Using scallop-edge shears, cut out circle ⅛ inch inside edge of adhesive; set aside.

6. Measure circumference and depth (top to bottom) of box sides. Add ½ inch to each dimension and cut a strip of mounting adhesive to match those measurements. **Note:** *If circumference measures more than 11 inches, cut two strips and butt ends together.*

7. Peel backing from one side and adhere strip to wrong side of satin. Cut out fabric along edges of adhesive, then trim one short end of strip with scallop-edge shears. Peel off remaining backing and adhere fabric around sides of box, aligning top edge of fabric with top edge of box; fold excess fabric onto bottom of box, clipping fabric as needed. Overlap short ends of strip with scalloped edge on top.

8. Peel remaining backing from satin circle (step 5) and adhere to bottom of box, covering edges of fabric from sides. ✂

Geometric Accents Bedroom Decor

Create this handsome bedroom set in a snap with bold fabrics and ready-made fringe. This is a great way to affordably update the look of your bedroom.

Designs by Debbie Williams

Project Notes

Purchasing fabric: If making the entire ensemble, the fabric totals are: 1¼ yards medium-weight fabric with small print; 1⅞ yards medium-weight solid purple fabric; ¾ yard fabric with large print; 1 yard solid beige fabric.

Coordinating fabrics: Fabric used for small lamp shade matches that used on clock and stool and should coordinate with fabric used on large lamp shade.

Tumble-dry all fabrics on the hottest appropriate setting to preshrink.

Measure and cut trims precisely. Tape over cutting marks and cut through tape, then apply seam sealant to ends. Let dry before carefully removing tape. Use craft picks to apply glue carefully to back of trims.

For wooden projects, sand wood smooth, then wipe off dust with a tack cloth. Apply sealer with a flat brush; let dry, then sand lightly and wipe off dust.

Stool

1. Stool comes unassembled. Trace around top of stool onto foam pad; cut foam on traced line. Lightly trace around top of stool onto back of print fabric; add 2½-inch margin all around oval and cut fabric on this outer line.

2. Place print fabric right side down on table. Lay cushion on inner oval. Place wood top down over cushion. Wrap fabric up around edges and staple to underside of wood, stapling first at one end and then at opposite end. Next staple center of one side, then center of other side. Continue stapling back and forth in this manner to distribute fabric evenly. After stapling is completed, tap staples with hammer until they are flush with wood surface.

3. Sand remaining wood pieces; wipe with tack cloth. Using flat brush, seal inner surface and all edges of legs, edges of leg brace and edges of

groove on underside of stool top with a coat of sealer; let dry. Paint sealed surfaces black; let dry. Apply iridescent glaze; let dry.

4. Iron adhesive onto wrong side of purple fabric. Trace legs onto paper backing; also trace entire leg brace, rolling brace on edge to opposite side. (Brace tracing should measure approximately 7 inches x 7½ inches.) Apply seam sealant as needed; let dry.

5. Beginning at floor edge, apply fused fabric to outer sides of legs and brace, trimming edges carefully as needed. To ensure that leg assembly fits in grooves, leave ⅛ inch of wood uncovered at top of legs. On ends of brace, leave ¼ inch of wood uncovered. Fit assembly into grooves to check fit; trim as needed before proceeding.

6. Trace oval edge and leg and brace grooves on underside of stool top onto tracing paper with pencil. Place

Materials

Stool

- 12½-inch x 7½-inch x 9-inch wooden stool
- 18-inch x 12-inch x 1-inch foam cushion
- 18-inch x 12-inch white poster board
- ¼ yard solid purple medium-weight fabric
- ½ yard fabric with small print
- 2-inch antique rose tassel fringe
- ½ yard heavy-duty fusible adhesive
- All-purpose sealer
- 1-inch glaze/wash paintbrush
- Black acrylic craft paint
- Red iridescent glaze
- Several craft picks
- Glass countertop or wooden cutting board
- Old pillowcase or muslin
- Rotary cutter and self-healing mat
- Acrylic ruler
- Razor knife
- Seam sealant
- Tracing paper
- Fine-grit sandpaper
- Tack cloth

- Heavy-duty home decor stapler with staples
- White glue
- Clothespins
- Removable tape

Clock

- 5-inch x 7-inch x 2-inch wooden arch clock
- Quartz clock movement for ¾-inch-thick surface
- All-purpose sealer
- Brown antiquing gel
- Glossy-finish interior/exterior varnish
- Size 12 shader paintbrush
- Stencil sponges
- Brush cleaner
- White glue
- 10-inch x 7-inch piece fabric with small print
- Pure gold ³⁄₁₆-inch rayon twisted satin cord
- Removable tape

Large Lamp

- 6-inch x 8-inch x 12-inch self-adhesive lamp shade
- Desired lamp base
- 2¼ yards natural-color ½-inch

Mandarin braid trim

- 1⅝ yards natural-color 2-inch flapper fringe
- Fabrics: ¾ yard fabric with large print; 1⅝ yards solid purple
- Chalk pencil
- 27-inch wine chair tie
- Rubbing alcohol
- Cotton swabs
- Removable tape
- White glue
- Craft picks

Small Lamp

- 4-inch x 10-inch x 6-inch self-adhesive lamp shade
- Desired lamp base
- 1¼ yards aubergine ostrich trim
- Fabrics: ½ yard fabric with small print; 1 yard solid beige
- Chalk pencil
- 27-inch moss green chair tie
- Rubbing alcohol
- Cotton swabs
- Removable tape
- White glue
- Craft picks

Cutting Edges

Panels and large pieces of woven fabric should always be cut following the lengthwise or crosswise grain of the fabric. These grains are stable and the shapes will maintain their shape.

To cut panels, first square off one end of the fabric. Line up a T-square or carpenter's square with the fabric's selvage edge and mark a line straight across the fabric. Use this line as the basis for cutting your first panel (Fig. 1).

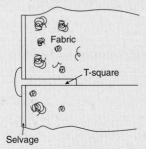

Fig. 1
Squaring Fabric Edges

Pillow Shams

Standard pillow sizes are as follows, but it's best to measure your pillow to be sure.

Standard

    20 inches x 26 inches

Queen

    20 inches x 30 inches

King

    20 inches x 38 inches

tracing paper pencil side down on poster board. Rub over traced lines firmly with pencil, transferring them to poster board.

7. Apply iron-on adhesive to clean side of poster board. Cut traced oval lines and grooves on poster board with scissors and razor knife. Apply purple fabric over adhesive; trim to ½ inch beyond edge of poster board. Cut a line down the center only of the grooves. Clip fabric edge at ¼-inch to

½-inch intervals; glue clipped fabric smoothly to underside of poster board. Let dry.

8. Align poster board with grooves on underside of stool top. Apply glue to grooves. Place brace through fabric-covered poster board and into slot. Assemble legs by leaning leg and placing the outer fabric side into the slot first. Slide poster board away from underside of tool enough to apply glue around legs and brace. Apply glue around perimeter. Use pins to hold poster board against cushion fabric while glue dries. Apply weight to glued areas around legs and brace.

9. When dry, place stool upright and apply tassel fringe around lower edge of cushion. Apply tape, cut and seal as directed in Project Notes. When dry, cut end to fit precisely and glue in place. Hold all fringe in place with pins while drying.

Clock

1. Place tracing paper over front of clock. Trace inner arch shape with pencil. Measure perimeter of arch precisely with measuring tape. Measure twisted cord to fit around arch; tape, seal and cut as directed in Project Notes. Set aside cord and paper pattern.

2. Prepare wood as directed in Project Notes.

3. Using stencil sponges, apply antiquing gel to base and arch edges. Use flat brush to apply gel to hard-to-reach areas under base. Lightly remove excess gel with clean sponge; let dry for 1 hour.

4. Apply two coats of varnish with a clean, dry, flat brush, letting varnish dry between coats.

5. Cut traced arch shape from tracing paper. Pin to fabric and cut out, adding ¼ inch all around. Repeat to make second fabric arch.

6. Using a paintbrush, apply a thin, even coat of glue to front and adjacent routed edge of clock. Press fabric arch in place over glue; press firmly and smooth fabric. Glue cord over cut edge of fabric, pressing it into routed groove. Glue remaining fabric and trim to back of clock; let dry.

7. Using razor knife, cut hole for clock movement. Insert clock movement according to accompanying instructions.

Large Lamp

1. Remove adhesive from metal parts of lamp shade with cotton swabs and rubbing alcohol.

2. Referring to instructions accompanying lamp shade, cover shade with print fabric.

3. Seal end of fringe with seam sealant or tape to keep it from unraveling; let dry. Measure fringe to fit around bottom edge of shade. Apply seam sealant to ¼-inch area on either side of where fringe will be cut, but do not cut at this time; let dry. Without cutting, begin gluing fringe around bottom of shade, applying glue to about 2 inches at a time, and holding fringe to shade with spring clothespins. After 3 or 4 hours, when glue has begun to set, carefully remove clothespins. When completely dry, carefully cut fringe through sealed section so ends will meet neatly; glue remaining fringe in place.

4. Measure Mandarin braid to fit around top and bottom edges of shade. Using same procedure as in step 3, glue braid over top of fringe and around top of shade.

5. Measure from top of lamp base around to other side, keeping tape measure against shape of base. Add 16 inches to this measurement, then divide total by 2. Note this measurement.

6. Fold solid purple fabric into quarters, wrong side out; mark center with a pin. Fold fabric once more in half, forming a triangle. Pin layers together to prevent shifting.

7. Beginning at triple fold, measure from pin toward cut edges and mark with a chalk pencil. Mark at 1- to 2-inch intervals across to single fold, forming a curve. Cut fabric through all layers along curve.

8. Measure diameter of base at bottom; divide by 2 to find radius. Measure from bottom of base to electrical cord; add this figure to the radius for cord position. Measure from center marking pin and mark cord position with chalk pencil.

9. Measure perimeter of largest part of electrical cord plug. Divide by 2, then add ¼ inch for length of plug and cord opening. Mark the plug opening, centering it over cord position mark. The direction of the cutting line should go from center mark pin toward cut edge of fabric.

10. Keep center of fabric marked. Unfold to reveal circle. Press fabric and place on table covered with protective surface. Apply generous amount of seam sealant to cord/plug opening and cut edge of fabric circle. When dry, place cord opening over cutting mat and cut with razor knife.

11. Place fabric circle right side up on table. Measure 8 inches from edge all around and mark with pins. Turn fabric wrong side up. Fold cut edge toward center at pin-marked line.

12. Place lamp base on center of fabric; run cord through opening for cord and plug. Tie chair tie loosely around top of lamp base. Removing pins as needed, carefully pull fabric up through tie, forming a cuff above tie. (Cut edge of cuff should remain under tie). Evenly distribute fabric gathers around base. Remove pins and adjust tie as needed; tie in knot or bow.

Small Lamp

Follow procedures for making large lamp, substituting small lamp materials. Use print fabric for shade and beige fabric for base. ✂

Lights On!

It's easy to cover any size lamp shade with fabric when you make a pattern first using pattern tracing cloth or tracing paper.

1. Locate the seam. If there isn't one, draw a straight line from the bottom to the top of the shade.

2. Using a large piece of tracing cloth or paper, line one straight edge up with the seam or drawn line and tape in place. Wrap the paper around the shade, overlapping the starting end, and tape to secure.

3. Use a fine-tip marker to trace the upper and lower edges of the shade and the seam line or marked line (Fig. 1).

4. Remove the paper and cut along the traced lines for a pattern.

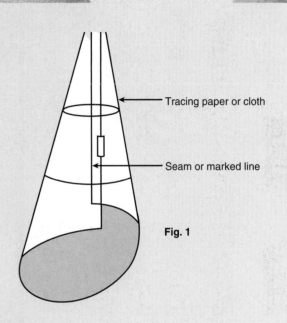

Tracing paper or cloth

Seam or marked line

Fig. 1

Making Welting

Plain cotton cording, available by the yard in the home decor department of fabric stores, is inexpensive yet sturdy and ideal for covering with bias fabric strips to create welting.

Choose a diameter that's proportionate to the size of your project. You'll want a ¼- to ¾-inch diameter for most home decor applications.

Purchase or make continuous bias-cut fabric strips equal to the length of the seam or edge to be finished, plus several inches for an overlap. The strips should be wide enough to wrap closely around the cording, plus 1 inch for seam allowances.

Cut strips of fusible web or adhesive in the same dimensions. Fuse the adhesive to the wrong side of the bias strip; remove the paper. Wrap the fabric strip, right side out, around the cording. Align the fabric edges and fuse together up to the cording edge; it's not necessary to fuse the fabric to the cording (Fig. 1).

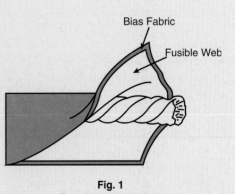

Bias Fabric

Fusible Web

Fig. 1
Fuse layers to cording.

Playful Pals Cornice

Cavorting critters and bright colors make this a playful addition to any child's room. Complete the cornice easily using Styrofoam brand foam and iron-on adhesive.

Design by Annabelle Keller for Dow

Cornice

1. Referring to layout diagram, cut pieces for cornice ends and top from one sheet of Styrofoam using a serrated knife waxed with paraffin or a table saw. Second piece of Styrofoam is used as is, uncut, for front of cornice.

2. Assemble ends and top: Referring to Fig. 1, apply hot glue to three wooden picks and insert into edge of top, leaving ¾ inch protruding. Apply plastic-foam adhesive to edge between the picks and hot glue to the picks themselves, then press end securely onto top; let dry. Repeat to assemble other end of cornice.

3. Attach front to top/end assembly, gluing picks into edges of Styrofoam every 3 inches. Apply plastic-foam adhesive to spaces between the picks; partially press into top/end assembly. Apply hot glue to a few spots along edge between picks and quickly press front and top/end together securely; let dry.

Covering & Final Assembly

1. Cut a piece of batting 23 inches x 54 inches. Wrap batting from 1½ inches

Materials

- 2 (12-inch x 36-inch x 1-inch) sheets Styrofoam® brand foam
- 30 (3-inch) wooden floral picks with wires removed
- Crib-size piece of polyester batting
- 44- to 45-inch-wide fabrics: ⅝ yard animal print for center panel; 1⅝ yards solid gold for top, borders and lining
- 2 packages emerald large piping
- ¼ yard heavy-duty fusible adhesive
- 2 (5-inch) angle brackets with screws
- 6 large T-pins
- Plastic-foam adhesive
- Permanent fabric adhesive
- Fine-tip permanent marker
- Serrated knife
- Small piece paraffin
- Table saw (optional)
- Hot-glue gun with needle nozzle
- Rotary cutter and self-healing mat

inside top to inside bottom and 1½ inches inside from side to side. Trim away excess batting at mitered corners. Hot-glue batting inside cornice near edge.

2. From print fabric, cut one piece 37 inches x 10 inches and two pieces 9½ inches x 10 inches.

3. Center fabric panel: Press ½-inch hems in long edges of larger fabric panel. Center fabric across front of cornice and hot-glue in place, wrapping excess fabric around edges at sides.

4. End panels: Press ½-inch hems in top and bottom edges of smaller fabric panels, and along the right edge of one and the left edge of the other. Align pressed side edges at front corners and top to bottom with front panel and wrap unpressed edges to inside back of cornice; hot-glue to secure.

5. Piping: Cut two 55-inch pieces piping. Align raw edges with hemmed edges of center panel; glue in place with fabric adhesive, wrapping approximately 1½ inches to inside of cornice on each side, top and bottom.

6. Gold borders: From gold fabric, cut an 11-inch x 55-inch strip for top and top border and a 5-inch x 55-inch strip for bottom border. Press ½-inch hem in one long edge of each piece.

Centering both top and bottom pieces, use fabric adhesive to glue fabric over raw edges of piping, leaving only the corded portion showing. Miter all corners, trimming away excess fabric, and hot-glue approximately 1½ inches of the gold fabric inside cornice.

7. Lining: From gold fabric, cut one strip 55¾ inches x 5¼ inches to line top and sides, and one strip 34¼ inches x 11¼ inches to line front. Press ¼-inch hems in two short edges and one long edge of each strip. Center and hot-glue hemmed edges of longer strip approximately 1 inch from open edges of sides and top. Press ¼-inch hem in all sides of shorter strip; hot-glue to back of cornice front, covering raw edges of first piece and adjusting hem on end as needed for a good fit.

8. Following manufacturer's instructions, apply fusible adhesive to wrong side of a piece of remaining print fabric. Cut out desired additional animal motifs; remove paper backing and fuse motifs carefully on cornice, using tip of hot iron.

9. Mount angle brackets on wall; rest completed cornice on brackets. ✁

Prints Charming

If you're going to use a large-print fabric for pillows or cushions, purchase extra fabric to allow you to center a large motif on each pillow or cushion.

You'll also want to purchase extra yardage of print or plaid fabrics for projects where you want them to match at the seam lines. Generally it isn't necessary for small overall designs or prints, but it adds a professional touch for larger motifs.

It's especially important for projects like duvet covers and window treatments where the entire fabric expanse is seen at the same time.

To determine the amount of extra fabric you'll need, multiply the number of seams to be matched by the length of the fabric repeat. For example, if you want to match two seams and the fabric has a 12-inch repeat, you'll need an extra 24 inches, or ⅔ yard of fabric.

Bedtime Story

To make bedspreads, duvet covers and dust ruffles, it's important to correctly determine the yardage. Standard mattress dimensions (width x length) are as follows:

Twin	39 inches x 75 inches
Full	54 inches x 75 inches
Queen	60 inches x 80 inches
King	78 inches x 80 inches

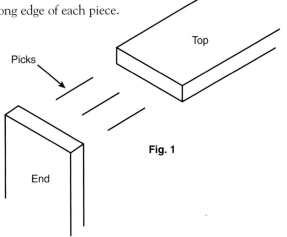

Fig. 1

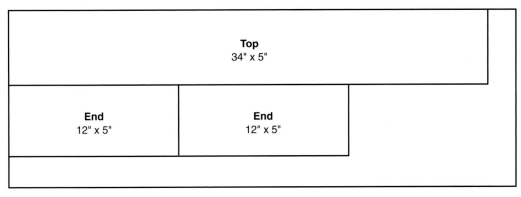

Layout Diagram

Ice-Cream Friend

Use felt and Styrofoam to make this cheerful friend for a young girl's bedroom. She'll add a warm and caring touch to a bureau or shelf!

Design by Debra Quartermain for Dow

Instructions

1. Using serrated knife to cut Styrofoam throughout, cut smaller egg in half lengthwise for arms; cut 4-inch ball in half for ice-cream scoops. Cut 1½-inch balls in half for feet and hands. Cut thin strip off one long side of larger egg for body (flattened side will be tummy side). The 2-inch ball will be head; flatten one side for bottom.

2. Referring to patterns, cut one body on fold and one overalls piece on fold from misty blue; one hair back, one set bangs and three braids on fold from light yellow; two arms on fold and one collar from baby pink; two shoe bottoms from walnut; and one cone cover from antique white parquet. Cut two 7-inch circles from white felt with sparkles (for ice-cream scoops); two 3-inch circles (for hands) and one 5-inch circle (for head) from regular antique white; two 3-inch circles walnut (for feet); and one 3-inch circle baby pink (for cherry).

3. Head: Center 2-inch Styrofoam ball on 5-inch circle antique white felt; bring edges over to flat side. Pin to hold at four points around circle. Adjust excess felt between pins. Glue felt in place; remove pins when dry.

4. Repeat step 3 with other Styrofoam half-balls and eggs, centering two small half-balls on 3-inch circles of antique white (hands) and two on 3-inch circles of walnut (feet); larger egg on misty blue (body) and smaller half-eggs on baby pink (arms). Pull felt edges onto flattened surfaces of foam and glue.

5. Thin paint slightly with water; lightly paint head and hands. Let dry.

6. Ice-cream cone: Wrap cone with antique white textured felt; glue in place, gluing down excess felt at top and bottom. Center circle of white felt with sparkles over rounded surface of large half-ball for scoop; apply a line of glue around bottom edge of half-ball, leaving ½ inch of felt hanging over. Repeat to make two ice-cream scoops. Glue flat surface of one scoop to top of cone; glue next scoop on top. Cover 1-inch Styrofoam ball with 3-inch circle baby pink for cherry; glue on top.

7. Overalls: Turn up bottom edge of overall strip ½ inch for cuff. Starting on flat side of body, glue overalls around body, meeting on flat side. Use craft knife to indent centerline of overalls.

8. Glue walnut shoe bottoms to flat sides of shoes; glue rounded surface of shoes to bottoms of legs.

9. Face: Cut a ¼-inch circle regular antique white felt for nose; pinch slightly and glue in center of face. Using sharp point of scissors, make small holes on either side of nose for eyes. Glue beads in eyes. Thread needle with 3 strands pink floss; pass needle from bottom of head out through face front at one end of mouth and back on other end of mouth to make smile. Tie floss ends underneath.

10. Hair: Fringe bangs; glue from one side of face to the other. Braid braids

Materials

- Styrofoam® brand foam shapes: 4-inch ball (ice-cream scoops), 2-inch ball (head), 2 (1½-inch) balls (hands, feet), 1-inch ball (cherry), 3¹³/₁₆-inch x 2¹³/₁₆-inch egg (body), 2⅜-inch x 1⅞-inch egg (arms), 6-inch x 2¹⁵/₁₆-inch cone (ice-cream cone)
- Felt: 9-inch x 12-inch sheet each regular antique white, baby pink, light yellow, misty blue and walnut; 9-inch x 12-inch sheet antique white parquet felt, 2 (9-inch x 12-inch) sheets white felt with iridescent sparkles
- 2 (5mm) black eye beads
- Embroidery floss: 18-inch lengths pink and blue
- Embroidery needle
- Light pink craft paint
- Small paintbrush
- Craft knife
- Pins
- Low-temperature glue gun
- Needle and white thread
- Serrated knife

together and tie ends with blue embroidery floss; glue over top of head along edge of bangs. Glue hair back in place.

11. Glue head to top of body; glue collar around neck.

12. With legs even with bottom of cone, glue flat side of body to cone. Glue arms to body, angling them up slightly. Glue hands to ends of sleeves and cone. ✄

Enlarge all cutting diagrams 125% for Ice-Cream Friend

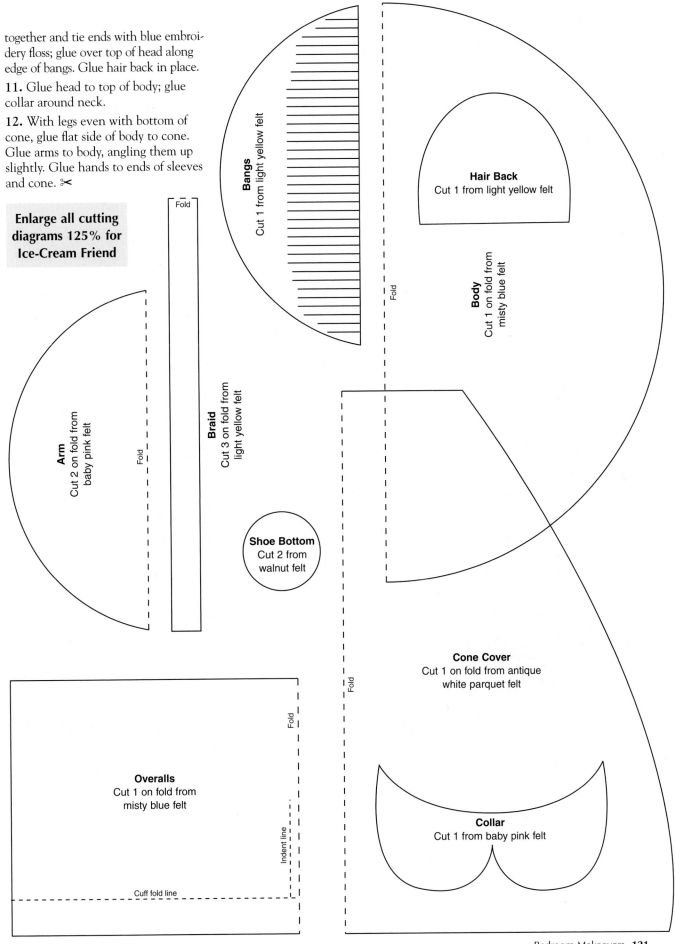

Fold

Bangs
Cut 1 from light yellow felt

Fold

Hair Back
Cut 1 from light yellow felt

Body
Cut 1 on fold from misty blue felt

Arm
Cut 2 on fold from baby pink felt

Fold

Braid
Cut 3 on fold from light yellow felt

Shoe Bottom
Cut 2 from walnut felt

Fold

Cone Cover
Cut 1 on fold from antique white parquet felt

Overalls
Cut 1 on fold from misty blue felt

Fold

Indent line

Cuff fold line

Collar
Cut 1 from baby pink felt

Outer Space Desk Set

Make an out-of-this-world set for a nephew or son with paint and fabric. With the wide variety of fabrics available, it's simple to customize sets.

Designs by Deborah Brooks

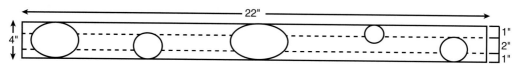

Fig. 1
Cut cardboard strip 22" x 4"

Materials

All Projects
- 1 yard planet/space print fabric
- Fusible adhesive
- Craft knife
- Craft glue
- Spatter brush

Stacked Boxes
- 3 square boxes
- Star-shaped wooden cutouts
- Decoupage glue
- Craft paints: black, green, light blue, orange, purple, white, yellow
- Flat paintbrush

Photo Album, Address Book & Desk Blotter
- Star picture frame
- Large photo album
- Small photo album
- Desk blotter
- Craft paints: light blue, white
- Spatter brush
- Low-loft batting
- Fabrics: 1½ yards solid black, ¼ yard yellow fabric
- 4-inch x 22-inch strip of cardboard
- 8 star-shaped wooden cutouts

Fabric Preparation

1. Launder fabrics without using fabric softener; press as needed.

2. Fuse adhesive onto backs of planet fabric and half the yellow fabric. Cut planet motifs from planet fabric and seven stars from fused yellow fabric.

Stacked Boxes

1. Boxes: Paint exterior of boxes—not lids—black. Let dry, then spatter with light blue. Let dry.

2. Decoupage cutout planets onto boxes as desired; let dry.

3. Using paintbrush handle dipped in white, apply dots of varying sizes around planets to create the appearance of distant stars.

4. Paint wooden stars yellow; let dry, then glue to sides of boxes.

5. Box lids: Paint each lid a different color. On samples, small lid is green, medium lid is orange and large lid is purple. Let dry.

Photo Album

1. Using star frame as template, trace star shape in upper right-hand corner of album cover, lining up points of stars against edges of cover. Trim cover to give upper right corner a star-shaped outline (do not cut out entire star).

2. Cut 15-inch x 25-inch piece batting; trim to fit around outside of album cover. Remove paper backing on album, exposing sticky surface. Insert screws; press on batting to cover.

3. Fabric cover: Spatter black fabric with light blue paint; let dry. Fuse planets and yellow fabric stars to black fabric. Measure album, then cut fabric to cover outside, clipping and notching fabric around star corner and other corners so that fabric will lie smooth.

4. Lining: Measure height and width of album; add a scant ½ inch to each dimension and cut black fabric to size. Fold under ¼ inch all around; press. Apply glue around edges on wrong side of fabric and press in place inside album. Install rings as manufacturer directs.

5. Star frame: Cover front of frame first with batting and then with unfused yellow fabric, wrapping excess fabric around edges to back of frame and clipping fabric as necessary. Insert picture in frame, then glue frame to upper right corner of album, matching star points on frame to star points trimmed in album cover.

6. Using paintbrush handle dipped in white, add clusters of dots of various sizes around stars and planets. Let dry completely.

Address Book

1. Cut batting to fit around outside of album cover. Remove paper backing on album, exposing sticky surface. Insert screws; press on batting to cover.

2. Fabric cover: Spatter black fabric with light blue paint; let dry. Fuse planets to black fabric. Measure album, then cut fabric to cover outside, clipping and notching fabric around corners so that fabric will lie smooth.

3. Lining: Measure height and width of album; add a scant ½ inch to each dimension and cut black fabric to size. Fold under ¼ inch all around; press. Apply glue around edges on wrong side of fabric and press in place inside album. Install rings as manufacturer directs.

4. Highlight planets with dots of white paint as in step 6 for photo album. Let dry.

Desk Blotter

1. Referring to Fig. 1 throughout, lightly draw a line across top and bottom of cardboard strip 1 inch from edges (dashed lines).

2. Dry-fit fused planet shapes on cardboard, overlapping lines drawn in step 1. Trace around planets. Set planet shapes aside.

3. Cut away 1-inch margins from top and bottom of strip, carefully trimming around planet shapes.

4. Cut batting to fit over cardboard; cover batting and cardboard with black fabric, clipping and folding edges to back and gluing so fabric lies smooth on front.

5. Spatter fabric-covered strip with light blue; let dry.

6. Fuse planets in place. Using paintbrush handle dipped in white, paint dots around planets; let dry.

7. Paint wooden star shapes yellow; let dry. Reserve four; glue remaining stars to strip.

8. From remaining black fabric, cut two strips each 5½ inches x 10 inches. Fold each in half, ironing under raw edges. Glue one across each bottom corner of blotter, folding ends to back and gluing securely.

9. Lightly spatter black fabric corners with light blue. Using handle of paintbrush dipped in white, add dots. Let dry.

10. Glue two yellow wooden stars to each bottom corner of blotter. ✂

Bathroom Accents

Whether you prefer the family's bathroom to be classically stylish, spotlessly modern or bright and whimsical, the techniques and accents featured in this chapter can easily be adapted to most fabrics and your own personal sense of style!

Charming Violets Bath Set

Shades of lavender ribbons and lace are delightful, especially when paired with silk flowers. You can easily coordinate this feminine set to match your home's decor.

Designs by Marian Shenk

Project Notes

Use fabric glue unless instructions specify spray adhesive or hot glue.

Tissue Box Cover

1. Measure sides of tissue box; add ½ inch to each dimension and cut four pieces of foam board that size. Assemble foam-board pieces into sides of tissue box cover, applying tape inside to hold them in place.

2. Measure foam-board box's height and circumference; add 1 inch to each dimension and cut a piece of multicolored fabric that size.

3. Spray box cover with cement. Lay fabric strip on box cover, aligning edge with bottom edge of box and with excess fabric extending beyond top of box. Press fabric into cement to cover box, folding under fabric edge at end where it overlaps. Neatly fold excess fabric at top inside box; glue in place.

4. Cut strip of orchid fabric 2½ inches

wide x circumference of box plus 1 inch. Fold under ½ inch along each long edge; press. Glue strip around bottom of box so that ½ inch of fabric is visible on exterior, folding under fabric edge at end, where it overlaps. Neatly fold remaining fabric over bottom edge to inside of box; glue in place.

5. Hot-glue lace around top of box; glue ¼-inch ribbon over lace.

6. Measure top of box from inner surface to inner surface of foam-board sides (piece will fit into top of box; it will not rest on top of sides); cut foam board to size. Cut 2½-inch hole in center for removing tissues.

7. Spray foam-board top with cement; lay on wrong side of multicolored fabric. Smooth fabric in place.

8. Trim excess fabric leaving 1-inch margin all around. Smoothly wrap excess fabric over edge to back, clipping as needed at corners, and glue fabric in place. Carefully clip fabric over center opening; fold fabric to inside, gluing in place.

9. Slip foam-board top into box cover;

Materials

All Projects

- 1 yard lavender multicolored print
- Spray-on adhesive
- Fabric glue
- Hot-glue gun
- Assorted laces, braids and ribbons, ¼–½ inch wide (samples included lavender ⅝-inch, lavender picot-edge ¼-inch, baby blue ¼-inch, and purple ⅛-inch satin ribbons, as well as white decorative trim and assorted 1-inch white flat and ruffled laces)
- Assorted complementary silk leaves and flowers removed from wire stems

Tissue Box Cover

- Boutique-style box of tissues
- White foam board
- Remnant of complementary solid orchid fabric
- Tape

Cosmetics Tray & Jars

- 8-inch x 10-inch gold picture frame (use a style in which glass and backing are held in place with spring clips, tacks or framing points; do not use a slide-in style of frame)
- Cylindrical cosmetic storage jars with lids
- Heavy white paper (optional)
- ¼-inch-wide heavy-duty fusible adhesive strips
- Small Battenburg doilies or appliqués (optional)

Lined Basket

- White with colored woven trim basket with handle
- Newspaper
- Adhesive-back hook-and-loop tape

Towels

- Washcloth and 2 hand towels
- ¼-inch-wide heavy-duty fusible adhesive strips
- Solid orchid fabric
- Coordinating ⅛-inch ribbon

Lamp Shade

- Lamp shade to cover
- ¼ yard coordinating solid fabric
- 5 yards coordinating ¼-inch ribbon (Lavender picot-edge ribbon was used on sample.)

set box cover on its top and apply hot glue inside to hold top in place.

10. Set box cover right side up. Hot-glue lace around center opening; hot-glue silk flowers and leaves to box as desired. Slip cover over box of tissues.

Tray

1. Remove glass and cardboard from frame; set aside spring clips. Measure cardboard; add 1 inch to each dimension and cut a piece of multicolored fabric that size.

2. Spray cardboard with cement and cover with fabric, smoothing excess to back and gluing it in place. Cover back with decorative paper or additional fabric, if desired, to conceal fabric edges.

3. Hot-glue a tiny Battenburg doily or piece of flat lace trim in one corner; top with small, flat silk flowers.

4. Replace glass in frame; under it, insert fabric-covered cardboard. Secure cardboard and glass in frame by tacking on metal framing points that came with frame.

Jars

1. If your jars do not come with paper liners, cut liners to fit from heavy white paper. Measure paper liners; add ½ inch to each dimension and cut pieces of multicolored fabric to that size.

2. Apply spray cement to paper liner; lay in center of fabric on wrong side. Fold excess fabric smoothly to back of paper; glue in place.

3. Cut another piece of fabric ½ inch bigger all around; "hem" top, bottom and one side using fusible adhesive strips. Spray back of covered paper liner with cement; press hemmed fabric in place, concealing fabric edges folded over in step 2.

4. Roll fabric-covered liner and slip inside jar.

5. Hot-glue tiny Battenburg doily or lace to front of jar; add silk flowers. Tie bow of ribbon or lace around jar lid's handle. Set jars on tray.

Basket

1. Make newspaper pattern by placing a sheet of newspaper inside basket and folding it at corners to make it fit. Remove paper from basket and cut away paper folds at corners.

2. Pin paper pattern to wrong side of print fabric. Cut out, adding ½ inch all around. Turn under excess around top; glue. Tack liner together at corners with glue. Test fit in basket.

3. Cut hook-and-loop tape in several pieces to arrange evenly around inside of basket. Peel adhesive backing from hook or loop pieces and press inside basket just below top edge. Peel backing from other pieces and press onto wrong side of fabric liner. Place liner inside and secure by pressing fasteners together.

4. Hot-glue lace around top of basket. Hot-glue ribbon trims to basket handles as desired (on sample, lavender ⅝-inch satin ribbon was glued on first; then ¼-inch baby blue ribbon was glued over it).

5. Tie bow around base of handle on one side, which will be back of basket (lavender ⅝-inch satin ribbon was used on sample); on front of basket, hot-glue silk flowers and leaves at base of handle.

Towel Set

1. Measure widths of towels and washcloth. For each towel and washcloth, cut a 5-inch-wide strip of print fabric that is twice towel or washcloth's width.

2. Fold strip in half lengthwise; press. Fold and pin tucks every ¼ inch down length of fabric.

3. Choose ribbon and/or lace to be applied across top of pleated fabric strip; measure its width. Cut a piece of fusible web the length of pleated fabric and not quite as wide as ribbon. Fuse webbing along top edge—raw edges—of fabric and press to hold pleats in place. Remove remaining backing and fuse lace or ribbon on top.

4. Glue pleats and lace along bottom edge of towel or washcloth so that pleats just conceal edge of towel; let dry.

5. For each towel and washcloth, cut a strip of solid orchid fabric measuring 1½ inches x width of towel or washcloth. Lay strip facedown; fold over ½ inch along one long edge, then ½ inch along other long edge; press. Secure folds with ¼-inch adhesive strips.

6. Lay orchid strip right side up across towel so that it overlaps top edges of lace and pleats; fuse in place with ¼-inch adhesive strips.

7. Glue coordinating ⅛-inch-wide ribbon to inner edge of strip (purple was used on samples); glue ribbon bow to lace at center of towel (⅝-inch lavender satin ribbon was used on samples).

Lamp Shade

1. Using pattern accompanying shade, cut print fabric. Spray outside of shade with cement and cover with fabric, smoothing it as you go.

2. Measure circumference of lamp shade's top edge; note measurement. Measure a point on shade about halfway down from top edge; note this measurement. Cut strip of solid fabric as long as the circumference and as wide as the measurement from top of shade. Measure and cut triangles from strip to fit around top edge of lamp.

3. Glue triangles in place. Glue on ¼-inch ribbon to cover two longer edges of triangles (lavender picot-edge ribbon was used on sample). Glue a small ribbon bow at the point of each triangle (lavender ⅝-inch satin ribbon was used to make bows on sample).

4. Glue braid or trim around top and bottom edges of shade (white trim was used on sample). Add small bows at top of shade, just below braid/trim and between triangles (baby blue ¼-inch satin ribbon was used on sample). ✂

Pressing Matters

Save yourself time and aggravation by covering your pressing surface with muslin or cotton before ironing fusible webs.

Also use a press cloth on top of the fabric you're pressing. This will prevent adhesive from getting on your iron or pressing surface, where it can be transferred to other fabrics.

Look for Teflon-coated press cloths to make the task even easier.

Spring Garden Hand Towels

Not just for guests or special occasions, these stenciled and blanket-stitched towels are so easy to make you'll want to use them every day.

Designs by Mary Ayres

Instructions

1. Cut two 4½-inch squares fusible adhesive; fuse to back of cotton fabric. Using pencil, lightly draw 4-inch square in center of each adhesive square.

2. Stencil flowers on squares, referring to directions for Stenciling with Brush under Painting Techniques in the General Instructions, page 174. On one square, stencil rounded flowers with baby blue deep; shade outer edges with true blue. On other square, stencil tuliplike flowers with baby pink deep; shade top edges with fuchsia. Stencil all leaves and stems with Hauser light green; shade along one edge of each with Christmas green. Let dry; lay paper atop painted designs and press with iron to set paints.

3. Cut out 4-inch squares with pinking shears. Peel paper backing from square with blue flowers; position on center front of blue towel with bottom edge of square 3¼ inches above edge of towel. Fuse square in place. Repeat with remaining square and pink towel.

4. Using 3 strands pink or blue floss to match color of towel, embroider blanket stitch around each square with loops between indentations in pinked edges. ✂

Materials

- Linen-look dish towels: 1 each pink and blue
- Heavy-duty fusible adhesive
- ⅛ yard pre-quilted cotton fabric or muslin
- 6-strand cotton embroidery floss: 1 skein each pink and blue
- Embroidery needle
- Flowers and tulips stencils
- Fabric paints: baby blue deep, baby pink deep, Christmas green, fuchsia, Hauser light green, true blue
- Stencil brushes
- Pinking shears
- Iron

Embellished Hand Towels

These hand towels are so pretty, it's hard to believe there's no sewing involved. You'll love the decorative accent they add to any bathroom in your home.

Designs by Carol Zentgraf

Lace-Edge Towel

1. Cut a 4⅜-inch-wide strip from adhesive sheet equal in measurement to towel's width plus 2 inches. Center along towel's bottom edge; fuse. Turn excess to back and fuse to wrong side.

2. Center and position gathered lace trim along bottom edge of adhesive and 1-inch flat trim along top edge. Center 3½-inch lace between trims, slightly overlapping.

3. Using Teflon press cloth, fuse trims to adhesive. Turn lace ends to back of towel; fuse.

Woven Ribbon & Fringe Towel

1. Center and glue fringe along towel's bottom edge. Turn ends to back and glue to wrong side of towel.

2. Center and glue ribbon in place, overlapping top edge of fringe trim; fold ribbon ends to back and glue to wrong side of towel.

Lace Flower & Fringe Towel

1. Arrange flower lace trim in a pleasing wavy line across towel, aligning ends with towel edges. Use liquid fusible web to fuse flowers in place, one at a time.

2. Center fringe along towel's bottom edge; glue in place with permanent fabric adhesive. Fold fringe ends to back and glue to wrong side of towel. ✂

Materials
Lace-Edge Towel
- Hand towel
- Lace trims equal in length to width of towel plus 2 inches: 1-inch-wide flat off-white, 1-inch-wide gathered off-white, 3½-inch-wide flat ecru
- Heavy-duty fusible adhesive sheet
- Teflon press cloth

Woven Ribbon & Fringe Towel
- Hand towel
- 2½-inch woven ribbon equal in length to width of towel plus 2 inches

- 5½-inch bullion fringe equal in length to width of towel plus 2 inches
- Heavy-duty fusible adhesive sheet
- Permanent fabric adhesive

Lace Flower & Fringe Towel
- Hand towel
- Lace flower trim equal in length to 1½ times width of towel
- 4-inch fringe equal in length to width of towel plus 2 inches
- Liquid fusible web
- Permanent fabric adhesive

Timeless Style Bath Ensemble

Give your bathroom a makeover with this stylish set. Self-adhesive pieces make it possible to update a room in a day or less.

Designs by Carol Zentgraf

Materials

Shower Curtain

- 54-inch-wide home decor fabric: 4 yards plus 1 repeat for curtain; and ¾ yard coordinating print, plaid or check for borders
- Plastic shower curtain liner
- 12 large grommets
- Grommet tool
- Water- or air-soluble fabric-marking pen
- ½-inch-wide fusible adhesive tape
- Heavyweight stick-on fabric stabilizer

Tissue Box Cover

- Purchased plastic tissue box cover for boutique-style box of tissues
- Home decor fabrics: 8-inch square of one fabric plus 8-inch x 26-inch strip of complementary fabric
- Batting: 6-inch square plus 6-inch x 24-inch strip
- 1½ yards coordinating tassel fringe
- 26 inches ½-inch-wide gimp
- Permanent fabric adhesive

Wastebasket

- Self-adhesive wastebasket
- Home decor fabric to cover wastebasket (check wastebasket instructions for amount)
- Length of coordinating tassel fringe equal in measurement to twice the perimeter of wastebasket's top edge plus 2 inches
- Length of coordinating gimp trim equal in measurement to the perimeter of wastebasket's bottom edge plus 2 inches
- Permanent fabric adhesive

Shower Curtain

1. Cut fabric for curtain into two 72-inch lengths, matching fabric repeat.

2. Using fusible adhesive tape, fuse panels together along matched edges. Trim selvage to edge of fused seams.

3. Trim outer edges evenly so curtain measures 76 inches wide.

4. Upper border: Cut two 7-inch x 54-inch strips fabric, coordinating prints or plaids. Cut two 3-inch x 54-inch strips stabilizer. Remove backing; adhere stabilizer to each side of curtain's upper edge.

5. Fuse short ends of fabric strips together. Press strip in half lengthwise, wrong sides facing. Apply fusible tape to right side of long edges; do not remove backing. Press edges under ½ inch.

6. Insert upper edge of curtain into border fold, aligning center seams. Trim border edges even with curtain edges. Remove paper backing; fuse border edges in place.

7. Lower border: Cut two 13-inch x 54-inch strips fabric, coordinating prints or plaids. Fuse short ends of fabric strips together. Press strip in half lengthwise, wrong sides facing. Apply fusible tape to right side of long edges; do not remove backing. Press edges under ½ inch.

8. Insert bottom edge of curtain into border fold, aligning center seams. Trim border edges even with curtain edges. Remove paper backing; fuse border edges in place.

9. Turn under and fuse a doubled 1-inch hem down each side of curtain so curtain measures 72 inches x 72 inches.

10. Attach grommets: Place curtain on flat surface. Lay plastic shower curtain liner on top, aligning top and sides. Using holes in liner for guides, mark curtain for grommet placement with fabric-marking pen. Attach grommet at each mark.

11. Position liner inside curtain; hang both from shower rod with shower curtain rings.

Tissue Box Cover

1. Glue batting square to top of tissue box cover, applying glue along center opening and edges. Cut out center opening. Glue batting strip around sides of box, applying glue along top and bottom edges.

2. Center fabric square over top of box; glue edges to box sides and let dry. From inside box, slit fabric in center opening. Clip fabric in opening from slit to box cover as needed; evenly fold fabric edges around opening to inside of box cover and glue inside cover.

3. Align fabric strip with top of box sides. Glue one short edge of fabric strip down center of one side of tissue box cover. Wrap fabric around box, gluing top edge in place. Turn under remaining fabric and overlap at starting point; glue in place. At bottom, turn extra fabric over edge to inside of box cover and secure with glue.

4. Glue a row of tassel fringe around upper edge of box cover; glue a second row just below it, staggering positions of tassels as much as possible. Glue one row of gimp trim around bottom edge. Insert box of tissues in cover.

Wastebasket

1. Following instructions accompanying wastebasket, use label as pattern to cut fabric and adhere it to wastebasket.

2. Glue one row of tassel fringe around top of wastebasket just below curved lip and another row around lip itself. ✂

Toile Baskets & Bowl Set

Display your bathroom necessities in style in this fashionable set. Toile fabric coordinates well with many decors and makes a stylish statement.

Designs by Barb Chauncey

Materials
Lined Baskets

- 2 nesting baskets (samples measure 8¾ inches W x 4 inches H x 6½ inches deep, and 12¼ inches W x 6 inches H x 10½ inches deep)
- ⅔ yard toile print fabric
- ⅔ yard cotton batting
- Lightweight cardboard
- Hot-glue gun

Shaped Bowl

- Glass or vase with flat 2⅝-inch base
- 9-inch circle toile fabric
- 9-inch circle muslin
- 9-inch circle aluminum mesh
- 2 (9-inch) circles heavy-duty fusible adhesive
- ¾ yard small lip cord to coordinate with fabric
- Hot-glue gun

Baskets

1. Trace around bottom of baskets on cardboard; cut out ⅛ inch inside traced lines. Check fit inside bottom of baskets; trim as needed.

2. Trace around cardboard shapes onto batting; cut out ¼ inch inside traced lines. Center batting on cardboard; tack in place with hot glue.

3. Lay cardboard with batting on wrong side of fabric over desired portion of pattern; trace and cut out ¾ inch outside traced lines.

4. Lay cardboard in center of fabric shape, batting facing wrong side of fabric. Tack fabric edges to back of cardboard at each end and in center of each side. Clip fabric around curves and glue fabric to back of cardboard, taking care not to pull fabric too tight so as to pucker cardboard.

5. Measure circumference around outside rim and depth of basket. Cut a piece of fabric measuring circumference plus 1½ inches x depth plus 1½ inches. Press as needed.

6. Turn under one long edge ¼ inch; tack with hot glue. Align this edge, right side up, with bottom edge of rim on outside of basket; glue fabric to basket rim, beginning in a spot that is neither too conspicuous nor right next to the basket handle.

7. To go around handle, hold fabric right over handle and cut a "Y" in fabric just as big as opening needed to go around handle (see Fig. 1). Turn fabric edges back from cuts and glue to wrong side of fabric to make opening with a finished edge. Lay it around handle and glue down edges. Continue gluing fabric around basket rim. To finish, fold under raw edge where fabric overlaps beginning point. Secure seam with hot glue all the way down inside basket.

8. Smooth fabric down sides inside basket, distributing excess fabric evenly. Glue fabric to bottom of basket around edge.

9. Apply hot-glue to bottom of covered cardboard; push into bottom of basket.

Bowl

1. Adhere adhesive circles to backs of toile and muslin circles; this should keep edges from raveling, so be sure adhesive extends to edges of fabric all around.

2. Hot-glue lip of trim to wrong side

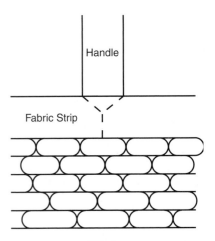

Fig. 1
Cut Y along dashed lines;
fold back to wrong side and
glue; fit opening around handle.

of muslin circle, gluing ends of trim together to keep them from unraveling.

3. Remove backing from adhesive; layer toile, mesh and muslin circles and fuse together. Let cool.

4. Turn glass or vase with base up. Center fabric circle over base and form sides of bowl by pushing fused layers downward on outer edge of circle. Make uniform ruffles around edge as you shape fabric-mesh bowl. Remove bowl from glass or vase and complete shaping as desired. ✂

Great Glues

In addition to being a wonderful timesaver, the right glue can perform a multitude of tasks.

Fabric glues and permanent fabric adhesives are strong and best used for adhering small areas; applying trims, bindings, buttons, beads and embellishments; for bonding heavy fabrics; and for fabrics that aren't heat resistant.

Most fabric glues and adhesives have a strong bond, dry clear on most fabrics and are permanent once dry. For the best results, wash fabric to remove any sizing before use and always test on a scrap of fabric first.

Some dry more quickly and hold a stronger bond than others, so experiment with different brands until you find your favorite.

Underwater Fantasy Set

Swimming fish and beautiful underwater scenery are a great addition to any bathroom. Your family and guests will marvel over this delightful bathroom set and only you have to know how easy it is to make.

Designs by Deborah Brooks

Materials

All Projects

- Fabrics: 1 yard undersea print with tropical fish theme, 6-inch squares hunter green and kelly green
- Fusible adhesive
- Craft knife

Tray

- 8-inch x 16-inch piece contrasting fabric for background
- 8-inch x 16-inch picture frame
- 4 (2-inch) wooden ball knobs
- Acrylic paints to coordinate with print fabric: blue, green, orange, red, white, yellow
- Paintbrushes: splatter brush and flat brush
- Wood glue
- Glossy coating/sealer

Shower Curtain

- Drop cloth
- Roll of paper table covering
- Fabric shower curtain
- Spray paints for fabric: Caribbean blue, royal blue
- Black matte-finish dimensional fabric paint
- Spray bottle with water

Hand Towel

- Coordinating hand towel

Prepare Fabric Shapes

1. Launder and dry all fabrics without using fabric softener; press as needed.

2. Fuse fabrics to fusible adhesive. Cut out sea creatures, using craft knife to carefully trim background fabric from all areas. Set shapes aside.

3. Cut kelly and hunter fabrics into squiggly strips of various lengths to resemble seaweed and grasses.

Tray

1. Take frame apart, reserving all pieces. Glue a ball to each corner on back of frame for tray legs; place large book or other heavy object on top of frame until glue is dry.

2. Paint frame and ball legs white with flat brush; let dry.

3. Lightly splatter frame with other colors of paint; let dry.

4. Coat frame and feet with glossy coating/sealer; let dry.

5. Arrange fabric shapes on background fabric. Peel off backing and fuse shapes in place.

6. Clean glass from picture frame. Reassemble frame, inserting panel with fused underwater scene under glass.

Shower Curtain

1. Place drop cloth on floor or other large area in a place where it can remain undisturbed for at least 24 hours. Lay paper table covering over drop cloth; it will absorb moisture and keep it from puddling under the shower curtain.

2. Lay shower curtain over paper; mist shower curtain with water from spray bottle.

3. Starting at top, spray curtain with Caribbean blue, applying a solid coat across top and gradually applying color in an increasingly random and lighter fashion as you approach bottom of curtain. Starting at bottom of curtain, repeat process with royal blue spray paint, applying solid coat across bottom and increasingly random and lighter color as you approach the top. Let dry completely, at least 24 hours.

4. Arrange fish and coral cutouts on shower curtain; peel off backing and fuse in place. Add sea grass and seaweed.

5. Highlight shapes on curtain with black matte-finish dimensional paint; let dry completely.

Hand Towel

Arrange fish and coral cutouts in center of hand towel near bottom edge; peel off backing and fuse in place. ✂

The Hole Story

You can use grommets and eyelets in myriad ways for home decor applications. They are available in metal tones and colors, in a variety of sizes.

Grommets and smaller eyelets are set by using grommet or eyelet pliers, and extra-large eyelets are set using an eyelet tool and hammer. Follow the manufacturer's instructions to apply any of these notions, especially noting the recommendations for fabric thickness.

Use grommets and eyelets for shower curtains and drapery headers, for lacing effects and as decorative elements.

No-Sew Bath Caddy

Treat your overnight guests to luxury with scented soaps and body wash stored in this easy no-sew nautical shower bag.

Design by June Fiechter

Materials

- 2 ecru-striped dish towels
- Fabric glue
- Coordinating print, checked or solid fabrics: 5-inch x 7-inch piece raspberry, 3-inch x 6-inch piece and 2 (1½-inch x 14-inch) strips blue, 8-inch square taupe
- 3 (⅞-inch) wooden clothing buttons
- 12 inches hemp cord or fine jute twine
- Needle and thread
- Heavy-duty fusible adhesive

Instructions

1. Launder and dry towels. Lay one on top of the other, wrong sides facing, with shorter edges at top and bottom. Holding bottom edges of towels together, fold up in half, making ends even at top; secure side edges of all layers with fabric glue.

2. Fuse adhesive to backs of all fabrics including 1½-inch x 14-inch blue strips; set strips aside for now.

3. Referring to pattern, trace pieces on backing paper of adhesive, using raspberry for sails, blue for pennant and boat and taupe for background. Cut out each piece; peel backing off. Peel backing from all pieces, including strips.

4. Position background, boat, pennant and sail on front of caddy; fuse in place with iron.

5. Straps: Peel backing from blue strips. Fold strips in half lengthwise and press, sealing adhesive sides together. Glue one end of each strip to back top edge of caddy about 3 inches in from sides. Slit buttonhole

in other end of each strap about ½ inch from edge.

6. Sew two buttons on top front layer opposite where straps are anchored. Button straps to front. Sew remaining button to boat for life preserver.

7. Tie hemp cord in bow; glue to center front of boat. ✂

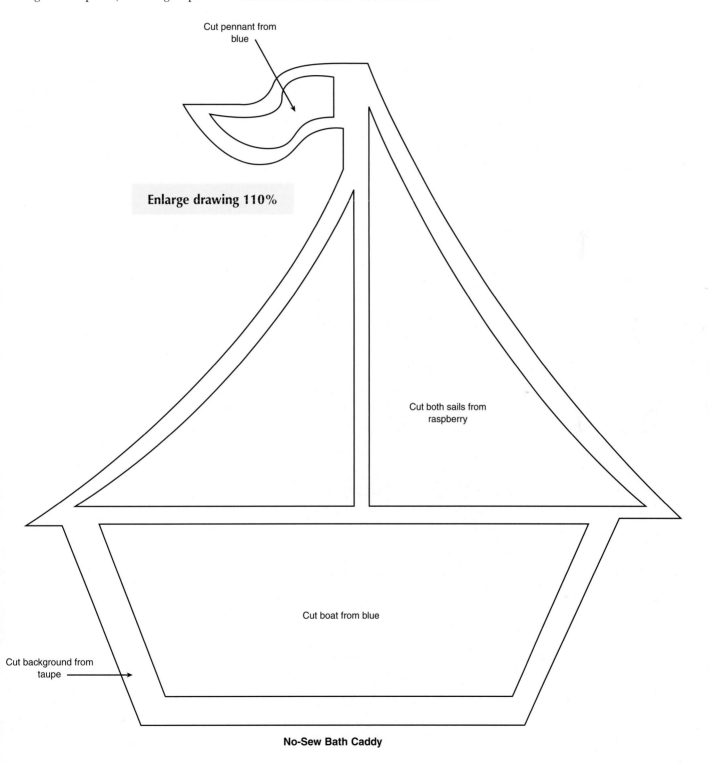

Cut pennant from blue

Enlarge drawing 110%

Cut both sails from raspberry

Cut boat from blue

Cut background from taupe

No-Sew Bath Caddy

Floral Seat Cover

Adding floral accents to a toilet seat is a perfect way to update your bath. Coordinate with matching accessories and you've economically remodeled a room!

Designs by Lorine Mason

Materials

- Toilet seat with lid
- Desired fabric
- Heavy-duty fusible adhesive
- Laminating liquid
- Sponge
- Stamping/embossing heat tool (optional)
- Fine-grit sandpaper

1. Choose design elements from fabric to decorate lid. Fuse adhesive onto wrong side of fabric and cut out desired design(s).

2. Remove paper backing and press design(s) onto lid, overlapping them as desired.

3. Sponge laminating liquid over fabric designs and lid; liquid should saturate fabric and be sponged evenly over entire lid. Take care when sponging around fabric edges. Let dry.

4. Repeat step 3.

5. Lightly sand surface to remove any raised fibers; wipe off dust.

6. Apply a final coat of laminating liquid to top and sides of lid; let dry. ✂

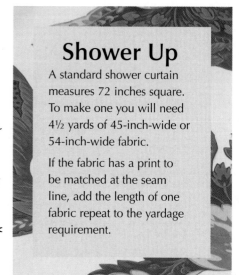

Shower Up

A standard shower curtain measures 72 inches square. To make one you will need 4½ yards of 45-inch-wide or 54-inch-wide fabric.

If the fabric has a print to be matched at the seam line, add the length of one fabric repeat to the yardage requirement.

Getting Started

Ready to create? The first step is to explore the wonderful array of fabrics and products that will make your no-sew endeavors fun and easy.

Select Fabrics

Whether you decide to use home decor or fashion fabrics or want to create your own unique fabric designs with paint, dyes and other embellishments, fabric selection is the first step in planning your project.

Choose Other Products

Once you've chosen the perfect fabric, it's time to select the fusible product or other no-sew product that suits your project needs. Consider the fabric texture and fiber content, the project end use and whether or not it will need laundering, then select the most appropriate products.

Consider Technique

The technique you'll be using is also a factor. For seams and edge finishes, a fusible web or adhesive tape may be most suitable, while the same adhesive in a larger piece would be more efficient for applying a large appliqué.

Glues are wonderful for applying embellishments, but may not result in a perfectly straight seam when used to bond seam allowances.

Holiday Home

Decorating your home for the holidays is a big part of the season's excitement and fun! The simplicity of the no-sew projects in this chapter will help you make your holiday home spectacular with plenty of time to spare!

Stained Glass Poinsettia Set

Fuse simple fabric appliqués to achieve the sheer elegance of stained glass in this coordinating set. Display this in your living room for stylish, eye-catching holiday decor.

Designs by Karen de la Durantaye

Materials

Each Project

- Fabric-marking pencil
- Poster board
- Masking tape
- Permanent fabric adhesive
- Tracing paper

Table Runner

- Fabrics: 1⅜ yards ivory; ⅛ yard each burgundy, dark green and light green; 2-inch x 7-inch piece gold
- ¼ yard 90-inch-wide cotton batting
- 1½ yards heavy-duty iron-on adhesive

Pillow

- 12-inch-square pillow form
- Fabrics: ⅜ yard ivory; ⅛ yard each burgundy, dark green and light green; 1½-inch x 2-inch piece gold
- 9-inch square cotton batting
- ¼ yard heavy-duty iron-on adhesive
- 2 yards iron-on adhesive quilter's edging

Tree Skirt

- Fabrics: 4¼ yards ivory; ¼ yard each burgundy, dark green and light green; 2-inch x 14-inch piece gold
- 9-inch square cotton batting
- ¾ yard 90-inch-wide cotton batting
- 1¼ yards heavy-duty iron-on adhesive
- 2 (15-yard) rolls iron-on adhesive quilter's edging

Poinsettia Square

1. Cut 9-inch square batting and 11-inch square ivory fabric.

2. Center batting square on top of fabric; fold excess fabric over edges of batting; press.

3. Draw 8¾-inch square on back of iron-on adhesive sheet; referring to manufacturer's instructions throughout, peel off backing and fuse adhesive onto another piece of ivory fabric. Cut out ivory square and fuse on top of batting square, sandwiching batting between layers of ivory fabric.

4. Using a pencil, trace poinsettia pattern onto tracing paper. Mark each pattern piece with its number and color.

5. Transfer pattern to poster board: Place tracing paper on poster board, traced side down; secure with masking tape. Retrace lines with pencil, marking each piece with its number and color.

6. Cut out poster-board pattern pieces. Trace around each piece onto a sheet of iron-on adhesive; mark each piece with number and color.

7. Fuse pieces 1G–3G to gold fabric; fuse pieces 4B–12B to burgundy; fuse pieces 13DG–18DG to dark green; fuse pieces 19LG–23LG to light green; cut out.

8. On poinsettia square, use fabric-marking pencil to draw diagonal lines from corner to corner to create a large X across square.

9. Place tracing-paper pattern right side up on poinsettia square, aligning corners of design with marked lines on square. Tape pattern in place on one side only.

Using pattern as a guide, position each appliqué on the square. Peel off paper backing and slide each pattern piece into position under tracing paper.

10. When all pieces are in place, carefully remove tracing paper and fuse poinsettia appliqués in place.

Filler Square

1. Cut 6-inch square batting and 8-inch square light green fabric.

2. Center batting square on top of fabric; fold excess fabric over edges of batting and press.

3. Draw 5¾-inch square on back of iron-on adhesive sheet; referring to manufacturer's instructions throughout, peel off backing and fuse adhesive onto another piece of light green fabric. Cut out light green square and fuse on top of batting square, sandwiching batting between layers of light green fabric.

Table Runner

1. Referring to preceding instructions, make a total of four poinsettia squares and three filler squares.

2. Buttons: Cut three small circles from batting and three from poster board; glue together. Cut three large circles from ivory fabric. Place a small circle, batting side down, in center of each large fabric circle. Run a bead of glue along back edges of small circle; fold edges of large circle to back of small circle. Repeat with remaining circles.

3. Assembly: Line up poinsettia squares point-to-point with each poinsettia pointing in a different direction. Position filler squares between poinsettia squares

as shown; glue filler squares to poinsettia squares. Glue a button over points of poinsettia squares where they meet.

Pillow

1. Cut 9-inch square batting and 11-inch square ivory fabric. Apply quilter's edging along all four edges on wrong side of fabric square.

2. Center batting square on top of fabric. Fold excess fabric over edges of batting; press.

3. Follow steps 4–10 for poinsettia square to apply poinsettia to fabric side of fabric/batting square.

4. Cut two 13-inch squares from dark green fabric. On right side of one square, use fabric-marking pencil to draw diagonal lines from corner to corner to create a large X across square.

5. Apply quilter's tape along all four edges on backside of poinsettia panel. Place poinsettia panel in center of pillow square marked with X, aligning corners of panel with chalk lines; pin in place.

6. Fold under ¼ inch along one edge of each green pillow square; press. On one green square, apply quilter's edging to right side along three edges that were not folded under.

7. Fuse pillow squares together, right sides facing and matching folded-under edges; turn right side out.

8. Apply quilter's edging along one folded edge inside pillow. Insert pillow form. Align open edges and iron over them to fuse pillow closed.

Tree Skirt

1. Skirt sections: Use photocopier to enlarge pattern for skirt section 250 percent before cutting. From batting, cut eight skirt sections as shown; from ivory fabric, cut 16 skirt sections, adding ½-inch seam allowance along all sides.

2. Center batting atop a fabric section; fold ½-inch seam allowance over edges of batting; press. This will be front of section.

3. Fold under seam allowances on a second fabric section; press. Apply quilter's edging tape along folded edges on wrong side of fabric; peel off backing, position fabric on top of fabric/batting section, wrong sides facing, and fuse. (This is back of section.) Repeat to make a total of eight skirt sections.

4. Follow steps 4–7 for poinsettia squares to make pieces for a total of eight poinsettias.

5. Using marking pencil, draw a horizontal line on front of each skirt section from point to point and a vertical line from top center to bottom point.

6. Place tracing-paper design right side up on skirt section, aligning corners of design with chalk lines on skirt section. Tape it down only on one side. Referring to steps 9 and 10 for poinsettia square, fuse poinsettia design in place on skirt section; repeat with remaining sections.

7. Skirt assembly: From ivory fabric, cut seven 2-inch x 36-inch strips; on each strip, fold under ½ inch along both long sides so that edges meet in center; press. Fold under one short end ½ inch; press.

8. Apply quilter's edging tape along both long edges on wrong side.

9. Position two sections side by side, butting up against one another. Peel off paper backing from a strip and center it over adjoining edges of the two skirt sections; fuse in place. Turn ends of joining strip to back of tree skirt; fuse in place, turning under top end where ends of strip overlap.

10. In this manner, attach remaining skirt sections until all are joined. ✄

Embossing Velvet

Embossed velvet is beautiful for pillows, throws and holiday decorations. Best of all, all you need is a rubber stamp and an iron to create this designer-look effect. Follow these pointers to ensure success:

• Read the fiber content on the fabric bolt to select the appropriate velvet fabric for embossing. Silk, rayon and rayon/acetate velvets work best; don't use nylon or polyester velvets.

• Choose a rubber stamp with a wooden backing and large, bold design without tiny lines or details.

• Never press your finished embossed velvet projects with steam or the embossing will disappear.

Here's How ...

Work on a heat-resistant surface and have a spray bottle of water at hand. Emboss as follows:

1. Place the stamp right side up on the work surface.

2. Place the fabric right side down on top of the stamp and lightly mist the wrong side of the fabric with water.

3. Press a medium-hot dry iron directly on top of the fabric and stamp without shifting or sliding the iron (Fig. 1).

4. Hold the iron in place for 20–30 seconds, then lift it straight up, being careful not to slide it. Let fabric cool.

5. Repeat to create multiple embossed impressions.

Fig. 1
Place velvet right side down over stamp; mist fabric and press directly over stamp.

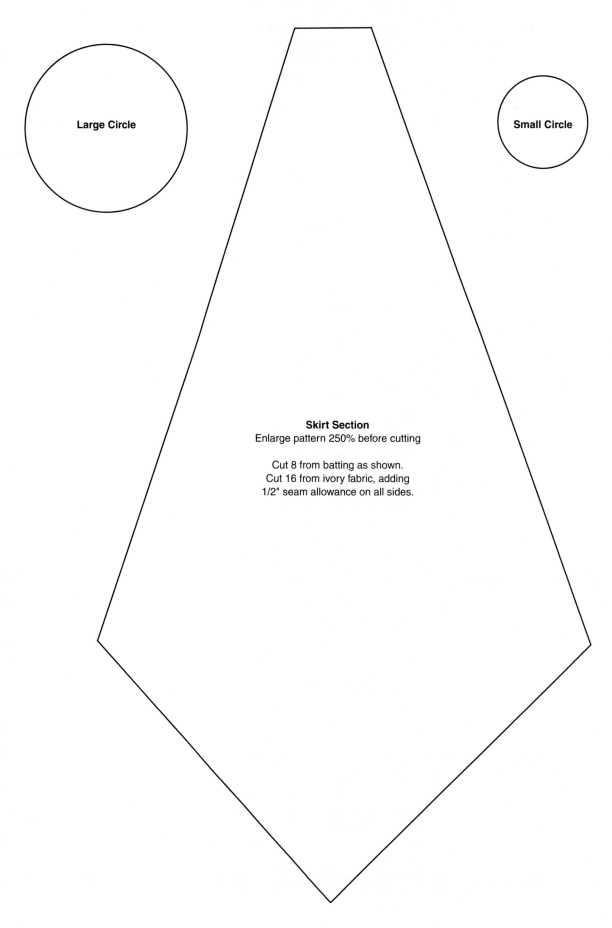

Large Circle

Small Circle

Skirt Section
Enlarge pattern 250% before cutting

Cut 8 from batting as shown.
Cut 16 from ivory fabric, adding
1/2" seam allowance on all sides.

Enlarge drawing on this page 110% for actual size

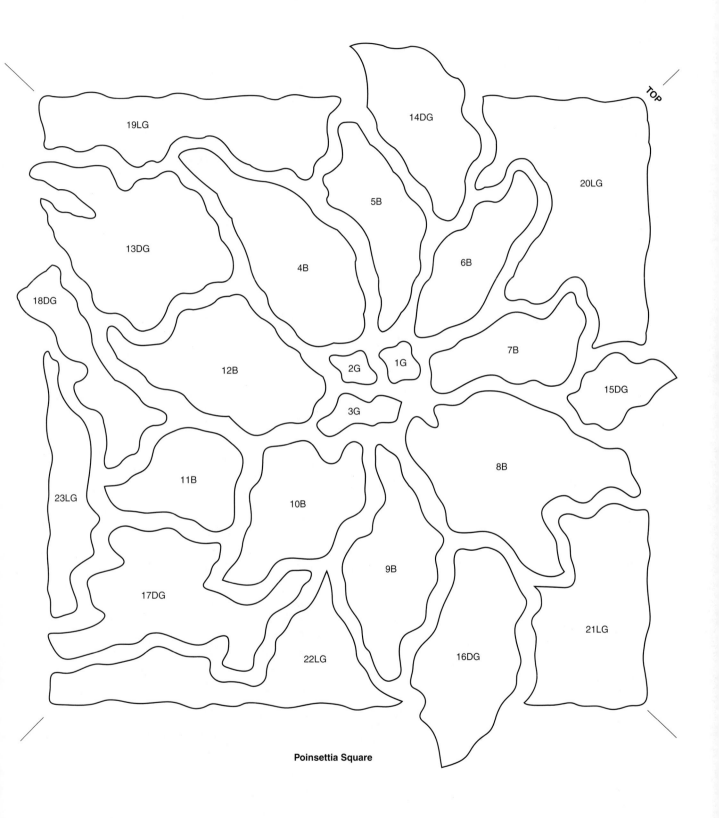

Poinsettia Square

Poinsettia Elegance Mantel Skirt

Add glitter and jingle to your mantel for extra Christmas spirit. Easy no-sew techniques combined with eye-catching embellishments make a decorative seasonal piece.

Design by Marian Shenk

Materials

- 1¾ yards white/silver fabric
- ½ yard 90-inch-wide off-white quilt-backing fabric
- ½ yard Christmas print fabric with large poinsettias
- Iron-on adhesive
- Washable fabric glue
- 2½ yards ⅜-inch-wide flat metallic gold lace
- 1½ yards ⅜-inch-wide red ribbon
- 5 gold brass bells on a cord
- Gold metallic fabric paint

Instructions

1. From white/silver fabric cut one piece 17½ inches x 67½ inches; cut an identical piece from the off-white backing fabric.

2. Fold the white/silver fabric in half and then into thirds to divide fabric into sixths. Secure layers with pins, then round off bottom edge with scissors to create scalloped edge. Repeat with off-white backing fabric, using a template of the scallop if needed to obtain an identical curve.

3. Open fabrics; press. Lay white/silver fabric on top of off-white backing fabric, right sides facing. Glue together along edges of sides and scallops with fabric glue; let dry.

4. Turn mantel cover right side out; press.

5. Apply gold lace along scalloped edges with fabric glue; let dry.

6. Iron adhesive onto wrong side of poinsettia print following manufacturer's instructions. Cut out six poinsettias; peel off paper backing and iron one poinsettia onto white/silver side of each scallop.

7. Outline poinsettias with gold paint.

8. Cut a small slit in the center bottom of each indented point between scallops; insert cord from a bell up inside mantel cover, leaving about 2 inches of bell cord showing. Secure bell cords with fabric glue; let dry.

9. Cut ribbon into six pieces; tie each in a bow. Using fabric glue, glue one to cover at each bell cord.

10. Turn ¼ inch of white/silver fabric and off-white backing fabric to inside along straight edge; close with fabric glue; let dry. ✂

Creating Bias Strips

Bias strips can be used for binding edges or covering cotton piping to make welting. Use premade bias tape or binding or you can make your own from the lightweight woven fabric of your choice.

If you only need a small amount of strips, use a clear ruler and rotary cutter to cut bias strips across the fabric bias. For larger projects where multiple yards of bias binding are needed, it's easiest to create continuous binding strips by seaming and cutting a square of fabric as follows:

1. Determine the bias strip width you want to cut. For binding, double the finished width you'll need and add 1¼ inches for seam allowances. To cover piping, wrap a scrap of fabric loosely around the piping and pin it in place. Mark the fabric close to the piping on both sides, remove the fabric and measure between the marks. Add 1¼ inches for seam allowance to this measurement for the cut width you'll need (Fig. 1).

2. Cut a perfect square; the larger the square, the more strips it will yield. To determine the size of the fabric square you'll need, first figure the number of bias strip yards a piece of fabric will yield: Multiply the fabric width by the fabric length, then divide this number by the desired cut strip width. Divide again by 36 inches.

For example, to calculate how many yards of 1½-inch-wide bias strips an 18-inch square of fabric will yield, figure as follows: 18 inches (width) x 18 inches (length) = 324 inches; 324 inches divided by 1½ inches (strip width) = 216 inches; 216 inches divided by 36 inches (inches per yard) = 6 yards of bias strips.

3. Fold the square in half diagonally and mark the fold line. Cut the square in half along the marked line. Number the pieces as shown (Fig. 2).

4. Use a ¼-inch seam allowance to fuse edges 1 and 4 together with right sides facing. Press the seam to one side. Place the fabric on a flat surface with the diagonal edges at the sides. Using

continued on next page

a yardstick and tailor's chalk, begin at one diagonal edge and mark the strip width along the edge. Repeat to mark strips across the fabric width. Cut away any excess fabric beyond the final marked line (Fig. 3).

5. With right sides facing, offset sides 2 and 4 by one strip width and fuse the edges together using a ¼-inch seam allowance; press them to one side. The resulting fabric tube will appear slightly twisted (Fig. 4).

6. Begin at one offset end and continuously cut along the marked lines to the opposite offset end (Fig. 5).

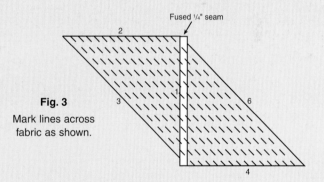

Fig. 3
Mark lines across fabric as shown.

Fig. 1
Measure from fold to pins, double measurement and add 1¼".

Fig. 2
Cut square diagonally and number every edge.

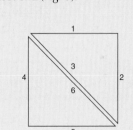

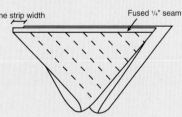

Fig. 4
Join sides 2 and 4 in ¼" seam offset by one strip width.

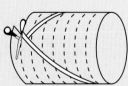

Fig. 5
Cut along marked lines.

Holiday Tree Skirt

The shine of Christmas lights and piles of presents will look fabulous on top of this cheery tree skirt. Use fabric that matches the theme of your tree.

Design by Marian Shenk

Instructions

1. Cut 41-inch circle from red velveteen and another from dark red print for lining; cut a 4-inch circle in the center of each.

2. Fold each circle in half; cut along fold from one edge to center hole.

3. Using chalk fabric marker and referring to pattern for scallop, draw a scalloped border around velveteen circle; on sample, six scallops divide tree skirt into six equal sections. Bottoms of scallops should rest 3½ inches from tree skirt's outer edge. Glue flat braid over marked line.

4. Turn under all edges of both pieces ¼ inch; press as needed.

5. Position twisted-cord edging along outer edge between top and lining; secure edging and fabric with fabric

Materials
- Fabrics: 1¼ yards each red velveteen and dark red print; fat quarter of green; ¼ yard red print; scrap of gold lamé
- 18 (½-inch) red berries
- 3 yards ¼-inch-wide flat gold metallic braid
- 4 yards gold twisted-cord edging
- Fusible web
- Washable fabric glue
- Metallic fabric paints in bottles with writer tip: green, gold
- Flat round acrylic jewel cabochons: 3 red, 3 green
- 1 yard fine gold cord
- Light-color chalk fabric marker

glue. Let dry. Glue edges of velveteen and lining together along slit in side and center opening.

6. Trace 18 leaves, six ornaments and six ornament caps onto paper side of fusible web. Fuse ornaments to wrong side of red print fabric, ornament caps to gold lamé and holly leaves to green.

7. Holly leaves: Cut out leaves; peel off backing and arrange as shown at points of braid; iron to fuse leaves in place. When cool, outline leaves and add veins with green paint; let dry.

8. Holly berries: Glue three red berries in center of each cluster of holly leaves.

9. Ornaments: Cut six 4-inch pieces of fine gold cord; loop each piece over one of the berries in each cluster and extend ends straight down so ornament will appear to hang from holly; glue cord ends in place. Arrange a red ornament and a gold lamé cap over ends of cord; iron to fuse in place. When cool, outline ornament and cap with gold paint. Glue a red or green cabochon near top of each ornament. ✂️

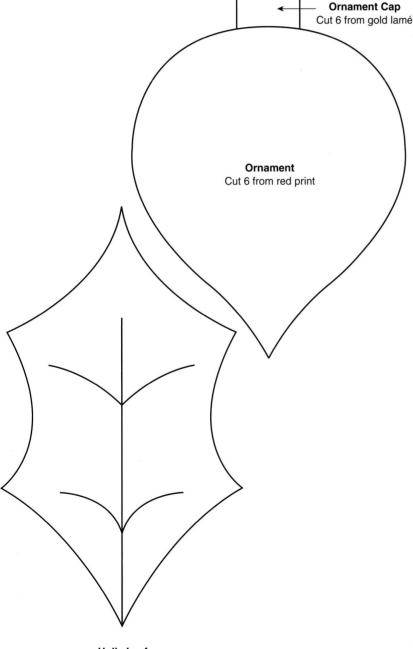

Ornament Cap
Cut 6 from gold lamé

Ornament
Cut 6 from red print

Holly Leaf
Cut 18 from green

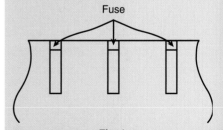

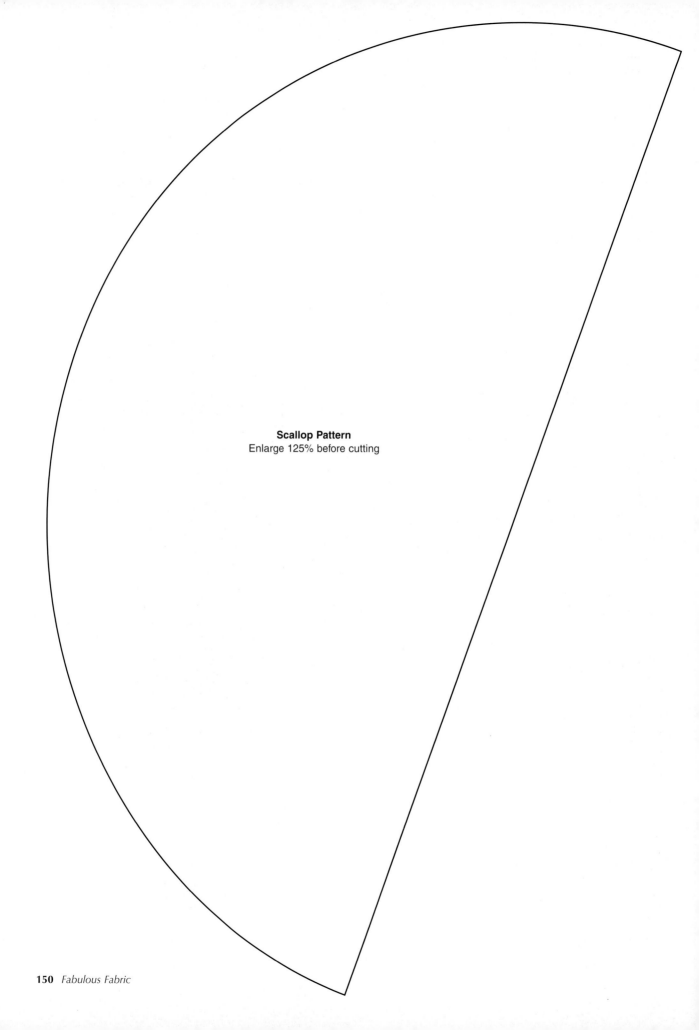

Scallop Pattern
Enlarge 125% before cutting

Lacy Holiday Table Runner

Adding elegance to your home is simple by embellishing fabric with lace and ribbon. Make this piece with the holiday-themed fabric of your choice.

Design by Mary Cosgrove

Instructions

1. Cut two 64-inch pieces scarlet ribbon (or long enough to fit long edges, allowing ½ inch extra at each end for turning under). Working on a surface protected with plastic, glue each piece along long edge of lace fabric to cover cut edge; turn under ½ inch at each end and glue to back.

2. Position poinsettia fabric in center of lace panel; secure with pins as needed. Apply a bead of glue along cut edges of poinsettia fabric; position dark gold trim all around edges to glue fabric to lace and keep edges from fraying.

3. Remove plastic after you have finished gluing; turn runner over to allow glue to dry completely. ✂

Materials

- 63-inch x 16-inch piece ivory lace fabric with scalloped edging on short ends
- 9½-inch x 44-inch piece poinsettia-print fabric
- 4 yards ⅝-inch-wide scarlet satin ribbon
- 1 pack (4 yards) dark gold 4mm trim
- Permanent fabric adhesive
- Plastic wrap or plastic trash bags

Patchwork Ornaments

Gather up your Christmas fabric scraps and create a set of these festive ornaments. Pretty floral and corded embellishments add to the antique feel of this set.

Designs by Marian Shenk

Materials

- Scraps of green and red Christmas fabrics
- Fine-point marking pen
- Blunt knife
- 3-inch plastic foam ball
- 1 yard ½-inch-wide gold trim
- Silk flowers: 2 small poinsettias, 3 holly leaves
- ⅜-inch gold bead
- 5-inch piece gold cord
- Hot-glue gun
- Pin

Instructions

1. Referring to pattern, cut three shapes from red Christmas fabric and three from green.

2. Using marking pen, draw three lines all the way around ball across top and bottom, spacing them evenly to divide ball into six equal sections, or wedges, like an orange.

3. Using a blunt knife and starting at the top, press edges of one fabric section into ball along drawn lines. Continue this process all around ball, alternating red and green sections, making sure all raw edges are tucked into ball.

4. Pin end of gold braid at top of ball, leaving half of pin protruding. Wrap braid around ball three times to cover all edges of each section.

5. Fold gold cord in half; knot ends together. Remove pin; using point of scissors, poke ends of braid and knot of cord loop into ball, leaving loop protruding for hanger.

6. Hot-glue holly leaves and one poinsettia into top hole; glue remaining poinsettias at bottom where braids overlap. Glue gold bead in center of bottom poinsettia. ✂

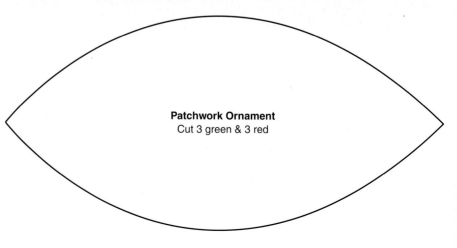

Patchwork Ornament
Cut 3 green & 3 red

Victorian Star Stocking

Blanket stitches in a contrasting color add a casual touch to this Victorian-style stocking. Hang it up for decoration only or try filling it with small gifts or accents.

Design by Mary Ayres

Materials

- ⅜ yard yellow/gold wool fabric or felt
- Cotton print fabrics: scraps in complementary red and green
- Gold jingle bells: ⅝-inch and 5 (⁵⁄₁₆-inch)
- ¾ yard 1¼-inch-wide wire-edge gold ribbon
- Red embroidery floss
- Embroidery needle
- Iron-on adhesive
- Permanent fabric adhesive

Instructions

1. Retrace pattern for stocking foot, adding a 5½-inch x 12-inch rectangle to top to create complete stocking pattern. Cut two stockings from gold wool or felt, reversing one.

2. Cut two 5-inch x 6-inch rectangles iron-on adhesive; following manufacturer's instructions, fuse to wrong side of red and green fabrics. Referring to patterns, cut one cuff from fused green fabric and one star from fused red. Peel off paper backing; fuse cuff to stocking front with top and side edges even; fuse star 1 inch below cuff.

3. Sew a ⁵⁄₁₆-inch jingle bell to each point of star with red embroidery floss. (Or, glue jingle bells to star after embroidery is completed.)

4. Using 3 strands floss, blanket-stitch across top edge of stocking back and stocking front. Pin stocking halves together and blanket-stitch together down side, around toe, across bottom, around heel and back up other side.

5. Hanger: Cut a 6-inch piece ribbon; fold in half, ends even. Stitch or glue ribbon ends to top back of stocking front. Stitch or glue ⅝-inch jingle bell to front of stocking on top of ribbon ends.

6. Tie remaining ribbon in a bow; trim ends even. Stitch or glue to point of cuff. ✂

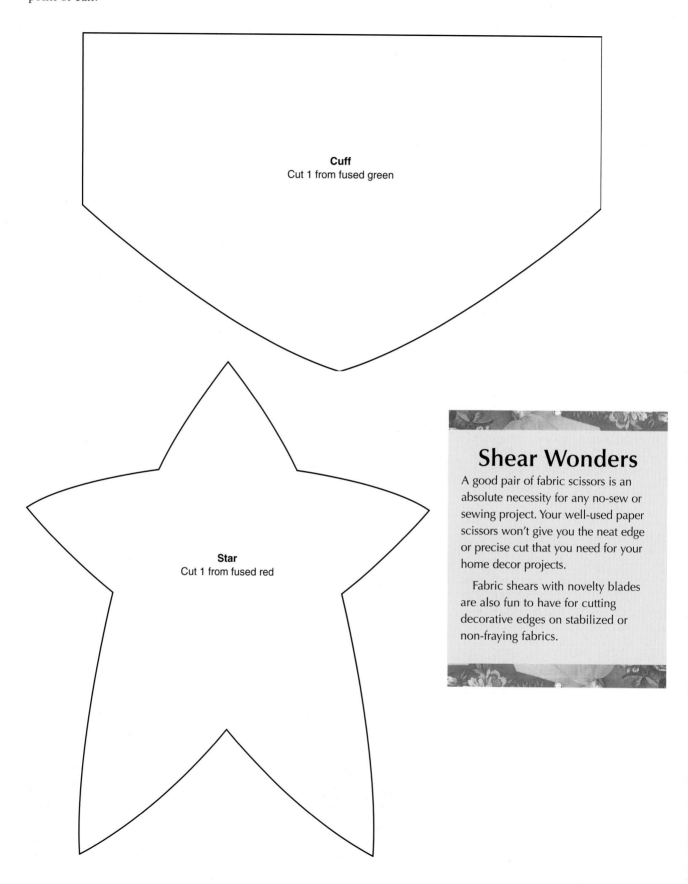

Cuff
Cut 1 from fused green

Star
Cut 1 from fused red

Shear Wonders

A good pair of fabric scissors is an absolute necessity for any no-sew or sewing project. Your well-used paper scissors won't give you the neat edge or precise cut that you need for your home decor projects.

Fabric shears with novelty blades are also fun to have for cutting decorative edges on stabilized or non-fraying fabrics.

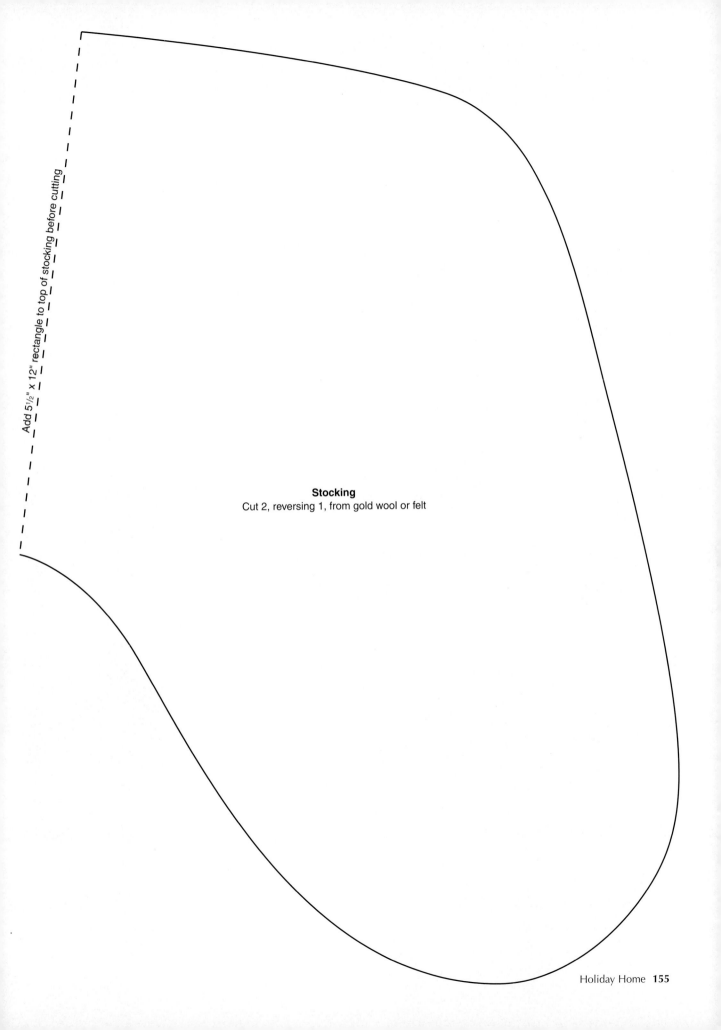

Add 5½" x 12" rectangle to top of stocking before cutting

Stocking
Cut 2, reversing 1, from gold wool or felt

Quilted-Look Wreath

Tuck rich-colored fabrics into foam and add metallic accents to make this classy wall hanging. You'll marvel over the quilted look of this piece that takes only a short time to complete.

Design by Annabelle Keller for Dow Chemical

Materials

- 12-inch x 36-inch x 1-inch sheet Styrofoam® brand foam
- Fabrics: ½ yard cream satin, ¾ yard green satin, ⅛ yard purple satin, ⅛ yard red rayon acetate velvet, ⅛ yard green rayon acetate velvet
- Trims: 1½ yards gold loop-edge trim; ½ yard gold swirl-style braid; 1⅝ yards gold bead edging; 2 yards metallic gold scalloped trim with sequins
- Assorted sequins, beads, charms, buttons or other trims of your choice
- Serrated knife
- Small piece paraffin or wax
- Tracing paper at least 15 inches square
- Transparent tape
- #10 artist's painting knife
- Holly rubber stamp
- 1 sheet 5-count plastic canvas
- Sawtooth hanger
- 6 round toothpicks
- Yardstick
- Black marking pen
- Straight pins
- Spray bottle with water
- Plastic foam glue
- Hot-glue gun

Embossing Velvet

Test process first on a scrap of velvet: Place stamp on ironing surface, image side up. Place velvet on stamp right side down; mist with water. Press with hot iron, avoiding steam vents, for 20–30 seconds, taking care not to move fabric and adjusting heat if velvet sticks.

Base

1. Using serrated knife lightly waxed with paraffin, cut Styrofoam sheet in half to make two 12-inch x 18-inch pieces.

2. Apply hot glue to one end of six wooden toothpicks. Referring to Fig. 1, insert toothpicks, glued ends first, halfway into one 18-inch edge of one piece of Styrofoam, spacing picks evenly. Apply plastic foam glue to edge between the picks and hot glue to the picks themselves, then press end securely onto one end of the remaining Styrofoam sheet; let dry.

3. Using waxed serrated knife, trim Styrofoam to make an 18-inch square. Lightly sand the edges as needed with a scrap of Styrofoam.

4. Using yardstick and marking pen, draw a 1½-inch border around 18-inch square. **Note:** *If your sheet is slightly undersized, adjust border width so that you will have a 15-inch square inside the border. Also draw diagonal lines at each corner.*

5. Fold a 15-inch square of tracing paper into fourths. Open sheet. Trace Dresden Plate pattern onto paper four times, positioning pattern's dashed lines on fold lines of paper to create complete pattern.

6. Center tracing paper inside border on Styrofoam, anchoring it with a few straight pins; score all lines, including border lines, with a sharp pencil.

7. Carefully remove tracing paper; cut center, one pointed section and one rounded section from paper. Carefully trim away remaining parts of Dresden Plate from background. Use these four pieces—center, pointed section, rounded section and background—as patterns.

Adding Fabric

1. Using patterns cut in step 7 for base and adding ½-inch seam allowances all around throughout, cut center and background pieces from cream satin.

2. From red velvet, cut one piece 4½ inches x 18 inches. Referring to instructions for embossing velvet, emboss velvet with 5-count plastic canvas. Let cool, then cut four pointed sections so that mesh pattern runs diagonally.

3. From green velvet, cut four pointed sections; emboss each with holly stamp.

4. From purple satin, cut eight rounded sections.

5. Tucking: Starting with center background piece, center fabric between marked lines. Using artist's knife, feel scored lines and tuck seam allowances into Styrofoam. Repeat with pieces for Dresden Plate design. Position outer background piece and hold in place with a few pins while tucking, clipping seam allowances as necessary.

Finishing & Assembly

1. Center back of wall hanging on wrong side of 24-inch square of green satin. Fold excess fabric to the front and tuck into scored lines.

2. Hanger: Center and glue sawtooth hanger 1 inch below top back edge. Apply glue to tips of nails; push securely through holes in hanger into Styrofoam.

3. Trims and embellishments: Cut trims to fit and glue in place, first dividing segments with lengths of the loop-edge trim. Glue swirl-style braid around edge of inner circle, overlapping ends ½ inch and

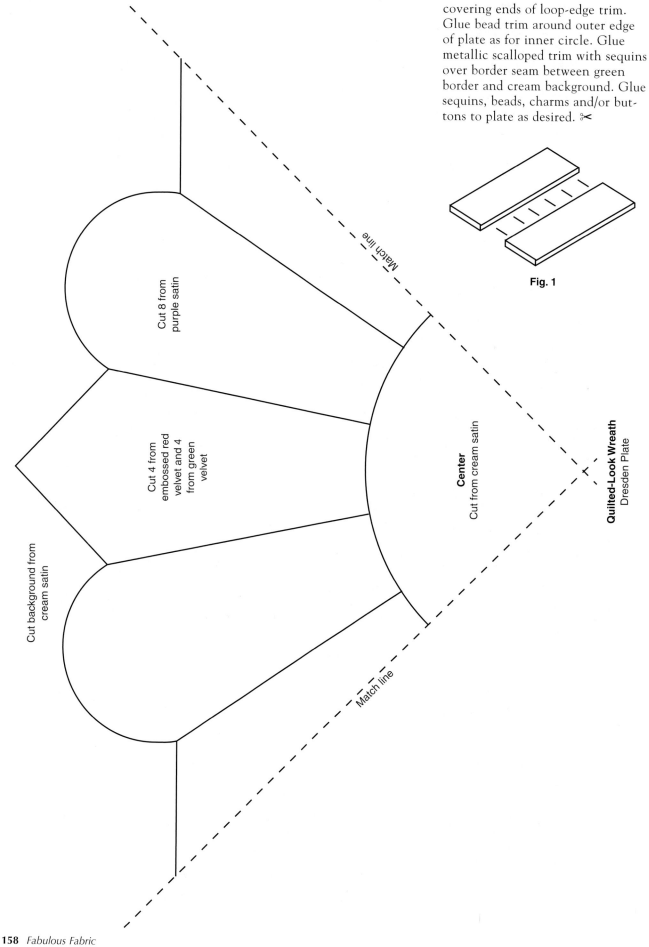

covering ends of loop-edge trim. Glue bead trim around outer edge of plate as for inner circle. Glue metallic scalloped trim with sequins over border seam between green border and cream background. Glue sequins, beads, charms and/or buttons to plate as desired. ✂

Fig. 1

Quilted-Look Wreath
Dresden Plate

Cut 8 from purple satin

Cut 4 from embossed red velvet and 4 from green velvet

Cut background from cream satin

Center
Cut from cream satin

Match line

Match line

Old-Fashioned Greeting Cards

Decorate blank cards with fabric of your choice for charming personalized holiday cards. You'll never want to send store-bought cards again.

Designs by Ann Butler

Materials

- Selected fabric
- Fusible fabric adhesive
- Blank cards with matching envelopes
- Dimensional paints: deep red, metallic gold

Instructions

1. Following manufacturer's instructions, fuse fabric adhesive onto wrong side of fabric; let cool.

2. Cut desired shapes from fabric; peel off backing and iron onto front of card and envelope as desired.

3. Embellish fabric designs with dimensional paints; let dry. ✂

Making Wired Edges

Wire can add a whimsical wavy touch to the hem of a fabric skirt or to a pillow flange or ruffle. It's also ideal for edging fabric ribbon for ties or bows.

For a wired hem, cut spool wire equal to the hem length plus 1 inch. Center the wire in the fold of the hem and fuse the hem in place. Bend the wire ends into the fabric on the wrong side, trimming if necessary. Shape the hem into waves as desired.

Wire a pillow ruffle or flange, before attaching it to the pillow panels. Insert the wire in the fold on the wrong side. Use very narrow fusible tape to fuse the fold around the wire.

To wire the edges of purchased ribbon or a fabric strip to be used for a bow or tie, fuse ¼-inch-wide adhesive tape along each edge on the wrong side. Leaving the paper in place, press ⅛ inch along each edge to the wrong side. Remove the paper backing, insert wire in the fold and fuse in place. Bend the wire ends to the wrong side and clip.

Winter Cheer Gift Bags

Present your gifts with a personal touch by adding seasonal fabric to inexpensive paper bags. You'll enjoy the holiday season even more by delighting others with your creativity.

Designs by Ann Butler

Materials
- Paper gift bags
- Selected fabric
- Complementary raffia or fabric scraps
- Complementary buttons
- Fusible fabric adhesive
- Craft glue
- Pinking shears

Instructions

1. Following manufacturer's instructions, fuse fabric adhesive onto wrong side of fabrics; let cool.

2. Cut desired shapes from fabric using pinking shears; peel off backing and iron onto front of gift bag as desired.

3. Tie a bow for each gift bag from raffia or strips of fabric; glue to gift bag. Glue button in center of bow. ✂

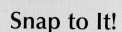

Snap to It!

Like grommets and eyelets, decorative snaps can be used for practical as well as decorative applications. Look for them in assorted metal tones and colors, in a variety of sizes. You will need a special snap-setting tool to add these decorative snaps.

Rows of Lace

Whether you want to add rows of lace or trim to create a wide border as shown on the Lace-edge Towels on page 129, or cover an entire panel for a pillow or Christmas stocking, it's fast and easy when you use a sheet of fusible adhesive.

1. Cut the fusible adhesive sheet to the size of the desired border or panel. Remove the paper from one side of the adhesive sheet and fuse it to the background fabric.

2. Remove the remaining paper backing and position the trims as desired.

3. Follow the adhesive sheet manufacturer's instructions to fuse the trims in place.

Sugarplum Grapes Door Hanger

Greet family and friends with the cheery tinkle of bells this holiday season. This glittery home decor piece can be used year-round.

Design by Bev Shenefield

Materials

- 26 (30mm) jingle bells
- Glossy-finish plum spray paint
- Spray adhesive
- Clear glitter
- 3–4 purple chenille stems
- 1 yard green ribbon
- Wooden skewers
- Grape acrylic craft paint
- #4 flat paintbrush
- Block of plastic foam

Instructions

1. Suspend each bell from the tip of a skewer. Spray jingle bells with plum paint, then stick skewer in block of plastic foam to hold bells upright until they dry. **Note:** *Weight foam block at bottom by inserting four skewers so that they extend out from sides of block near bottom edge; weight down these skewers with cans, phone book, etc., to hold plastic foam block securely in place. When dry, touch up as needed.*

2. Spray each bell with adhesive, then roll in glitter.

3. Join jingle-bell grapes into a cluster with chenille stems, winding them in and out and adding new stems as needed. When satisfied with the shape, form excess chenille stem into a hanger at the top. **Note:** *If purple chenille stems cannot be found, paint them grape with #4 paintbrush; this can be done before or after assembly. If done after assembly, paint any parts that are visible. The tighter the stems are wound, the less touch-up will be needed.*

4. Wrap ribbon around stem and a couple of grapes at top of cluster; tie in a double bow and trim ends. ✄

Gingerbread Boy Basket Liner

Present your freshly baked holiday goodies in a basket lined with this charming piece featuring happy gingerbread boys.

Design by June Fiechter

Materials

- Faux suede fabric
- Fabric glue
- Lace-trimmed red-and-white check place mat
- Puff paints: white, red, blue, green, black
- Pink acrylic craft paint
- Paintbrush

Instructions

1. Referring to pattern, trace four gingerbread boys onto faux suede; cut out. Glue one to each corner of place mat.

2. Add designs to gingerbread boys with puff paints: Outline with blue; add buttons with green, eyes with black and heart with red; add eyebrows and icing across arms and legs with white. *Note: Keep paint designs small to allow for growth when it is puffed. Puff paints as directed by paint manufacturer.*

3. Dot on cheeks with paintbrush handle dipped in pink paint; let dry. ✂

Gingerbread Boy
Cut 4 from faux suede

Seams Great

Use a ½-inch seam allowance to construct home decor projects unless otherwise indicated in the project instructions.

To seam fabric pieces together, use ½-inch or ⅜-inch fusible web or adhesive tape. Following the manufacturer's instructions, adhere the tape to the right side of one fabric piece seam allowance, along the edge for ½-inch tape or ⅛ inch from the edge for ⅜-inch tape. (Fig. 1).

Fig. 1

Remove the paper backing from the tape. Position the remaining fabric piece, aligning the edges right sides together, and fuse in place. Press the seam allowance to one side. (Fig. 2).

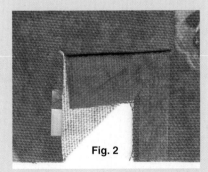

Fig. 2

To piece fabric strips together for ties, bands or binding, follow the instructions above to piece the short ends of the strips with right sides together.

Overlapping Seams

For heavy, nonfraying fabrics, such as leather and suede, an overlapping seam will reduce bulk and have a nicer finished appearance than a traditional seam. The edges can be cut straight or with a novelty edge for a decorative effect.

Test first to determine if heavy-duty adhesive film or permanent fabric adhesive works best on your fabric. Let each test sample dry, then pull on the seam to determine if the bond is stable.

On the right side of one piece, apply the fusible film or a thin, even layer of adhesive to the seam allowance. With the right side up, overlap the remaining piece ½ inch and bond together, following the manufacturer's instructions for the adhesive product. (Fig. 3).

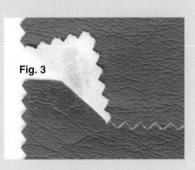

Fig. 3

Gingerbread Buddies

These cheery gingerbread friends will add a loving touch to your home during the Christmas season. They're so simple to make; you could even give some as gifts!

Designs by Helen Rafson

Ornaments

1. Trace two gingerbread B's, one heart B and two strap A's onto fusible webbing; cut pieces apart. Following manufacturer's instructions, fuse pieces with gingerbread patterns to wrong side of tan print fabric, heart pattern to wrong side of check fabric, and strap patterns to wrong side of white fabric; cut out. Cut also two gingerbread A's from stiffened green felt and one heart A from red felt.

2. Using fine-tip marker, draw running stitch around tan gingerbread pieces and red felt heart; add mouths to gingerbread.

3. Dip paintbrush handle into black paint; dot on eyes. Dip handle into red; dot on cheeks. Let dry.

4. Fuse tan print gingerbread shapes to green felt gingerbread shapes.

5. *Girl:* Fuse straps in place as shown. Cut a piece of lace measuring 1⅛ inches across top and 1¾ inches across bottom; cut a second piece measuring 1½ inches across top and 2⅛ inches across bottom. Glue shorter piece of lace atop longer piece as shown for skirt; let dry.

6. *Boy:* Using jewel adhesive, glue buttons down front as shown; let dry.

Materials

Each Project
- Fusible webbing
- Acrylic craft paints: lamp black, calico red
- Small paintbrush
- Black permanent fine-tip marker
- Craft glue
- Jewel adhesive
- Seam sealant

Ornaments
- Fabrics: tan print, white, red-and-white check
- Stiffened felt: red, kelly green
- 4 inches ½-inch-wide white eyelet lace
- Ribbon: 10½ inches ⅛-inch-wide white satin; 11 inches ⅜-inch-wide red check
- Flat buttons: 3 (¼-inch) white; ⁷⁄₁₆-inch red

Candy Cane Holder
- Fabrics: tan print, white
- Kelly green stiffened felt
- 2 inches ½-inch-wide white eyelet lace
- 5⅜ inches ⅛-inch-wide white satin ribbon
- 2 (¼-inch) flat white buttons
- ¼-inch masking tape
- 6-inch candy cane

7. Cut ribbon in half; tie each piece in a bow. Trim ends at an angle; treat with seam sealant; let dry. Glue bows to necklines as shown; let dry.

8. Fuse red check heart onto red felt heart. Using jewel adhesive, glue red button onto heart; let dry.

9. Glue heart to gingerbread buddies as shown; let dry.

10. *Hanger:* Glue ends of red check ribbon to back of gingerbread buddies; let dry.

Candy Cane Holder

1. Trace one gingerbread D and two strap B's (if making girl) onto back of fusible webbing; cut individual pieces apart. Following manufacturer's instructions, fuse gingerbread pattern to wrong side of tan print and strap patterns to wrong side of white fabric; cut out. Cut also one gingerbread C and one candy cane strip from stiffened green felt.

2. Using fine-tip marker, draw running stitch around tan gingerbread; add mouth.

3. Dip paintbrush handle into black paint; dot on eyes. Dip handle into red; dot on cheeks. Let dry.

4. Fuse tan print gingerbread onto center of green felt gingerbread shape.

5. Depending on whether you are making a boy or girl, add details:

Girl: Fuse straps in place. Cut a piece of lace to measure 1 inch across top and 1½ inches across bottom; glue on as shown; let dry.

Boy: Using jewel adhesive, glue buttons down front as shown; let dry.

6. Tie ribbon in a bow. Trim ends at an angle; treat with seam sealant; let dry. Glue on at neckline; let dry.

7. Turn gingerbread shape over. Center candy cane on back; place felt candy cane strip across candy cane and press down. Glue down ends of strip, keeping candy cane in place; secure felt with masking tape until glue dries, then remove tape. ✂

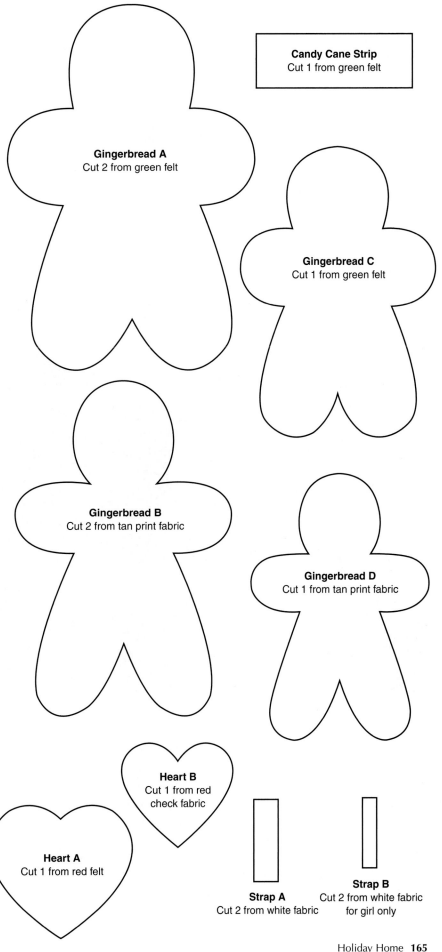

Candy Cane Strip
Cut 1 from green felt

Gingerbread A
Cut 2 from green felt

Gingerbread C
Cut 1 from green felt

Gingerbread B
Cut 2 from tan print fabric

Gingerbread D
Cut 1 from tan print fabric

Heart B
Cut 1 from red check fabric

Heart A
Cut 1 from red felt

Strap A
Cut 2 from white fabric

Strap B
Cut 2 from white fabric for girl only

Christmas Stars Table Covering

Serve holiday meals in style on this delightful hand-painted table covering. Using a purchased tablecloth and a compressed-sponge stamp, you can complete this piece in no time!

Design by Annie Lang

Materials

- 68-inch x 52-inch flannel-backed green plastic tablecloth
- 5-inch square compressed sponge
- Silver-leafing pen
- Patio paints: cloud white, geranium red, pot o' gold metallic
- Paintbrushes: #10 round, #0 liner, ½ deerfoot stippler
- Blow dryer

Instructions

1. Remove wrinkles from tablecloth with a blow dryer.

2. Referring to pattern, cut star from compressed sponge.

3. *Using ruler and pencil, mark a border strip all around tablecloth:* Mark one line 12 inches from hem, and a second line 8 inches above the first line.

4. Place a puddle of gold paint on palette. Dip sponge star into paint; on a second clean palette, work paint into sponge by tapping it up and down, working paint evenly into sponge.

5. Position sponge star along bottom edge of inner guideline. Gently press sponge down onto tablecloth surface, then pull straight up to stamp a gold star.

6. Leaving approximately ½ inch between stars, repeat steps 3 and 4 to sponge stars along inner guideline.

7. Repeat steps 3–5 to add a second border of stars along bottom edge of outer guideline. Let dry.

8. Load stippler with white paint, then gently stipple along both guidelines around star tips. *To stipple:* Gently pounce loaded brush along line using an up-and-down motion. Let dry.

9. Load liner with red paint; referring to Fig. 1, make small, loose, roping lines around white stippled garland, making sure strokes follow in the same direction. Let dry.

10. Use tip of silver-leafing pen, loosely outline each star; add dots between stars and around each corner with end of round paintbrush; let dry. ✂

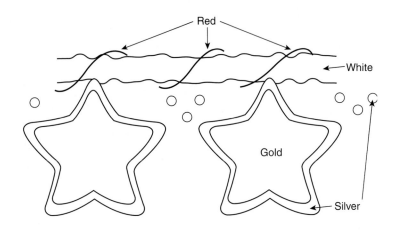

Fig. 1

Christmas Stars
Table Covering
Cut 1 from compressed sponge

Pillow Perfection

A pillow made from panels cut as perfect squares or rectangles will have floppy corners after a pillow form is inserted or stuffed with polyester fiberfill. This clever cutting technique of tapering the edges to the corners will result in perfect corners after the pillow is assembled and stuffed.

Cut two pillow panels in the desired measurements. Fold one panel into fourths, right sides together, and pin the edges to secure. Mark the distance halfway between the corner and the edge on two raw edges. Make another mark ½ inch from the corner and draw a line to connect the three marks (Fig. 1).

Cut on the marked lines through all layers. Open the trimmed panel and use it as a guide to shape the second panel.

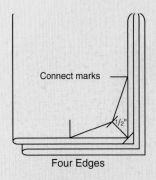

Fig. 1
Pillow Corners
Fold panel in half twice;
mark halfway between corner
along raw edges. Mark ½" in
from raw edge corner and
connect to side marks.

Holly & Pinecone Stool

The understated rustic charm of this piece will add a warm touch to your holiday decor. It's versatile enough to display anywhere in your home.

Design by June Fiechter

Materials

- Wooden stool
- 9-inch x 12-inch piece batting
- Complementary fabrics: 14-inch x 16-inch piece green; 7¼-inch x 9¾-inch piece purple; 6¼-inch x 8½-inch piece off-white; scraps of preceding fabrics plus brown and tan (sample uses green, purple and off-white even-weave fabrics, and brown and tan lightweight synthetic suede)
- Fine metallic braid in colors to match fabrics
- Embroidery needle
- Staple gun
- Fabric glue
- Wood stain

Instructions

1. Using stool top as a guide, trim green, purple and off-white fabric rectangles into ovals of even proportions; reserve fabric scraps.

2. Referring to pattern, trace pattern pieces onto fabric scraps, using green for holly leaves and purple for berries. Trace complete pinecone segments onto brown, and tips of segments only on tan; trace highlights for berries onto off-white.

3. Cut out pattern pieces. Glue tan tips onto corresponding brown pinecone segments; glue off-white highlights onto berries. Glue all pieces onto off-white oval as shown.

4. Using matching fine metallic braid and embroidery needle, blanket-stitch around each pinecone segment, berry and leaf; backstitch vein down center of each leaf.

5. Glue off-white oval in center of purple oval; blanket-stitch around edge with matching fine metallic braid. Glue purple oval in center of green oval; blanket-stitch around edge.

6. Stain all surfaces of stool except for top; let dry completely.

7. Cut batting to fit top of stool; glue in place.

8. Carefully center fabric over batting; turn stool over and rest on clean, firm surface. Stretching fabric gently and evenly, secure fabric to stool by stapling along underside, positioning staples about ½ inch from edge of stool. **Note:** *To stretch fabric evenly, apply staples alternating from side to side and top to bottom, not in a continuous line.*

9. Trim excess fabric from back of stool; treat edges with fabric glue and let dry.

10. Complete assembly of stool, following manufacturer's instructions. ✂

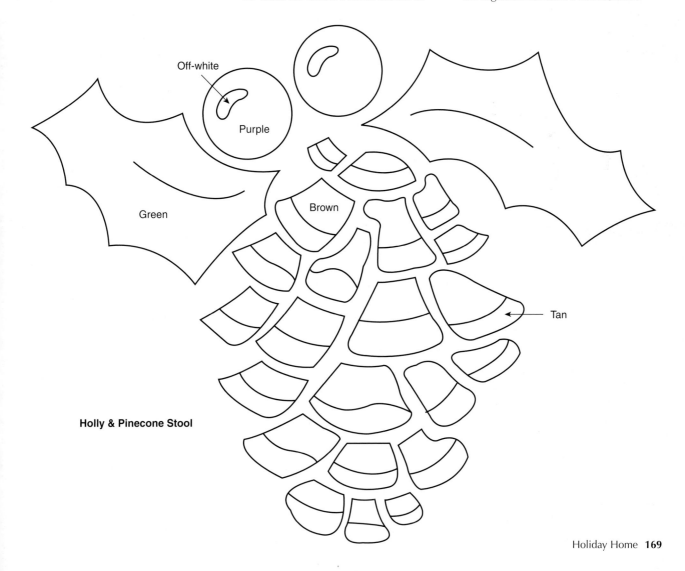

Holly & Pinecone Stool

Off-white

Purple

Green

Brown

Tan

Sources

Casual Living

Southwest Set
Denver Fabrics suede cloth; brown bead fringe #BP11077-10 from Hirschberg Schutz; Create-A-Craft double-stick fusible tape from The Warm Co.; Pellon Wonder Under; batting from Fairfield Processing; Sharpie marker; and Americana paints and DuraClear varnish, all from DecoArt, were used to complete these projects.

Embellished Lamp Shades
Fabri-Tac permanent fabric adhesive and Liqui-Fuse Liquid Fusible Web from Beacon; Trimtations bead and feather/bead trims from Expo International; Hollywood Trims ostrich fringe and tasseled fringe from Dritz; silk dupioni fabrics from Jackman's Fabrics; and PeelnStick double-sided adhesive from Therm O Web were used to complete these projects.

Flower Power Throw Pillow
Crafters Pick fabric glue from API; Fiskars pinking shears; and So Soft fabric paint and paint writer #DAS80 from DecoArt were used to complete this project.

Woven Heart Accent Pillow
Pellon Wonder Under, Crafter's Pick fabric glue and Jewel Bond glue from API; and a Sharpie permanent marker were used to complete this project.

Stamped Suede Home Decor Set
Stamp Décor leaves and medallions and FolkArt paint, all from Plaid; Steam-A-Seam 2 fusible web and fusible tape from The Warm Co.; and Fiskars rotary cutter were used to complete these projects.

Floral Elegance Doily
Doily #078-10 from Wimpole Street Creations; Scotch Magic and Double Stick tapes from 3M; and Stencil Magic delicate vine farmes and accents stencil #95-664-0018, floral colors Stencil Paint Crème Variety Pack #99-234-0056-998, brushes and Ceramcoat brush cleaner, all from Delta, were used to complete this project.

Reversible Table Runner
3M adhesive spray; Unique Stitch fabric glue from W.H. Collins; Quick Bias tape from Clover Needlecraft; and HeatnBond fusible tape from Therm O Web were used to complete this project.

Fabric Armchair Caddy
Armchair organizer #2720 from BagWorks; Steam-A-Seam II iron-on adhesive from The Warm Co.; and Gem-Tac adhesive from Beacon were used to complete this project.

Tapestry Rug
Ultrahold Fusible Adhesive Tape from Therm O Web was used to complete this project.

Living Room Cornice
STYROFOAM® brand plastic foam from Dow; Traditional poly-fil batting from Fairfield Processing; Capulet Stripe decorator fabric from Waverly; Dritz Fray Check seam sealant; Hold the Foam plastic foam and Fabri-Tac permanent fabric adhesives from Beacon; Craft & Floral Pro Glue Gun with needle nozzle and Crafty Magic Melt general-purpose oval glue sticks were used to complete this project.

Decorative Switch Plate & Outlet Covers
Fabri-Tac Permanent Fabric Adhesive and Liqui-Fuse liquid fusible web from Beacon; and PeelnStick double-sided adhesive from Therm O Web were used to complete these projects.

Fall Harvest Pumpkins
Warm & Natural Batting from The Warm Co.; and Crafter's Pick The Ultimate!, fabric glue and Jewel Bond glue from API were used to complete this project.

Blooming Box
Papier-mâché box from D&CC; Ceramcoat Satin Decoupage Medium, Satin Exterior/Interior Varnish and Sparkle Glaze, all from Delta; Glass, Metal & More permanent glue from Beacon; and 18KT Gold leafing pen from Krylon were used to complete this project.

Falling-Leaves Boxes
Falling Leaves fabric from Cranston Home Fashions was used to complete this project.

Rose-Covered Memory Box
Hoffman California Fabrics; Rainbow Felt Classic from Kunin; Ceramcoat paint and stencil sponge from Delta; Wrights gimp; and Kids Choice! Glue from Beacon were used to complete this project.

Home Office Ensemble
Fabri-Tac permanent fabric adhesive from Beacon; Conso bullion fringe; Covington Fabrics damask; and HeatnBond Ultrahold fusible adhesive tape from Therm O Web were used to complete this project.

Blue Leather Adornments
Leather Factory Trim Pack, Fiebing's Leathercraft Cement, Staz On solvent ink pad Tsukineko; and All Night Media rubber stamps from Plaid were used to complete these projects.

Leather Trimmed Boxes
Premium Trim Pack and Leathercraft cement from The Leather Factory; Staz On solvent ink pad from Tsukineko; and Square Stripes rubber stamps from All Night Media were used to complete these projects.

Entertaining in Style

Leaf Ensemble
Wonder Under Heavy Duty fusible web from Pellon; and Steam-A-Seam 2 fusible adhesive tape from The Warm Co. were used to complete these projects.

Autumn Twist Table Covering
DecoArt Patio Paints and Krylon 18K gold leafing pen were used to complete this project.

Reversible Place Mats
Sprayment and Unique Stitch fabric adhesive from 3M were used to complete these projects.

No-Sew Fabric Trivets
"Chives" stamp from Rubber Stampede and vine stamp from Posh Impressions were used to complete these projects.

Lace Candle Mats
Sprayment and Unique Stitch fabric adhesive from 3M and HeatnBond fusible adhesive from Therm O Web were used to complete these projects.

Floral Motif Kitchen Set
HeatnBond Ultrahold Iron-On Adhesive from Therm O Web; Duncan Enterprises' Chunky Stamps violet/violette #CHS18612 from Duncan Enterprises, Tulip Soft Brushable Fabric Paints and Tulip Paint Sponges; and TrimTations Designer Accents #1R1896 royal from Expo International were used to complete these projects.

Flower Button Coasters & Basket Liner
Warm & Natural needled cotton batting from The Warm Co.; HeatnBond Ultrahold Iron-On adhesive from Therm O Web; and Fabri-Tac adhesive from Beacon were used to complete this project.

Fruit Kitchen Tea Set
Janlynn apron; Anita's rubber stamps from Sugarloaf Products Inc.; Fabrico craft ink stamp pad from Rubber Designs; and Encre Pigment Ink Textile Markers #TC-4000 from Kuretake were used to complete these projects.

Appliquéd Fruit Towels

HeatnBond Ultrahold Iron-On adhesive from Therm O Web and Fabri-Tac adhesive from Beacon were used to complete these projects.

Stenciled Fern Dish Towels

Dish towels from Wimpole Street Creations; HeatnBond Ultrahold Iron-On Adhesive from Therm O Web; fern stencil #26776 from Plaid Stencil Decor; and Americana acrylic paints from DecoArt were used to complete these projects.

Stamped Canvas Shelf Unit

Rubbermaid 4 Shelf Cart #75505; SoSoft fabric paints from DecoArt; HeatnBond Ultrahold Iron-On Adhesive Tape from Therm O Web; and Rubber Stampede Fancy Fern rubber stamp were used to complete this project.

Dining Side Table & Linens

HeatnBond Ultrahold Iron-On adhesive and tape from Therm O Web were used to complete these projects.

French Country Picnic Set

HeatnBond Ultrahold Iron-On adhesive and tapes from Therm O Web and place mats from Rubbermaid were used to complete these projects.

Bulletin Board

Styrofoam brand plastic foam; Dritz button covers #215–24 and #17 ball-point pins from Prym-Dritz; Wrights braid; Extra-Loft batting from Fairfield Processing; Sakura Identi-Pen; and Hold the Foam! and Fabri-Tac adhesives from Beacon were used to complete this project.

Bag Holder Trio

Papier-mâché boxes from D&CC; Soft & Bright batting and Steam-A-Seam 2 iron-on adhesive from The Warm Co.; and Gem-Tac craft cement and Fabri-Tac fabric adhesive, both from Beacon, were used to complete these projects.

A Lifetime of Memories

Father's Day Card

Warm & Natural's Steam-A-Seam fusible tape and Steam-A-Seam 2 Double Stick Fusible Web Sheets from The Warm Co. were used to complete this project.

Mitten Card & Pin

Paper Reflections card and envelope from DMD Industries; Pellon Wonder Under and Heavy Duty Wonder Under fusible webs and Fusible Fleece; ZIG Millennium 005 black writer from EK Success Ltd.; Kreinik Metallics Balger fuchsia #024 fine #8 braid; and Gem-Tac adhesive from Beacon were used to complete these projects.

Child's Party Invitation

Warm & Natural's Steam-A-Seam 2 Double Stick Fusible Web Sheets from The Warm Co. were used to complete this project.

Baby Photo Album Covers

HeatnBond Iron-On Adhesive from Therm O Web; ZIG Memory System Millenium 05 marker from EK Success Ltd.; Kids Choice glue from Beacon; and McGill Punchline hole punch were used to complete projects.

Memories Set

Peel n Stick double-sided adhesive tape from Therm O Web, large cream #815 ribbon roses (#10-2009) from Offray; and The Ultimate Glue craft glue and fabric glue, both by Crafter's Pick, were used to complete these projects.

Denim Scrapbook

Colorfast Printer Fabric Sheets and Warm & Natural's Steam-A-Seam fusible tape and Steam-A-Seam 2 Double Stick Fusible Web Sheets from The Warm Co. were used to complete this project.

Fabric-Covered Photo Album

HeatnBond Ultrahold iron-on adhesive from Therm O Web and Fabri-Tac fabric adhesive from Beacon were used to complete this project.

French Country Frame Set

Frames from Lara's Crafts; and Gem-Tac and Fabri-Tac craft and fabric adhesives from Beacon were used to complete this project.

Cork Memo Board

Frame from Plaid Essentials; Warm and Natural needled cotton batting from The Warm Co.; Americana paint from DecoArt; and Gem-Tac and Fabri-Tac craft and fabric adhesives from Beacon were used to complete this project.

Bedroom Makeovers

Fringed Bedroom Ensemble

Fabrics from Waverly's American Rose Collection, Romantica #666732, Melrose Strip #667044 and Garden Beauty #666692 (all in sorbet color); acetate loop fringe #009115 (color #S25), Princess Collection tassel fringe, gimp trim and chair tie and fusible shirring tape, all from Conso; Steam-A-Seam 2 adhesive fusible tapes from The Warm Co.; decoWrap No-Sew Pillow Forms from June Tailor; and Fabri-Tac permanent fabric adhesive from Beacon were used to complete these projects.

Floral Accent Bedroom Set

Frame: glass packaged with cardboard backing from Silverwood Products, Pellon Wonder-Under and Fusible Thermolam Plus were used to complete this project. **Window shade:**

Pellon Décor Bond fusible backing and Warm and Natural's Steam-A-Seam 2 fusible web tape were used to complete this project. **Swag:** Warm and Natural's Steam-A-Seam 2 fusible web tape was used to complete this project. **Wastebasket:** Pellon Wonder-Under, Fusible Thermolam Plus and Stabilizer #50 were used to complete this project.

Antique Crazy Quilt Set

Keep A Memory mounting adhesive and HeatnBond Lite iron-on adhesive from Therm O Web, Fabri-Tac permanent adhesive from Beacon Adhesives, and lingerie bag from Wimpole Street Creations were used to complete these projects.

Floral Stenciled Accessories

Flower stencil #BL-76, stencil brushes #B-4 and Shiva Oil Paint Sticks, all from American Traditional Stencils; and Hollywood Lights lamp shade were used to complete these projects.

Spring Tulips Valance

Napkins and Battenburg shapes from Wimpole Street Creations and HeatnBond Ultrahold Iron-On Adhesive and Adhesive Tape from Therm O Web were used to complete this project.

Wildly Floral Painted Sheet Set

Design Master Spray Colortools, available at most art/craft supply stores, and ZIG Textile Markers from EK Success Ltd. were used to complete these projects.

Safari Sheet Set

Ceramcoat acrylic paints and Ceramcoat textile medium from Delta and Chunky Rubber Stamps from Duncan Enterprises were used to complete these projects.

Asian Influence Display Banner

Canvas banner #4001 from BagWorks Inc.; jacquard ribbons from Europa Imports; Genuine Shell Buttons from JHB International Inc.; Fabri-Tac and Gem-Tac adhesives from Beacon; and TrimTations beaded fringe #IR1896DBR from Expo International were used to complete this project.

Natural Elegance Valance

Envelope Pillow Covers #3114 from BagWorks Inc.; place mats from World Market; jacquard ribbon from Europa Imports; Genuine Shell Buttons from JHB International Inc.; and Fabri-Tac and Gem-Tac adhesives from Beacon were used to complete this project.

French Country Toile Boxes

Keep a Memory mounting adhesive from Therm O Web, Fabri-Tac adhesive from Beacon and Fiskars scallop-edge fabric shears were used to complete these projects.

Geometric Accents Bedroom Set

Stool: Wooden oval stool #97648 from Walnut Hollow: antique rose #616 ChainLink Tassel Fringe from Prym-Dritz; HeatnBond Ultra-Hold Iron-On Adhesive from Therm O Web; Ceramcoat all-purpose sealer, acrylic paint and iridescent glaze, all from Delta; Forster craft picks; C-Thru Ruler; Sobo glue from Delta; and Scotch Removable Magic Tape from 3M were used for this project. **Clock:** Arch clock #53201 and quartz movement #TQ700P from Walnut Hollow; Ceramcoat all-purpose sealer, antiquing gel, gloss exterior/interior varnish, stencil sponges, brush cleaner and Sobo glue, all from Delta; pure gold #303 Rayon Twist Satin Cord from Prym-Dritz; and Scotch Removable Magic Tape from 3M were used for this project. **Large lamp:** Self-adhesive lamp shade #1246 from Woodstock Wire Works; Mandarin Braid trim, Chainette Flapper Fringe and wine #504 Deco chair tie, all from Prym-Dritz; Scotch Removable Magic Tape from 3M; Sobo glue from Delta; and Forster craft picks were used for this project. **Small lamp:** Self-adhesive lamp shade #1241 from Woodstock Wire Works; Hollywood Trims aubergine ostrich trim and moss #924 Deco tie from Prym-Dritz; Scotch Removable Magic Tape from 3M; Sobo glue from Delta; and Forster craft picks were used for this project.

Playful Pals Cornice

STYROFOAM® plastic foam from Dow; Traditional poly-fil batting from Fairfield Processing; Wrights Max-Piping; HeatnBond Ultrahold Iron-On Adhesive from Therm O Web; and Hold the Foam plastic-foam and Fabri-Tac permanent fabric adhesives from Beacon were used to complete this project.

Ice-Cream Friend

STYROFOAM® from Dow; and Rainbow Felt Classic, antique white Parquet textured felt and white Snowfelt with iridescent sparkles, all from Kunin, were used to complete these projects.

Outer Space Desk Set

Cranston Fabrics planet fabric, HeatnBond Iron-On adhesive from Therm O Web, Woodsies stars from Forster, and Pres-On star picture frame and large and small photo albums from Create-A-Binder were used to complete these projects.

Bathroom Accents

Charming Violets Bath Set

3M Spra-Ment; Unique Stitch fabric glue from W.H. Collins Inc.; cosmetic storage jars from Sears; HeatnBond Ultrahold fusible adhesive strips from Therm O Web; Velcro adhesive fastener tape; and lamp shade from JoAnn Fabrics were used to complete these projects.

Spring Garden Hand Towels

Towels from Wimpole Streets Creations, HeatnBond Ultrahold fusible adhesive from Therm O Web, Plaid Simply Stencils flower stencil #28239, and So Soft Fabric Paints from DecoArt were used to complete these projects.

Embellished Hand Towels

Teflon pressing cloth from June Tailor; Ultrahold Permanent Adhesive Sheet from Therm O Web; and Fabri-Tac permanent fabric adhesive and Liqui-Fuse liquid fusible web from Beacon were used to complete these projects.

Timeless Style Bath Ensemble

Waverly fabrics Swan Lake #666740, Tea Rose Plaid #648510 and Melrose Stripe (amethyst) #667042; Dritz grommets and grommet pliers; self-adhesive wastebasket from Hollywood Lights; ½-inch Steam-A-Seam 2 fusible adhesive tape from The Warm Co.; Totally Stable stick-on stabilizer from Sulky; Princess Collection tassel fringe #10078 and gimp trim #H18 from Conso; and Fabri-Tac permanent fabric adhesive from Beacon were used to complete these projects.

Toile Baskets & Bowl Set

Surebonder Best Stik hot glue from FPC Corp., Amaco Aluminum Studio Mesh, HeatnBond Ultrahold fusible adhesive from Therm O Web, and Wright's Small Lip Cord were used to complete these projects.

Underwater Fantasy Set

Crazy fabric from Cranston Fabrics, HeatnBond fusible adhesive from Therm O Web, and Gloss DuraClear coating/sealer from DecoArt were used to complete these projects.

No-Sew Bath Caddy

Dish towels #DTL-E1 from Wimpole Street Creations, Crafter's Pick Fabric Glue from API, Craftwood buttons from Darice, Razor Knife #9362-8097 from Fiskars, and HeatnBond Ultrahold fusible adhesive from Therm O Web were used to complete these projects.

Floral Seat Cover

HeatnBond Ultrahold fusible adhesive and ¾-inch tape from Therm O Web and Liquid Laminate from Beacon were used to complete these projects.

Holiday Home

Stained Glass Poinsettia Set

Warm & Natural needled cotton batting from The Warm Co.; HeatnBond Ultrahold iron-on adhesive and Quilter's Edge from Therm O Web; and Fabri-Tac permanent adhesive from Beacon were used to complete these projects.

Poinsettia Elegance Mantel Skirt

HeatnBond fusible adhesive from Therm O Web; Unique Stitch stitchless fabric adhesive; and Tulip Scribbles fabric paint from Duncan were used to complete this project.

Holiday Tree Skirt

HeatnBond from Therm O Web; Unique Stitch fabric adhesive from W.H. Collins; and Tulip Scribble paints from Duncan were used to complete this project.

Lacy Holiday Table Runner

Nature's Celebration fabric #8814 from Hoffman California Fabrics; Offray craft ribbon; dark gold #425 4mm Carat Madeira from Madeira; and Fabri-Tac permanent adhesive from Beacon were used to complete this project.

Patchwork Ornaments

STYROFOAM® plastic foam from Dow was used to complete these projects.

Victorian Star Stocking

HeatnBond Ultrahold fusible adhesive from Therm O Web and Fabri-Tac adhesive from Beacon were used to complete this project.

Quilted-Look Wreath

STYROFOAM® brand plastic foam from Dow; gold trim #10113, gold trim #46192, trim #99123 and trim #46837, all from Trimtex Co.; and Sakura Identi-Pen were used to complete this project.

Old-Fashioned Greeting Cards

Steam-A-Seam adhesive from The Warm Company and Tulip dimensional paints from Duncan were used to complete this project.

Winter Cheer Gift Bags

Steam-A-Seam adhesive from The Warm Co. and Crafter's Pick The Ultimate! Glue from API were used to complete this project.

Sugarplum Grapes Door Hanger

Fibre-Craft jingle bells; Krylon rich plum gloss spray paint from Sherwin-Williams; Elmer's Craft Bond Multipurpose Spray Adhesive; Glitterex Corp. Crystal Clear Glitter; Garbo #3716 ribbon from Offray & Son; and Ceramcoat acrylic paint from Delta were used to complete this project.

Gingerbread Boy Basket Liner

Place mat from Wimpole Street Creations;

Tulip Puff Paints from Duncan; and Crafter's Pick Fabric Glue from API were used to complete this project.

Gingerbread Buddies

HeatnBond Ultrahold from Therm O Web; Eazy Felt from CPE Inc.; ZIG Memory System marker from EK Success Ltd.;

Americana acrylic paints from DecoArt; La Petite white buttons from Blumenthal Lansing Co.; and Kids Choice Glue and Gem-Tac adhesive from Beacon were used to complete these projects.

Christmas Stars Table Covering

Americana patio paints from DecoArt and a

Krylon silver leafing pen were used to complete this project.

Holly & Pinecone Stool

Wooden stool from Walnut Hollow; batting from Fairfield Processing; Crafter's Pick Fabric Glue from API; and Kreinik Fine (#8) Braid were used to complete this project.

Designer Index

American Traditional Stencils
Floral Stenciled Accessories

Mary Ayres
Antique Crazy Quilt Set
Cork Memo Board
Floral Motif Kitchen Set
French Country Toile Boxes
Stenciled Fern Dish Towels
Spring Garden Hand Towels
French Country Frame Set
Victorian Star Stocking

Deborah Brooks
Outer Space Desk Set
Falling-Leaves Boxes
Underwater Fantasy Set

Ann Butler
Old-Fashioned Greeting Cards
Winter Cheer Gift Bags

Barb Chauncey
Toile Baskets & Bowl Set

Jeanne Cody
Safari Sheet Set

Mary Cosgrove
Lacy Holiday Table Runner
Rose-Covered Memory Box

Carol Dace
Flower Button Coasters & Basket Liner

Karen de la Durantaye
Stained Glass Poinsettia Set

June Fiechter
Flower Power Throw Pillow
Gingerbread Boy Basket Liner
Holly & Pinecone Stool
No-Sew Bath Caddy

Annabelle Keller
Bulletin Board
Playful Pals Cornice

Living Room Cornice
Quilted-Look Wreath

Annie Lang
Autumn Twist Table Covering
Christmas Stars Table Covering
Spring Tulips Valance
Wildly Floral Painted Sheet Set

Chris Malone
Appliquéd Fruit Towels
Fabric-Covered Photo Album

Mary Lynn Maloney
Asian Influence Display Banner
Natural Elegance Valance

Lorine Mason
Dining Side Table & Linens
French Country Picnic Set
Floral Seat Cover
Stamped Canvas Shelf Unit

Barbara Matthiessen
Blue Leather Adornments
Leather-Trimmed Boxes
Stamped Suede Home Decor Set

Janice McKee
Burgundy Satin Table Ornament
Fabric & Fiber Greeting Cards
No-Sew Fabric Trivets

Samantha McNesby
Treasure Balls

Debra Quartermain
Ice-Cream Friend

Helen Rafson
Gingerbread Buddies
Baby Photo Album Covers

Judith Sandstrom
Fruit Kitchen Tea Set
Leaf Ensemble

Bev Shenefield
Memories Set
Woven Heart Accent Pillow
Fall Harvest Pumpkins
Southwest Set
Sugarplum Grapes Door Hanger

Jane Schenck
Fabric-Covered Bedroom Set

Marian Shenk
Holiday Tree Skirt
Lace Candle Mats
Charming Violets Bath Set
Patchwork Ornaments
Poinsettia Elegance Mantel Skirt
Reversible Place Mats
Reversible Table Runner

Jacqueline Stetter
Child's Party Invitation
Denim Scrapbook
Father's Day Card

Angie Wilhite
Mitten Card & Pin

Debbie Williams
Geometric Accents Bedroom Decor
Floral Elegance Doily

Barbara Woolley
Fabric Armchair Caddy
Blooming Box
Bag Holder Trio

Linda Wyszynski
Floral Motif Kitchen Set

Carol Zentgraf
Timeless Style Bath Ensemble
Fringed Bedroom Ensemble
Decorative Outlet & Switch Plate Covers
Home Office Ensemble
Embellished Hand Towels
Embellished Lamp Shades
Tapestry Rug

General Instructions

Materials

In addition to the materials listed for each craft, some of the following supplies may be needed to complete your projects. No doubt most of these are already on hand in your "treasure chest" of crafting aids. Gather them before you begin working so that you'll be able to complete each design quickly and without a hitch!

General Crafts

- Scissors
- Pencil
- Ruler
- Paper
- Tracing paper
- Craft knife
- Heavy-duty craft cutters or wire nippers
- Newspapers to protect work surface
- Safety pins

Painted Items

- Paper towels
- Paper or plastic foam plate or tray to use as a disposable paint palette for holding and mixing paints
- Plastic—a garbage bag, grocery sack, etc.—to protect work surface
- Water or other recommended cleaning fluid for rinsing and cleaning brushes

Fabric Projects

- Iron and ironing board
- Press cloth
- Basic sewing notions and supplies
- Rotary cutter and self-healing mat
- Air-soluble markers
- Tailor's chalk

Using Transfer & Graphite Paper

Some projects recommend transferring patterns to wood or another material with transfer or graphite paper. Read the manufacturer's instructions before beginning.

Lay tracing paper over the printed pattern and trace it carefully. Then place transfer paper transfer side down on wood or other material to be marked. Lay traced pattern on top. Secure layers with low-tack masking tape or tacks to keep pattern and transfer paper from shifting while you work.

Using a stylus, pen or other implement, retrace the pattern lines using smooth, even pressure to transfer the design onto the surface.

Painted Designs

Disposable paper or plastic foam plates, including supermarket meat trays, make good palettes for pouring and mixing paints.

The success of a painted project often depends on the care taken in initial preparations, including sanding, applying primer and/or applying a base coat of color. Follow instructions carefully.

Take special care when painting adjacent sections with different colors; allow the first color to dry so that the second will not run or mix. When adding designs atop a painted base, let the base coat dry thoroughly first.

If you will be mixing media, such as drawing with marking pens on a painted surface, test the process and your materials on scraps to make sure there will be no running or bleeding.

Keep your work surface and your tools clean. Clean brushes promptly in the manner recommended by the paint manufacturer; many acrylics can be cleaned up with soap and water, while other paints may require a solvent. Suspend your paintbrushes by their handles to dry so that the fluid drains out completely and bristles remain straight and undamaged.

Work in a well-ventilated area when using paints, solvents or finishes that emit fumes; read product labels thoroughly to be aware of any potential hazards and precautions.

Painting Techniques

Base-coating: Load paintbrush evenly with color by dabbing it on palette, then coat surfaces with one or two smooth, solid coats of paint, letting paint dry between coats.

Dry-brushing: Dip a dry round-bristle brush in paint; wipe excess paint off onto paper towel until brush is almost dry. Wipe brush across edges for subtle shading.

Shading: Dip brush in water and blot lightly once on paper towel, leaving some water in brush. Dip point of brush into paint. Stroke onto palette once or twice to blend paint into water on bristles so that stroke has paint on one side gradually blending to no color on the other side. Apply to project as directed.

Stenciling with brush: Dip dry stencil brush in paint. Wipe brush on paper towel, removing excess paint to prevent seepage under stencil. Brush cutout areas with a circular motion, holding brush perpendicular to surface. When shading, brush should be almost dry, working only around edges. Use masking tape to hold stencil in place while working. ✂

Technique Index

Index

Buyer's Guide

Projects in this book were made using products provided by the manufacturers listed below. Look for the suggested products in your local craft- and art-supply stores. If unavailable, contact suppliers below. Some may be able to sell products directly to you; others may be able to refer you to retail sources.

3M Center
Consumer Relations
Bldg. 304-01-01
St. Paul, MN 55144-1000
(800) 537-9514

Aleene's
Div. of Duncan Enterprises
5673 E. Shields Ave.
Fresno, CA 93727
(800) 237-2642
www.duncan-enterprises.com

Amaco
American Art Clay Co. Inc.
4717 W. 16th St.
Indianapolis, IN 46222-2598
(317) 244-6871
www.amaco.com

American Traditional
Stencils
442 First New Hampshire
Turnpike
Northwood, NH 03261-9754
(800) 278-3624
www.americantraditional.com

API/The Adhesive
Products Inc.
520 Cleveland Ave.
Albany, CA 94710
(510) 526-7616
www.crafterspick.com

BagWorks
3301 S. Cravens Rd., Bldg. C
Fort Worth, TX 76119
(800) 365-7423
www.bagworks.com

Beacon Adhesives/
Signature Marketing
125 MacQuesten Pkwy. S
Mount Vernon, NY 10550
(914) 699-3400
www.beacon1.com

Conso Products Co.
P.O. Box 326
513 N. Duncan Bypass
Union, SC 29379
(800) 845-2431
www.conso.com

Covington Fabrics
15 E. 26th St. – 20th floor
New York, NY 10010-1590
(212) 689-2200
www.covington-industries.com

Crafter's Pick by API
520 Cleveland Ave.
Albany, CA 94710
(510) 526-7616
www.crafterspick.com

Cranston Fabrics/
Cranston Print Works Co.
2 Worcester Rd.
Webster, MA 01570-1652
(508) 943-0520
www.cpw.com

Create-A-Binder
1020 S. Westgate Dr.
Addison, IL 60101
(800) 323-1745
www.pres-on.com

C-Thru Ruler Co./
Deja Views
6 Britton Dr.
Bloomfield, CT
06002-3602
(800) 243-8419
www.cthruruler.com

Darice Inc.
Mail-order source:
Bolek's
330 N. Tuscarawas Ave.
Dover, OH 44622
(330) 364-8878

D&CC/
Decorator & Craft Corp.
428 Zelta
Wichita, KS 67207
(800) 835-3013

DecoArt
P.O. Box 386
Stanford, KY 40484
(800) 367-3047
www.decoart.com

Delta Technical
Coatings Inc.
2550 Pellissier Pl.
Whittier, CA 90601-1505
(800) 423-4135
www.deltacrafts.com

Denver Fabrics
(866) 996-4573
www.denverfabrics.com
df@denverfabrics.com

DMD Industries Inc./
The Paper Reflections Line
2300 S. Old Missouri Rd.
Springdale, AR 72764
(800) 805-9890
www.dmdind.com

Dow Flora Craft/
Dow Chemical Co.
(800) 441-4369

Dritz/Prym-Dritz Corp.
P.O. Box 5028
Spartanburg, SC 29304
(800) 255-7796
www.dritz.com

Duncan Enterprises
5673 E. Shields Ave.
Fresno, CA 93727
(800) 438-6226
www.duncan-enterprises.com

EK Success Ltd.
125 Entin Rd.
Clifton, NJ 07014
(800) 524-1349
www.eksuccess.com

Europa Imports Inc.
1528 Montague Expressway
San Jose, CA 95131
(408) 324-1944
www.europatrimmings.com

Expo International Inc.
5631 Braxton Dr.
Houston, TX 77036
(800) 542-4367
www.expointl.com

Fairfield Processing Corp.
P.O. Box 1157
Danbury, CT 06813-1157
(800) 243-0989
www.fairfieldprocessing.com

Fiebing
421 S. 2nd St.
Milwaukee, WI 53204-1612
(414) 271-5011

Fiskars Inc.
7811 W. Stewart Ave.
Wausau, WI 54401
(800) 950-0203, ext. 1277
www.fiskars.com

Forster Inc./
Diamond Brands
1800 Cloquet Ave.
Cloquet, MN 55720
(218) 879-6700
www.diamondbrands.com

FPC Corp.
355 Hollow Hill Dr.
Wauconda, IL 60084
(847) 487-4583
(800) 860-3838
www.surebonder.com

Hirschberg Schutz
650 Liberty Ave. #2
Union, NJ 07083
(908) 810-1111

Hoffman California Fabrics
25792 Obrero Dr.
Mission Viejo, CA 92691
info@hoffmanfabrics.com
www.hoffmanfabrics.com

Hollywood Lights
800 Wisconsin St.
Eau Claire, WI 54703

Jackman's Fabrics
(800) 758-3742
www.jackmanfabrics.com

Janlynn Corp.
P.O. Box 51848
34 Front St.
Indian Orchard, MA
01151-5848
(800) 445-5565
www.janlynn.com

JHB International Inc.
1955 S. Quince St.
Denver, CO 80231
(303) 751-8100
www.buttons.com

June Tailor
P.O. Box 208
2861 Highway 175
Richfield, WI 53076
(800) 844-5400
www.junetailor.com

Kreinik Mfg. Co. Inc.
3106 Lord Baltimore Dr., #101
Baltimore, MD 21244
(800) 537-2166

Krylon/Sherwin-Williams
31500 Solon Rd.
Solon, OH 44139
(800) 797-3332
www.krylon.com

Kunin Felt Co./
Foss Mfg. Co. Inc.
P.O. Box 5000
Hampton, NH 03842-5000
(603) 929-6100
www.kuninfelt.com

Kuretake Co. Ltd.
Unit 6 Colemeadow Road
North Moons Moat
Redditch, Worcestershire
B98 9PB England UK
www.kuretake.co.jp/uk

Lara's Crafts
590 N. Beach St.
Fort Worth, TX 76111
(800) 232-5272
www.larascrafts.com

Leather Factory
P.O. Box 50429
Fort Worth, TX 76105
(817) 496-4414
(800) 433-3201
www.leatherfactory.com

Madeira Threads
30 Bayside Ct.
P.O. Box 6068
Laconia, NH 03246
(800) 225-3001

McGill Craftivity
Mail-order source:
Alpine Imports
7106 N. Alpine Rd.
Rock Island, IL 61111
(800) 654-6114

C.M. Offray & Son Inc./
Lion Ribbon Co. Inc.
Route 24, Box 601
Chester, NJ 07930
(800) 551-LION
www.offray.com

Pellon Consumer Products
3440 Industrial Dr.
Durham, NC 27704
(919) 620-7457

Plaid Enterprises Inc.
3225 Westech Dr.
Norcross, GA 30092
(800) 842-4197
www.plaidonline.com

Posh Impressions
22600 Building A
Lambert Street, #706
Lake Forest, CA 92630
(800) 421-7674
www.poshimpressions.com

Rubber Designs
16604 Music Grove Ct.
Rockville, MD 20853
(301) 570-8853
www.rubberd.com/fabrico.htm

Rubber Stampede Inc.
P.O. Box 246
Berkeley, CA 94701
(800) 423-4135
www.rstampede.com

Sakura Hobby Craft
2444 205th St., A-1
Torrance, CA 90501
(310) 212-7878
e-mail: craftman@earthlink.net

Silverwood Products
6301 Forbing Rd.
Little Rock, AR 72209
(501) 664-7416
www.silverwoodproducts.com

Sugarloaf Products Inc.
P.O. Box 348
Lithonia, GA 30058
(770) 484-0722
www.sugarloafproducts.com

Sulky of America
3113 Broadpoint Dr.
Punta Gorda, FL 33983
www.sulky.com

Therm O Web
770 Glenn Ave.
Wheeling, IL 60090
(847) 520-5200
www.thermoweb.com

Trimtext Co.
400 Park Ave.
Williamsport, PA 17703

Tsukineko Inc.
17640 N.E. 65th St.
Redmond, WA 98052
(800) 769-6633
www.tsukineko.com

Walnut Hollow Farms Inc.
1409 State Rd. 23
Dodgeville, WI 53533-2112
(800) 950-5101
www.walnuthollow.com

Warm & Natural/
The Warm Co.
954 E. Union St.
Seattle, WA 98122
(800) 234-WARM
www.warmcompany.com

Waverly Fabrics
www.waverly.com

Wimpole Street Creations
Mail-order source:
Barrett House
P.O. Box 540585
North Salt Lake, UT
84054-0585
www.barrett-house.com

Woodstock Wire Works Inc.
300 N. Seminary Ave.
Woodstock, IL 60098-0759
(800) 435-8083
E-mail: Kitiinc@aol.com

Wrights
P.O. Box 398
West Warren, MA 01092
(413) 436-7732, ext. 445